D0205803

Cultural Hegemony
and
African American
Development

Cultural Hegemony and African American Development

Clovis E. Semmes

PRAEGER

Westport, Connecticut
London

Copyright Acknowledgments

The author and publisher are grateful to the following for allowing use of their material:

Philip Cohran. Interviews with the author, March 1, 1979, and March 8, 1979. Used by permission.

Clovis E. Semmes (Jabulani K. Makalani). "Toward a Sociological Analysis of the Renaissance: Why Harlem?" *Black World* 25 (February 1976): 4-13, 93-97. Used by permission.

Clovis E. Semmes. "The Role of African-American Health Beliefs and Practices in Social Movements and Cultural Revitalization." *Minority Voices* 6, no. 2 (1990): 45-57. Used by permission.

Clovis E. Semmes. "The Dialectics of Cultural Survival and the Community Artist: Phil Cohan and the Affro-Arts Theater." *Journal of Black Studies*. In press. Used by permission.

Library of Congress Cataloging-in-Publication Data

Semmes, Clovis E.
    Cultural hegemony and African American development / Clovis E.
  Semmes.
      p.   cm.
    Includes bibliographical references and index.
    ISBN 0-275-93923-5 (alk. paper)
    1. Afro-Americans—Intellectual life. 2. Afro-Americans—Social
  conditions. 3. Afrocentrism.   I. Title.
  E185.86.S46   1992
  305.896'073—dc20   92-16205

British Library Cataloguing in Publication Data is available.

Library of Congress Catalog Card Number: 92-16205
ISBN: 0-275-93923-5

First published in 1992

Praeger Publishers, 88 Post Road West, Westport, CT 06881
An imprint of Greenwood Publishing Group, Inc.

Printed in the United States of America

The paper used in this book complies with the
Permanent Paper Standard issued by the National
Information Standards Organization (Z39.48-1984).

10 9 8 7 6 5 4 3 2 1

To Jean, Jelani, Maia, and Sala

Contents

Introduction   ix

1   Foundations of Knowledge in
African American Studies   1

2   The Frazerian Paradigm   41

3   The Dialectics of Harold Cruse   71

4   The Problem of Legitimacy   93

5   Culture, Economics, and the
Mass Media   111

6   Religious Fragmentation
and Social Cohesion   139

7   Toward a Theory of African
American Health   171

8   Revitalization Tendencies   195

9   A Concluding Comment   251

Bibliography   255

Index   265

Introduction

The purpose of this work is to provide a way of seeing and understanding the intellectual tradition and body of knowledge called Black, African American, or Africana studies. I address, through a series of essays, such questions as: What organizing principles emerge that seem to direct the production of knowledge within the discipline? What are its logical as well as empirical underpinnings? How do we properly locate the parameters of the discipline? What are its major theoretical and conceptual issues and why?

African American studies is emerging as a distinctive discipline that draws strength from many sources. Because of the way the discipline has come into existence, scholars have had to enter the field through other, more traditional (i.e., Eurocentrically focused) disciplines. Nevertheless, as one becomes immersed in the tradition, it takes on a life of its own and acquires a very distinctive substance and form. As a body of knowledge, Black, African American, or Africana studies is tied to explicating social and historical processes that affect the status and development of people of African descent on a global scale. It is in this context that this emerging discipline is able to provide universals for understanding the human experience in general.

When considering the status and development of African Americans, the study of Black issues has been posed in racial or class terms and not in terms of cultural process. This means that either racial or economic factors have been posited as the driving forces behind a distinctive experience of domination and oppression experienced by both African Americans and an African diaspora. This work proposes that such an either/or approach must be replaced by a focus on the impact of social organization and culture on one another and the resulting implications for institutional development. Most would agree, however, that the experience of domination has shaped and continues to shape the development of African Americans and the African diaspora.

Additional theoretical efforts have emerged that identify the Afrocentric parameters of the discipline. These efforts are useful in that they give fuller expression to the role of perspective and historiography in creating and defining a body of knowledge. Afrocentric theory, however, is not definitively delineated, monolithic, or fully developed. It requires additional examination, critique, and cultivation. The chapters in this work seek to extend Afrocentric theory development by linking such development to a fuller understanding of the motive forces and the epistemological foundations shaping the parameters of African American studies.

Several key elements become evident as a consequence of what has occurred in the formulation and reformulation of African American studies over the past two decades. First, there is a consistent focus on oppression and domination, or, as I would prefer, hegemony. Second, historical location or perspective is important in order to identify the emergence of provisional structures that define distinctive phases of African American development. Third, race and class oppression have arisen as important but not sufficient explanatory variables to account for the distinctive character of African American development. When and how race and class come into play are crucial. In addition, racial and class exploitation (and most recently, gender, which accounts for significant variation in the experience of hegemony) are not additive but combine in qualitatively distinctive ways, given a particular social context. Fourth, there is an underlying empirical and logical concern with cultural development: How have African cultures been altered? What are their continuing influences in the American context? How will African Americans emerge from domination and exploitation, and what will they become as a group? This idea of "becoming" necessarily brings into focus the problem of cultural development. Thus, in my view, in order to understand African American studies, we must develop and explicate a theory of culture, one that accurately describes African American reality. The basis for such a theory, I believe, involves recognition and elaboration of an important historical dialectic associated with the problem of cultural hegemony.

The fundamental thesis of this work is that cultural hegemony has become the metaproblem out of which epistemological, conceptual, theoretical, and critical issues emerge in African American studies. Cultural hegemony, the systemic negation of one culture by another, constitutes the major paradigmatic, historical, and structural phenomenon that has threatened African American institutional development and that has profoundly shaped this group's cultural strivings. Over time, the creation of institutions and culture among African Americans has been stimulated by the need to negotiate and respond to historical imperatives driven by the problem of systemic cultural negation. Social and revitalization movements, as well as the outpourings of creative intellectuals and artists, reflect varying degrees of a conscious and unconscious response to this problem. The structure of relationships that define cultural hegemony is dialectical, related to the specificities of a distinctive experience of exploitation and dehumanization, and calls into central importance the complex interactions between social organization and culture. Recognition of the dynamic historical imperatives emerging from cultural hegemony and its effects on African American development provides the essential basis for comprehending the African American cultural dynamic. Thus, I argue that social and humanistic inquiry in African American studies must be guided by an appreciation of these structural imperatives in order to generate meaningful research questions and to seek productive solutions to human problems.

Chapter One defines the relationship between cultural hegemony and the African American experience and establishes how this relationship creates distinctive and recurring problems for African American cultural and institutional development. It assesses current Afrocentric perspectives and examines to what extent these perspectives are logically and empirically based and comprehensive in scope. The chapter further illustrates how the problem of cultural hegemony contributes to a critical concern for analyzing the relationship between social organization and culture, for example, how changes in patterns of structured interaction affect norms, values, and beliefs, as well as the converse relationship.

Chapter Two analyzes the corpus of empirical works produced by sociologist E. Franklin Frazier. If we transcend the misconceptions concerning Frazier's work, we find that it reveals the underlying problem of cultural hegemony while setting forth an analysis of the pivotal interactions between social organization and culture. The themes of Frazier's works offer a cultural analysis that brings into focus the historical imperatives facing African American development.

Chapter Three illustrates the neo-Frazerian character of the work of social critic Harold Cruse. It also demonstrates that Cruse's work reveals important historical imperatives emanating from the problem of cultural hegemony. Cruse's conceptual formulations and critical analyses contribute to a theory of African American culture and are important for understanding African American developmental processes.

Chapter Four argues that universally human efforts to gain recognition and respect for intrinsic personal, institutional, and cultural expression are a perennial problem for African Americans linked to the problem of cultural hegemony. As such, it explores the role of legitimacy in psychological and social psychological adaptation, and inter-group and intra-group relations.

Chapter Five analyzes the relationship between the political economy of the mass media and African American aesthetic and artistic production. I argue that the expropriation of African American cultural products is a structural problem contributing to the tendency toward cultural negation. This problem is intensified by the internal contradictions of capitalism, characteristic of a posturban, postindustrial environment.

Chapters Six and Seven examine two important institutional forms, religion and health. Chapter Six argues that despite the central role and importance of religion in African American life, religious fragmentation and unresolved contradictions in sacred beliefs produce problems for cultural cohesion and institutional development. Chapter Seven shows that cultural hegemony can produce culturally maladaptive behavior. It examines how health is related to cultural viability and illustrates how such viability is systemically preempted for African Americans.

Chapter Eight looks at the significance of cultural revitalization tendencies, that is, diverse efforts by African Americans to create a more satisfying culture. These efforts reveal the collectively felt need to rehumanize one's existence and to transcend the debilitating and destructive capabilities of cultural hegemony.

Chapter Nine concludes with a comment on factors affecting the production of knowledge in African American studies and the implications for African American development.

Foundations of Knowledge in African American Studies

THE STRUCTURE AND ORIGINS OF CULTURAL HEGEMONY

The basic thesis of this work is that cultural hegemony has become the metaproblem out of which epistemological, conceptual, theoretical, and critical issues emerge in Black, African American, and Africana studies. I define cultural hegemony as the systemic negation of one culture by another. By this process I mean that the internal dynamics of one culture evolves in such a way that it calls into dissolution the independence, coherence, and viability of another culture to which it has a socio-historical connection. In a sense, the one culture bases its existence and well-being on the ability to absorb, redirect, or redefine institution building and symbol formation in the other.

The fundamental impetus behind cultural hegemony is the historical phenomenon of European expansion and contact, which resulted in the exploitation of Africa for its human, mineral, and agricultural wealth.[1] Even though economic gain was a driving force in the initiation of this process of exploitation, the way in which this exploitation was consummated involved the broader dimensions of race and culture. Racism emerged from an extant cultural complex of alienation, color prejudice and xenophobia and became operationalized as White supremacy.[2] An ideology of White supremacy emerged that rationalized the exploitation of non-White peoples, galvanized European class divisions, and strengthened European resolve to dominate non-Whites by any means necessary.

The seizure of African labor and wealth required the seizing of the African mind, and the transmutation and manipulation of culture became the vehicle to accomplish this end. Thus, the cultures of African peoples became, of necessity, objects to be dismantled for the purpose of more efficient exploitation and control. But even though catastrophic oppression brought about a process of objectification and dehumanization, the absolute negation of humanity was not possible because a damaged human spirit seeks to resurrect and reconstruct itself; it also seeks self-consciousness. Culture building may be impeded, but it does not stop. Consequently, reconstruction involves renewed historiography and reflectivity.

For African Americans, because of the self-generative character of the human spirit, a dialectic emerged that produced distinctive parameters for cultural reconstruction and hence the creation of new and relevant knowledge. This dialectic has manifested itself as the struggle between dehumanization and humanization, institutional negation and cultural revitalization, delegitimation and legitimation, and, borrowing from novelist Ralph Ellison, invisibility and visibility. The nascent and evolving characteristics of this cultural reconstruction seeks to transcend the dialectic created by cultural hegemony. The particulars of this dialectical process then become the key theoretical issues of the developing discipline and field of study known as Black, African American, or Africana studies.

Cultural hegemony, with its attendant internal dynamics and supremacist underpinnings, remains the problem behind the problem. Sustained exploitation of African peoples produced this type of oppression, and the racialist character of the imperialist group sought to shake its victims from their cultural foundations. The dominated were required to accept a world defined by their oppressor. Historical negation and distortion became central to the process of domination in order to weaken the ability of the victimized people to sustain a self-conscious and self-directed sense of origin, evolution, and purpose. The need was to force the victim to relinquish internal control (independence) in order to accept external control (dependence).

Through cultural hegemony, the perspective of the oppressed shifted to that of the imperial group. This rotation in perspective affirmed the legitimacy of the world view of the oppressor, which sought to present subordination as a normative order. The oppressed began to recognize the "right" of the oppressor to be dominant. This acceptance of subordination varied given the context and the circumstances but occupied significant psychic space in the oppressed's world view. Compared with the beginning stages of oppression, subordination was no longer determined by overwhelming violence and force but by the relative degree to which the subordinated group accepted the historiography, sacred beliefs, normative images, and social relationships that were now defined for them. A key element of cultural hegemony was that progress for the subordinated group meant the uncritical assimilation and regurgitation of the conquering culture. Creativity, criticism, theorizing, theologizing--in short, reality construction--were left to the oppressor. Cultural hegemony tends to preempt intellectual production and material production; it negates self-development.[3]

The relationship of the subordinated group to the imperial group is complicated by internal processes of stratification. All strata internal to the dominating ethnic or racial group are not equally involved in the subordinating process. Within the dominating "race" there are ruling classes, internal conflicts between the rulers and the ruled, and competition for ruling class ascendency among privileged groups. This means that strata within the dominating race may seek alliances with the dominated race in order to gain a better competitive position relative to other groups or strata within the dominating race.[4] Nevertheless, within an existing symbolic system of racial and cultural supremacy, members of the socially and historically defined dominating group are born into a cultural matrix that perpetuates their normative sense of racial superiority. The dominating group is not, as a matter of course, automatically capable of perceiving its own deeply felt and sacredly held beliefs in the right to dominate and to shape the ideological world of the dominated. As Franz Fanon would have us understand, the racist in a racist society is normal.[5] As a consequence, there must be a stimulus for the various strata of the dominating group to recognize and comprehend the racialist, supremacist, exploitative, mythological, and oppressive dimensions of the social reality they support and revere.

Stratification also comes into play for the oppressed group and is expressed for the African American through the prototypical plantation experience. The system of chattel slavery was essentially organized around the productive unit of the plantation. As slavery evolved from a purely economic institution to a social one, a system of stratification emerged that extended degrees of status and privilege to the slave population, and, no doubt, affected their life chances. The organization of work, the system of White supremacy and racial etiquette, and miscegenation (which involved the sexual exploitation of African women) all contributed to this status/stratification system. Field slaves roughly constituted the masses and lowest stratum. Domestic slaves, who were more likely to be of mixed parentage (the offspring of sexual unions between the slave owner and the enslaved African women), gained greater facility with the slave owner's culture because of their social closeness to whites (in terms of interaction), the functional requirement to raise the slave owner's children, and the responsibility and obligation to attend to the intimate personal and domestic affairs of the slave owner. This group, in a relative sense, also had access to better clothing, shelter, and food. Artisans, or African slaves who performed the skilled jobs on the plantation, held a similarly privileged status relative to the field slave.[6]

The point, however, is that the plantation structure eventually developed a stratification system that distributed status based roughly on color and physiognomy, levels of acculturation, and type of work. Because a premium was placed on "looking and acting white" (that is, acquiring European aristocratic culture), and because one's location in the organization of work offered real differences in the quality of life, a synthesis occurred between the status system based on color and culture and the job one performed.[7] These systems paralleled and reinforced one another. Gender also played a role, as it could determine the kind of work one performed. Also, sexual exploitation was an ever-present problem for women, and negation of masculine authority was a perennial problem for men. The way in which Black men and women were exploited often pitted them against one another as White male and female imperialists and supremacists attempted to define African male and female roles to meet their needs and to preserve their privileged status. One cannot overlook, however, the continuation of status determinants that African people brought with them from Africa and that were maintained within the slave community. These determinants included a high regard for elders, family, children, religious and spiritual leaders, and healers.[8]

The plantation experience remains an important prototype for understanding the character of cultural hegemony for African Americans. It accounts for the fusion of culture, race, and class in African American subordination. It explains the insidious nature of color stratification leading to racial self-hatred and intra-racial conflict, and it reveals the processes by which the superordinate group seeks to define the issues and people of importance for African American people. Also, we find the basis for understanding how a system of White supremacy differentially directs oppression based on gender and destroys male/female relationships among African Americans.[9] The complexities of these relationships continue to reveal themselves as subsequent historical phases (rural life, migration, urban life, and posturban life) transform the relatively undifferentiated status system of the plantation into more complex stratification configurations.

Even though the whole of the slave community was made subordinate, the system of status conferral created by plantation life permitted more efficient social control through differentiating a system of slave overseers and leaders selected and legitimated by the slave owners (ruling stratum). The mind set and consciousness of this imposed administrative and leadership stratum represented degrees of marginality. Marginality as a condition reflects the quality of psychic acculturation that ties the self-image and self-worth of the African to the dehumanizing world view of a normative White supremacist culture. This psychic enslavement is symbolized by the need for White approval. It represents the level of alienation that the African American has from the self and the degree to which the oppressed support their own oppression. Currently, the problem of marginality exists among all strata of African Americans and forms a central tension in Black life. In sum, however, the plantation experience and its prototypical relationships point to the way in which a new social context affected the preservation of old ideals (an African-based social heritage) in contradistinction to the emergence of ideals based upon an evolving White supremacist reality.

The emergence of a new social heritage was affected by the way in which an organized life developed among the slave population, and of necessity, religion played an integral part. Despite the debate over the degree of African culture retained among African slaves in the Americas, E. Franklin Frazier's classic work on the Black church clearly identifies the imperial role of European religion.[10] Frazier stated:

> It is our position that it was not what remained of African culture or African religious experience but the Christian religion that provided the basis of social cohesion. It follows then that in order to understand the religion of the slaves, one must study the influence of Christianity in creating solidarity among a people who

lacked social cohesion and a structured social life.[11]

Again, recognizing the survival of African expressive forms, LeRoi Jones (Amiri Baraka) concluded in his classic work, *Blues People*, that "the Christianity of the slave represented a movement away from Africa."[12]

Historian John Blassingame observed that

the white church quickly emerged as the key institution which had to be analyzed in order to understand the most critical aspects of Southern antebellum society. The pervasiveness of guilt among the planters, the acculturation of the bondsman, the evolution of marriage and family life in the quarters, the education, treatment and personality development of the slave all hinged, to some degree, on the activities of Southern white churches.[13]

Historian Albert Raboteau supported Blassingame when he asserted that "from the very beginning of the Atlantic slave trade, conversion of the slaves to Christianity was viewed by the emerging nations of Western Christendom as a justification for enslavement of Africans."[14]

Sterling Stuckey's extraordinary work, *Slave Culture*, affirms that cultural contradictions and ethnic negation were stimulated by the imposition of European Christianity on New World Africans, slave and "free." However, his analysis shows that cultural hegemony contributed to African ethnic homogenization, producing the potential for pan-African linkages among New World Africans. European religion was indeed a great force for cultural negation, but it first became Africanized before it was absorbed to the extent that it replaced an African consciousness but not an African spirituality. Stuckey does a masterful job identifying the nuances of African culture in the New World as Africanity persisted behind the oppressive veneer of European sacred, mythological, and supremacist symbol systems. This enduring Africanity, in my view, constituted the seeds of rebirth and rehumanization that produced, among other things, distinctive epistemological concerns. Further, this persistent Africanity, found most strongly among the folk, became a powerful stimulus for nationalist impulses.[15]

European Christianity, with its attendant ethnocentrism and racialist underpinnings, was central to the symbol imperialism that became a foundation for the establishment of cultural hegemony.[16] This phenomenon was buttressed by the profound role that religion has in the formation and maintenance of identity, the establishment of in-groups and out-groups, most notably by defining those people who are supposed to be chosen or validated by God and those who are not, and the relative power that sacred beliefs have in sustaining and perpetuating various patterns of social organization. God as an objectification of the self and religion as a projection of the natural order of things become extraordinary tools for cultural hegemony because the imperialist group uses religion to extend legitimacy to its exploitative and hegemonic designs.

European Christianity, despite its humanitarian traditions, has always had a central role in the genesis and perpetuation of racist ideologies, particularly White supremacy, and was used to galvanize imperial beliefs regarding the "right" of one people to exploit, rule, and oppress non-White peoples in general and African peoples in particular.[17] The effect of imposing one's religion on another, especially when the religion embodies and validates White supremacist thinking, is to convince the victimized Africans of their kinship with the oppressor while extending the idea of the "natural right" of the oppressor to rule. Acceptance by the victims is uneven, however, because there is variation in how the victims interpret the religion(s) of the oppressor. Nevertheless, as long as the right to define God remains with the imperial group and fundamental theological norms are not breached completely, the oppressing group will sustain significant power and legitimacy to define the identity and status of the oppressed. As a consequence, the victimized will even protect the power and privilege of their masters in their zeal to preserve the "sacred structures" that they now believe define the natural order of things, that is, God's will.[18]

Language, as the overt manifestation of cognitive processes, has an important role in the process by which cultural hegemony seeks to diminish the traditions of the dominated and to alter their previous ways of seeing and understanding phenomena. Slaves quickly learned that they could not speak their native languages--or speak freely, once they learned European languages--in front of their oppressors, who made every effort to control their consciousness and symbolic world. The negation and control of language required the expropriation of the power of self-definition, that is, the ability to define and create a world with one's self at the center. This process meant that social reality became expressed for the oppressed as a fundamentally dialectical tension--a psychic struggle that occurred as an obligation of the process of cultural hegemony, in contradistinction to the human process of self-definition and self-elevation. Thus, the survival of African linguistic structures, meanings, and stylistic forms of communication met head-on the forces of cultural hegemony.

African American language forms, in relationship to mainstream society, remain self-energizing, improvisational, and cryptic.[19] These forms flow from the character of the dialogue among African Americans and are shaped by African cultural survivals and the social realities of everyday life. However, as African American language forms are expropriated by mainstream America and wrenched of their original meaning and context, further linguistic innovation takes place. This process is similar to the experience of African American musicians, who perennially find their cultural products absorbed, negated, and redefined by a White-controlled music and communications industry. Garofola, for example, observed "a racist pattern . . . in American music whereby a style that is pioneered by black artists eventually comes to be popularized, dominated and even defined by whites as if it were their own."[20] The similarity between the processes affecting

African American language and music is not accidental, however, because language and music are structurally related in African culture and remain so in the American context, where African American expressive forms represent profoundly profitable and trend-setting contributions to American popular culture.

The above process of cultural absorption, negation, and redefinition prototypically emerged with the minstrel tradition. During the antebellum period, the minstrel tradition evolved from White performers imitating Black, primarily slave, performers on the plantations. However, because White performers and audiences viewed Black culture through the prism of their own ethnocentric world, which included the need to portray Africans as inferior, they transformed Black cultural products into distorted remnants of their original forms. The minstrel tradition, a comedic form of music, dance, and stylized repartee, which was done in blackface, depicted Blacks as grotesque distortions of humanity. The result, however, was that White performers delivered their versions of Black expressive culture to White audiences in ways that were acceptable to the White supremacist sensibilities imbedded in mainstream culture.[21]

The late and venerable anthropologist St. Clair Drake has observed that "since black communities have been, and are, relatively powerless, their cultural products are constantly being `co-opted' for ends other than those they set for themselves."[22] Because African Americans have essentially been cut off from ownership and control of mass media and institutions of ideation, their cultural products, particularly music, language, dance, and stylistic norms, are absorbed into the broader White-controlled commodity system, redefined, and used to advance the economic dominance of mainstream institutions at the expense of African American institutional and cultural development. In this example of cultural hegemony, African Americans lack sufficient control over the commercial use of their culture. They also lack sufficient capability to preserve progressive cultural traditions beyond the co-opting forces of commercial exploitation.

To reiterate, cultural hegemony, as a type of oppression, developed as a consequence of African enslavement by Europeans who sought cheap sources of labor to exploit the riches of newly found lands. The incentive to engage in slave trading grew as the economic demand for labor increased to mine precious metals and to develop systems of mass crop production, which provided raw materials for European manufacturers. The resulting triangular relationship between Europe, Africa, and the Americas gave tremendous stimulus to Western capitalism and Europe's industrial revolution, while dooming African peoples to underdevelopment and dependency.[23] Economic incentive stimulated an extant color prejudice and xenophobia with religious roots that emerged as a full-blown racist ideology of White supremacy and African inferiority. Thus, even though capitalism and industrialization resulted in internal class divisions among Europeans, there was the concomitant ideological and structural elevation of one "race" above another. Additionally, European enslavers practiced cultural imperialism in order to bring about accommodation and conformity among subjugated populations. African languages and religions were systematically suppressed. Talk and memories of an African past were discouraged to negate historical consciousness and to undermine the basis for unity.

In the above context and as the proportion of Africans born in the New World increased, a profound cognitive shift occurred that tended to dislocate Africans from their ethnic roots. However, the degree of dislocation varied and became a function of a number of factors affecting the level of social isolation from European cultural imperialism. The size of the plantation, the severity of the seasoning process, the length of the slave trade, the organization of work on the plantation, and the imposition of Roman Catholicism relative to Protestant variants of European Christianity (both carriers of European somatic norms, color prejudice, and supremacist thinking) were central among the factors affecting levels of African cultural survivals and consciousness.[24]

Thus, from the very beginning of the forced sojourn of Africans into the New World, the relationship between social organization and culture became central to understanding the relative penetration and potency of European cultural imperialism. Therefore, explicating the relationship between social organization and culture is fundamental to revealing the paradigmatic structure and process of cultural hegemony. Also, there developed a deep and pervasive tradition in European and Euro-American scholarship that distorted social science and historiography to construct and preserve the myth of White supremacy and African inferiority.[25] As a consequence, a countervailing struggle emerged to transcend the cognitive slavery of White supremacy. It is in this context that we locate the evolution of a Black intellectual tradition and African-centered thought.

AFRICAN-CENTERED THOUGHT

People, as a matter of course, place themselves at the center of their universe. They seek to understand others in terms of how they understand themselves. They also seek to understand how phenomena external to their shared sense of territoriality and experience affect their well-being and survival. Culture is the bond that provides a collective consciousness and a common center through which and from which these phenomena are observed and interpreted. Thus, given the cultural moorings of a people, they can be said to have a center, a perspective, and a world view.

Because of the problem of cultural hegemony, African Americans and the African diaspora have found the issue of perspective to be perennially problematic. Africans were shaken from their cultural foundations. The cataclysmic experience of chattel slavery, the basis for cultural hegemony, produced historical discontinuity and preempted normative culture building through a de-centering process.[26] Even though the experience of oppression and exploitation required movement away from an African center, it was this experience that produced the conditions for the emergence of an African-centered consciousness. Thus, the problem of perspective emerged as the fundamental issue shaping the evolution of a Black intellectual tradition. Again, we have the dialectic that I described earlier as African Americans sought to produce knowledge and culture but were structurally confronted with the contradictions spawned by racial and cultural oppression. The resulting historical imperatives generated the need to extend self-conscious attention to the idea of African-centered thought.

As I indicated previously, a major force in the decentering process was the imposition of European Christianity. In North America, by the nineteenth century, an increasing presence of second-, third-, and fourth-generation Africans born in the New World contributed to the decline of linguistic and cultural barriers to the acculturating force of European Christianity, particularly as the African slave trade began to wane.[27] In addition, European imperialists had always viewed the conversion of Africans to European Christianity as a justification for their enslavement.[28] They pushed slavery as a positive action that was sanctioned by biblical scriptures. The goal of the European enslaver was to sustain a social order and a system of production based on the mutual cooperation of master and slave.[29] Of course, Europeans had their debates over whether or not slavery was compatible with their Christian traditions, and whether conversion meant manumission.[30] The slave system won out, however, but religious proselytizing played the greatest role in acculturating the African.[31] The revivalism of the 1740s Great Awakening was one important impetus to European Christian proselytizing among the slave populations, and by the nineteenth century, a European Christian consciousness had gained a significant presence among African slaves.[32] Historian John Blassingame also points out that Europeans further encouraged the Christianization of African slaves to halt the Africanizing effects that slaves were having on European children. Further, the teaching of the English language to African slaves became synonymous with the teaching of European Christianity.[33] Thus, slave and master, although occupying different positions in the social structure, began to share a common theology (social heritage) through which to interpret their worlds.[34]

The contradictions, however, became too great as the slave system of White supremacy attempted to force African American slaves into the psychic space that it defined while maintaining an uncommon, separate, and subordinate social space for Black people. African Americans, slave and free, began to rediscover symbolic foundations for a redemptive African-centered consciousness. The irony of this rediscovery is that it occurred as a consequence of interpreting the biblical messages that were intended to bring conformity and docility. African American exegesis of biblical scriptures became the foundation for the rebirth of African-centered thought. Instead of learning to be good slaves by forgetting about Africa, some African Americans realized that many of the places discussed in the sacred text held in so high esteem by their White oppressors were in Africa and that many of the people were quite properly African. Biblical imagery permeated the sacred and secular oral expression of nineteenth-century African Americans, and many slaves drew parallels between their oppression and the myth of the Jewish flight from Egypt. However, it was the rediscovery of Africa (Egypt and Ethiopia) through the Bible and the idea that Ethiopia had prophetic significance that stimulated a revolutionary African consciousness.[35]

It was not long before some African Americans began to realize that the ancient Greeks and Romans owed a debt to Africa. For example, George Washington Williams' pioneering work, *History of the Negro Race in America*, published in 1883, devoted the first chapter to biblical analysis demonstrating the centrality of African people to the human family. In Chapter Two this work established the antiquity of African people, their Egyptian presence, their Asian presence, most notably in India and Japan, and their Greco-Roman presence. Williams argued for an African-centered historiography that saw civilization advance in Africa from the Ethiopians to the Egyptians to the Greeks and to the Romans. Speaking of the dynastic period, Williams stated, "We find that slavery was not, at this time, confined to any particular race of people," a clear effort to vindicate Black people from the White supremacist myth that Africans always existed in a perpetual state of servitude.[36] Earlier, in 1848, Henry Highland Garnet, using biblical and classical Greek references, established Egypt as a Black civilization. Garnet also argued for the importance of Ethiopia based upon its role in biblical prophecy, and he cited numerous examples of what he called "the ancient fame of our ancestors."[37]

As St. Clair Drake has convincingly argued, the Bible and its African referents gave African Americans the fuel to vindicate themselves. They were not inferior people with no past or accomplishments. Also, the Bible promised redemption. Drake observed that

Black people under slavery turned to the Bible to "prove" that black people, Ethiopians, were powerful and respected when white men in Europe were barbarians; Ethiopia came to symbolize all of African . . . [and] "Ethiopianism" became an energizing myth.[38]

Also, as suggested by Drake, a Black intellectual tradition had its roots in "vindicating the Negro," that is, African American efforts to correct stereotypes and set the record straight.[39] Thus, from its biblical roots, a pronounced tradition of scholarship, based initially on African American historical research that established an African frame of reference, began in the early nineteenth century, reached maturity in the 1890s, and has continued with episodic prominence to the present.[40] These nineteenth-century vindicationist efforts represented the rebirth of African-centered thought.

A current thrust in the direction of delimiting African American studies is the idea of Afrocentrism or, for some, Afrocentricity. The concepts of African-centered thought, an African world view, and an African-centered curriculum are also in use. Whatever nomenclature such efforts take in the future, they all evolved from a common vindicationist tradition, and they all involve, among other things, erecting corrective, reconstructive, and liberating scholarship around a way of seeing based upon recognition of one's distinctive location in socio-historical time, experience, and discourse. Because of the problem of cultural hegemony, the issue of perspective remains at the core of an evolving Black intellectual tradition. As a consequence, this tradition has placed greater scrutiny on the axiological dimensions of knowledge, with particular emphasis on the limits of scientistic thinking, the social and revolutionary implications of shifts in paradigms, and the particularistic and hegemonic aspects of Eurocentric knowledge as opposed to its universal claims.

Contemporary discussion of Afrocentrism or Afrocentricity might suggest that it is a recent concept as opposed to a evolving tradition that has taken various forms. I have already noted its nineteenth-century vindicationist roots, which gained maturity in the 1890s. This maturity reached greater development, prominence, and expression during the Harlem Renaissance of the 1920s. The Renaissance period of concentrated, self-conscious reflection was symbolized by Alain Locke's philosophy of the "New Negro." Locke, a leader of the Renaissance movement, spoke of the "Old Negro" as a creation of oppression and the "New Negro" as self-conscious and unashamed. This "New Negro" represented a shift toward self-definition and humanistic elevation. According to Locke, "the mind of the Negro seems suddenly to have slipped from under the tyranny of social intimidation and to be shaking off the psychology of imitation and implied inferiority."[41] Locke also observed that "up to the present one may adequately describe the Negro's `inner objectives' as an attempt to repair a damaged group psychology and reshape a warped social perspective."[42] Similar to Dubois's double-consciousness thesis, Locke recognized that "little social or self-understanding" could come from incorporating the perspectives of White America about Black people.[43]

The late 1960s' Black Power, Black Consciousness and Black Arts movements saw the reemergence of collective reflection on the critical importance of perspective in comprehending the African American experience. The corresponding Black Studies movement also stimulated Black scholars to redefine the substance and orientation of the academic disciplines in which they worked and were trained. In sociology such efforts were reflected in the publication of Joyce Ladner's anthology, *The Death of White Sociology*, in which she stated:

> The purpose of this anthology is to present a set of statements that attempt to define the emerging field of Black sociology and to establish basic premises, guidelines, concerns and priorities which can be useful to those who have an interest in understanding and applying these to their study and work.[44]

Robert Staples also made significant contributions toward defining a Black sociology in his book, *Black Sociology*. He argued that such a discipline proceeds from the premise that Blacks share a different physical environment or social experience.[45] Thus, Staples' recognition of the need to understand social reality from where Black people stand is again an expression of the problem of perspective.[46] Reginald Jones' anthology, *Black Psychology*, and Addison Gayle's anthology, *The Black Aesthetic*, were similar efforts to transcend the decentering effects of cultural hegemony.[47]

In the late 1960s Harold Cruse revisited the problem of perspective for Black historical research. He linked the issue of perspective to the question of which historical phases were most responsible for altering the character and context of African American culture.[48] In this sense, historical phases represented specific forms of social organization that transformed the lives of African Americans in distinctive ways. Despite the clear absence of African referents in Cruse's theorizing, his approach is decisively African-centered because it indicates that one must pay attention to key phenomena that affect the survival and development of African American people. Some may overlook Cruse's Afrocentrism because he argues for the centrality of the transformative power of the

American experience. However, Cruse's stance in terms of priority and his conscious attachment to a Black intellectual tradition makes him clearly African-centered. Borrowing from Karenga, Cruse's approach is unambiguously rooted in "the cultural image and human interests of African people."[49]

Finally, we should acknowledge that the epistemological concerns of the 1960s paralleled a struggle to build "Black universities." This struggle called for the creation of Black-controlled educational institutions that would maintain African-centered curriculums. The central ideals of this movement were to embody and convey knowledge that was psychologically liberating and politically and economically empowering. Among these efforts were The Institute of the Black World in Atlanta, Malcolm X Community College in Chicago, the Communiversity in Chicago, and Malcolm X Liberation University in Durham, North Carolina.[50]

Afrocentric or African-centered thought is solidly embedded within a history and tradition that can be understood by recognizing the internal dialectics and contradictions of cultural hegemony over historical time. Afrocentric or African-centered thought exists regardless of whether or not it is called Afrocentric or African-centered. It is the intellectual tradition and the historical imperatives to which it is attached that are important. In an earlier work in which I sketched out the foundations of an Afrocentric social science, I noted that Afrocentrism was the act of examining phenomena in terms of their relationship to the survival and prosperity of African peoples and that it is crucial to developing a social science approach within the context of African American studies as a discipline.[51] Again, the idea was to emphasize the importance of an epistemological center and such related historical imperatives as the need to transcend historical discontinuity, the need to engage in institution or culture building, the need to reconstruct a positive self-concept, and so on.

The development of the word "Afrocentric" was a product of the 1960s and 1970s ferment. For example, my own use of "Afrocentric" and

"Afrocentrism" was probably influenced by exposure to Professors Jacob Carruthers and Anderson Thompson during the mid-1970s at the Center for Inner City Studies in Chicago. These
scholars, and others, frequently spoke of an
Afrocentric or an African-centered world view.
However, Carruthers and Thompson, who were also
thoroughly steeped in the works of nineteenth-century vindicationist scholars, drew
heavily from contemporary vindicationist historians like John Henrik Clarke, Chancellor
Williams, Yosef ben-Jochannan, John G. Jackson,
Cheikh Anta Diop, and others. John Henrik
Clarke, for example, along with other Africana
historians, called for the "reconstruction of
African history and cultural studies along Afrocentric lines" as early as 1969.[52]

African-centered lexicon and theory developed
and sustained itself in other ways. Another context was an annual, national Black studies conference convened by Professor Armstead Allen and
held at Olive-Harvey College in Chicago. Since
1978 this invited conference has brought Black
scholars together from across the country to address themes central to Africana survival. Numerous institutions, publications, and independent Black scholars expanded the boundaries of
African-centered inquiry. One such institutional
formation was the publication, *Negro Digest*,
whose name later became *Black World*. This
monthly journal was published by Johnson Publications and, during its most significant period
as a scholarly organ, was edited by the late
Hoyt Fuller. *Negro Digest/Black World* was one of
the most important outlets for African-centered
discourse through the 1960s until its demise in
1976. There are other examples, but we need only
recognize the continuing presence of an enduring
African-centered intellectual tradition in numerous Black communities to which countless people have contributed and helped to develop.

Recognizing this tradition, we should not
confuse Afrocentric or African-centered nomenclature and the like with some recent discovery.[53] We do, however, need to identify the tradition's variegated expressions, contradictions,
and progressive and retrogressive aspects. For
example, Afrocentrism is not simply the inclu-

sion of African rhetoric in a linguistic sense, or the symbolic and prominent expression of traditional African cultures. African-centered thought has evolved, however, from its early vindicationist expressions. It has incorporated a much larger knowledge base, extended and refined its methodological tools, and penetrated the boundaries of a broader spectrum of disciplines. One must be careful not to limit the conception and construction of Afrocentric paradigms, for the Afrocentric or African-centered component of knowledge production acts as a guide for how to look and how to see, that is, where to put one's feet and where and how to begin inquiry. The dialectics of cultural hegemony stimulated the rebirth of African-centered thought, which, in addition to representing a shift toward a more normative world view devoid of mental enslavement, offers a broadly humanizing and liberating quality to the production of knowledge in general.

One important distinction that can be found in Afrocentric inquiry is the difference between a focus on African culture as the center or source of values and ideals and a priority focus on conditions that affect the survival and prosperity of African peoples, including the diaspora. The Africa-as-an-ideal focus involves embracing aspects of African cultures as a model for behavior. An African-people focus requires analysis of the experiences and conditions affecting the development of continental and diasporic Africans. The latter focus implies a concern for social and institutional development; the former stresses African values. These values may be considered central to an existing African American culture or personality, or their preservation or reintroduction may be considered necessary to stimulate and revitalize human development and liberation.[54] Thus, Afrocentric inquiry exhibits significant variation, and we must be careful not to place undue limits on its expression.[55]

Another issue facing African-centered formulations is the problem of metaphysical dualism. Metaphysical dualism is the tradition of dichotomizing essential qualities found in nature and in human interaction and embracing one or the other as reality or as universally dominant. In this sense, everything is posed as opposites that are essentially antagonistic. An alternative would be to understand these qualities not as conflicting opposites but as distinctively different but necessary manifestations of an interconnected reality. Indeed, we may find that a seemingly opposite quality is necessary in order to preserve the whole, as in the concepts of the male and female principles, which are necessary to perpetuate life.

This philosophical point of view has been posed as the unity of opposites and as an epistemological position that is wholly compatible with a Black, African-centered, or Afrocentric perspective. Unfortunately, this position has sometimes been used in a reactionary manner, that is, to stand in opposition to White culture and not as a critical and accurate assessment of Black culture. In fact, the Black Consciousness movement and Black Studies movement have been clouded and replete with metaphysical dualism, particularly in the social sciences, with the introduction of the Frazier/Herskovits debate, the race/class debate, the cultural nationalism/revolutionary nationalism debate, the conflict theory/equilibrium theory debate, and the weak family/strong family debate.[56] It is not the case that recognition of these disparate qualities is not valid; rather, to always assume that one or the other is the "truth" is retrogressive. Conceptually and paradigmatically, metaphysical dualism negates a much-needed focus suggested by the metaproblem of cultural hegemony, that is, a concern for analyzing the interaction between opposite qualities and for examining the context in which these interactions and subsequent transformations take place.

On a concrete level, we see metaphysical dualism expressed within some current Afrocentric claims. For example, there is the claim that African and African American cultures are more holistic than White cultures. However, some scholars contradict this claim by positioning themselves as the opposite of whatever they deem to be a characteristic of White culture. An example would be some of the discussion on African

American learning styles.[57] One argument is that because African Americans have retained African culture, they exhibit relational learning styles, but Euro-Americans exhibit analytic learning styles. Some Afrocentric theorists believe that this presumed propensity toward relational learning styles is positive because it validates that African cultural ideals have survived and have not been destroyed by the horrors and challenges of American slavery, racism, and oppression. The irony is that racist White scholars have said for years that Africans and African Americans do not have the capacity, culturally or genetically, for abstract and mathematical thinking, a characteristic, presumably, of an analytic orientation.[58]

If African and African American cultures are holistic, they should exhibit both relational and analytic orientations but, perhaps, in distinctive configurations. Thus, a more accurate analysis would reveal that a problem emerges when conditions, or as I would prefer, existing forms of social organization, create an imbalance in relational as compared with analytic development. Indeed, people probably have, on a random basis, a propensity toward one style or the other apart from culture or race. I do not want to suggest, however, that the analysis of learning styles does not have relevance for understanding African American academic achievement. I only want to caution against severe forms of reductionism that overly dichotomize social reality and that overlook alternative explanations.

Further, some Eurocentric social scientists have argued for the biogenetic basis of presumably inferior and negative personality traits among African Americans; some Afrocentric scholars, particularly psychologists and psychiatrists, have argued for the biogenetic basis of a positive African personality. Where these positive traits seem not to exist, Afrocentric theorists postulate that they have been altered by environmental and social conditions but nevertheless constitute normal (natural) components of a core African personality.[59] For example, one theory states that melanin is a key component of a persistent spirituality among African

Americans. However, biogenetic theories of Black personality have yet to be validated and fully elaborated. If, for example, the presence of melanin is a key factor in the African personality, what does this mean for African Americans who carry smaller quantities of melanin (light-skinned Blacks relative to dark-skinned Blacks)? And how has miscegenation affected the African personality? Also, in what ways do environmental or social conditions mask or alter a "true" African personality? The hypothesis that melanin provides the basis for a more elevated human personality is an important one for research but runs into the problem of metaphysical dualism without adequate validation. However, the idea of a biogenetic basis for a more elevated human personality among people of color stands Eurocentric racist thought on its head.

The confluence of African-centered scholarship, I believe, suggests that African values are either preserved through specific configurations of social organization or reconstructed through a process of self-conscious reflection, identification, and revitalization. Psychologist Naim Akbar has cautioned against oppositional reaction to racist Eurocentric postulates. Akbar has also stressed the universal quality of African-based ideals and that an Africentric model "does not exclude in its fundamental assumptions the possibilities for normative activity on the parts of people of other ethnic origins."[60] Thus, African ideals, which include an emphasis on collectivity, spirituality, harmony and balance, are available to others. The point, however, is that Western hegemony over non-White peoples reflects a deformed philosophy of human existence and human essence.

Transcending other purely biogenetic explanations, psychiatrist Frances Welsing gives some insight into the psycho-cultural and a psycho-social basis for the deformed philosophy of White supremacy, which she persuasively argues is rooted in Western (White) self-alienation. Welsing states: "The deep pervading fear of *white genetic annihilation* in the white psyche has caused a neurotic (unconscious) preoccupation with genes, genetic material, and those aspects of the human anatomy that either contain or transport the genetic material in the sexual act."[61] For Welsing, this fear of genetic annihilation by people who call themselves White, when confronted with the global majority of people with color, has contributed to a profound sense of inadequacy and aggression toward any people defined as non-White (which she says includes Jews and Gypsies).

AFROCENTRIC FORMS

I have suggested that the rebirth of African-centered thought was necessitated by the same social forces that prescribed its death, that is, the problem of cultural hegemony. Afrocentrism, Afrocentricity, and the like are efforts to grapple with the resulting problem of perspective. However, the particulars of the decentering process for African peoples in general and for African Americans in particular revolve around the issue of culture, its disorganization and its reconstruction. African American studies, taken in their totality, are about cultural analysis and contributing to a theory of culture regarding the survival and development of Africana people.[62] The evolution of African-centered thought reflects such a focus and is expressed in the breadth and diversity of Afrocentric forms. Thus, we need to identify the more prominent expressions of Afrocentric forms to cast further light on the internal dynamics of culture building and the metaproblem of cultural hegemony.

We have already identified a major division in African-centered thought: One trend focuses on the conditions of African survival and development, and the other is on ideals and values for behavior. Afrocentric forms frequently stress one or both of these concerns, but the variations are much greater. Major expression of these forms include the following: a Kemetic (or ancient Egyptian) focus, a world presence focus, a West African focus, a reconstructivist focus, a bicultural focus, and a White supremacy and comparative societies focus.

Also, we have observed the vindicationist tradition eloquently described by St. Clair

Drake.[63] This tradition, which sought to vindicate African people from the White supremacist myth that Black people contributed nothing to civilization and always lived in a state of static existence and perpetual servitude, became the foundation and stimulus for subsequent Afrocentric forms. The vindicationist tradition evolved from biblical exegesis to a reliance on the Greek classics, which gave unbiased recognition to Africa, to a growing reliance on an expanding body of archaeological data that clearly establish Africa as the cradle of civilization. Furthermore, African people are now without question civilizers and culture builders who had a profound impact on numerous world civilizations, including Europe and its Western edifice. From the vindicationist base came the Kemetic and world presence traditions.

Vindicationism necessarily did several things. It spawned a new historiography of world civilization building with Africa at the center. It placed the experience of chattel slavery within a context that clearly illustrated that 300 to 400 hundred years of slavery was but one episode in a continuous history of thousands (even millions) of years. As a consequence, vindicationism restimulated a key component of culture building, and that is the need to establish historical continuity and consciousness.

Kemet, the name of ancient Egypt, became a focal point because European scholars who were erecting the myth of White supremacy went to great lengths to define this civilization as non-African.[64] White scholars, but not all, were determined to deny that Kemetic people were Black, and, for all practical purposes, Kemet was effectively removed from African history. In modern times it was the late Cheikh Anta Diop who came to symbolize the charge to rescue Kemet from grave-robbing European imperialists.[65] However, Diop, despite his pioneering work, was part of an earlier international tradition. Nevertheless, Kemetic research and the rescue of Kemet for African history have become an essential component of the Afrocentric paradigm. However, Kemetic research has expanded well beyond its vindicationist roots. Its development has cast a much broader light on the role of Africa in world religions, science and technology, ethical discourse, and so on, and provides African peoples with a glimpse of what is needed to recover the elements of humanity ripped away by chattel slavery, colonialism, neocolonialism, segregation, apartheid, and racism.[66]

The Kemetic focus necessarily brought into sharper view the world presence focus. The world presence emphasis also had vindicationist roots because it challenged the White supremacist myth that African people never explored other lands, had the capacity to travel the oceans and seas (and, perhaps, skies), or carried enriching culture to other societies. Also, it established that Africans could come as peaceful settlers and as conquerors. Ivan Van Sertima's *They Came Before Columbus* symbolizes the contemporary world presence focus, but, again, his work stems from an earlier and broader tradition.[67] Works that look at the African presence in Asia and Europe or analyze the impact of the Moorish conquest of Spain on Western development are part of the world presence tradition. Blacks as carriers of culture, even during prehistoric periods, are integral features of this body of knowledge.[68] An important characteristic of the African world presence tradition is that it demonstrates how pervasive and broad-based African movement and interactions were on a global scale prior to the development of racial or chattel slavery.[69] This Afrocentric tradition signifies a pre-slavery African diaspora, in contradistinction to a postslavery diaspora spawned by European expansion and exploitation.

The West African focus points to the fact that Africans who were brought to the Americas in bondage were primarily from West Africa. Correspondingly, the question of cultural roots and cultural survival required an analysis of West African cultures. The West African traditions that survived seem to find their strongest expression in cognitive as opposed to material and institutional culture. This is understandable, since New World experiences quickly altered the material and institutional reality of Africans but could not affect deeply structured cultural components as easily. Linguistic studies that show the persistence of a West African syntax in

African American speech patterns, including fragments of a West African lexicon, and the application of African meanings to New World experiences have been central to the West African focus. The survival of African culture in music, dance, storytelling, religious culture, aesthetic, stylistic and expressive norms, and cognitive orientation have provided a rich and fertile ground for research.[70] They have also stimulated important theorizing toward the development of a Black psychology.[71] The ethics, values, and ideals of traditional African societies have also come under scrutiny as desirable if not extant components of African American culture.[72] They are either posed as key elements of an existing cultural matrix or as elements that must be reconstructed. These positions exist in some tension since all acknowledge that chattel slavery severely altered traditional West African cultures, not to mention the effects of other historical forces like migration, urbanization, integration, and posturban life. If properly understood, a key imperative of African American studies as a discipline is to provide cultural theory to assess such transformations. Nevertheless, the fact that one consensus holds that traditional West African cultures contain, for diasporic Africans, positive values and ideals that have been destroyed or submerged in the New World context, has led to the reconstructivist focus among Afrocentric forms.

The reconstructivist tradition is a historical imperative that acknowledges the fact that African institutions and ideals have been altered by European oppression and exploitation in such a way as to stifle human freedom and development. Thus, it is necessary to reconstruct African American culture in order to release its liberating and transformative potential. This imperative is at the root of cultural nationalism, in its secular and religious forms, and speaks to very deep cultural contradictions brought on by a history of domination. Episodic periods of self-conscious cultural reconstruction such as Moorish Science, the Harlem Renaissance, the Garvey Movement, the Nation of Islam, the Hebrew Israelite Nation, the Black Consciousness and Black Arts movements of the 1960s and 1970s, and the like are expressions of the reconstructivist imperative.[73] Maulana Karenga's Kawaida theory, which poses ethical principles and a model for what Black people should become, is a further example of this tradition.[74] Reconstructivism is self-conscious culture building. Today, as a continuation of this tradition, Afrocentric scholars are not only looking to traditional West African cultures as a source for redemptive ideals and values, but they are also looking to Kemet as the classical model for ethical discourse.[75] The reconstructivist imperative clearly points to the underlying forces of hegemony and the clash between a culture of slavery and a culture of liberation. The reconstructivist tradition embodies the problem of how the oppressed may rise above support for their own oppression.

Reconstructivism necessarily brings into focus the problem of biculturality, that is, the tension between living in a Black reality and a White-defined world.[76] African American culture is not wholly African but has been altered by the American milieu. Sometimes American culture is translated as White culture, but this is far from the truth. Europeans who came to the Americas had to adapt to a new environment, as did Africans, and American culture is as much a consequence of African influences as it is of European ones.[77] However, the problem for African Americans is the lack of institutional power that would give them the ability to define and express their cultural needs and goals.[78]

Also, there is the persistence of a slave culture, or that part of a shared American cultural experience that assigns legitimacy to Euro-American hegemonic norms. As I indicated earlier, Eurocentric religion, which played a strong role in the imperial process and in the establishment of White supremacy, is one aspect of this problem. Today mass media and other institutions of ideation continue to sustain the tension that exists within the reality of African American biculturality.[79] There is an extant system of rewards and punishments that discourages African American culture building and poses the problem of legitimacy, through which the behavioral processes of African Americans are systematically denied recognition and respect. Cedric Clark, now Sayed Malik Khatib, has written superbly on this issue in a classic analysis of the problem of legitimacy facing African Americans.[80]

The White supremacy and comparative societies focus is exemplified by the work of Dr. Frances Cress Welsing, who has developed a comprehensive theory of White supremacy. She observes that this is the only functional form of racism confronting African Americans.[81] Although her theory is not totally original, she is most identified with its elaboration and empirical verification. Welsing identifies White supremacy as a global problem facing all people who come to be defined as non-White. What is significant about Welsing's theorizing is that it poses White supremacy as a mental health problem that is based upon repressed feelings of fear and inadequacy. The behavioral logic of this repressed fear can only be understood by decoding the cultural symbols of Western (White) civilization. The White supremacy and comparative societies focus is a central and important Afrocentric form because it is clearly concerned with African survival while substantively directing itself toward an analysis of Western culture and global aggression. This focus highlights the reality that Black, African American, and Africana studies are structured by critical conceptual concerns and not by "Black" content. Also, Welsing's theory is one that illustrates an issue and an explanatory approach to which Eurocentric discourse has shown little propensity. Yet the basis, internal logic, and subsequent expression of White supremacy is a profound issue for most of the world's people. Finally, the global nature of White supremacy points to the critical importance of comparing Black (diasporic) societies and other non-White societies in order to understand the impact of and response to Western domination.[82]

The impetus behind each of the Afrocentric forms discussed above is the problem of cultural hegemony: the tendency by one culture to negate another for the purpose of exploitation and control. Thus, we have identified the hegemonic components of Eurocentric thought, but we may also posit the existence of nonhegemonic components. Consequently, the possibility for cultural tolerance and egalitarianism exists. Undoubtedly, there is a tradition of thought with Europe at its center in which we can assume the possibility exists for critical self-analysis, growth, transformation, and human liberation. This possibility we shall call a normative as opposed to a hegemonic alternative. In the case of Afrocentric thought, based upon the current socio-historical context, a hegemonic component is absent and is replaced by the problem of double-consciousness, the decentered state of cultural and psychic conflict brought on by the problem of cultural hegemony. For the African American, the impetus to recapture a center represents cultural reconstruction and movement toward a normative expression of knowledge. It is at this normative level that we may posit the possibility for greater inter-cultural harmony and for enlarging human knowledge for both Afrocentric and Eurocentric traditions. Moreover, the normative expression of Afrocentric thought signals transcendence of the dialectic of cultural hegemony.

SOCIAL ORGANIZATION AND CULTURE AS OBJECTS OF STUDY

Even though the representation of forms of thought are expressed as a dichotomy (normative versus double-consciousness), for African Americans there is one other significant analytical category: full acceptance of a European hegemonic consciousness. This is the state of total cultural negation, which we may refer to as assimilation. Returning to the plantation prototype, the level of African cultural negation was linked to the character of social organization. Sociological theorist Walter Wallace has keenly observed the importance of the interaction between social organization and culture for the study of African Americans.

Wallace noted that social organization and culture define the ways in which individuals and groups relate to one another. Social organization refers to habitual forms of interaction, and culture refers to regularities of shared subjective states. Despite their analytical distinctiveness, these concepts are related behaviorally. Wallace observed that many of the problems posed about African Americans argue for causal primacy for either social organization or culture.[83] For example, the question of whether White racism caused the enslavement of Africans or whether the enslavement of Africans caused White racism suggests that either subjective states (Western culture) contributed to a distinctive form or type of social organization (African slavery), or the reverse. Another issue is the primacy of race (culture) or class (social organization) in African American inequality. Further, the level and strength of surviving African culture is quite likely a function of the degree to which Africans were able to sustain a distinctive and supportive social organization.

Besides the interconnection between these two types of social phenomena, Wallace aptly noted that there are also levels of social phenomena. For example, there is the inter-personal (small groups), the inter-group or institutional, the inter-institutional or community, the inter-community or societal, and the inter-societal or international.[84] Social organization and culture are thus expressed at these various levels with diverse outcomes and possibilities. For example, when we pay attention to African American historical phases defined by slavery, rural life, urban and industrial life, and posturban life, we are focused on societal levels of social organization that may affect cultural forms at lower levels of social interaction. Institutionalized racism, for example, suggests that there are societal-level structures that perpetuate racial inequality despite the absence of prejudice at lower levels of social interaction. As I indicated previously, cultural negation, one side of the cultural dialectic of cultural hegemony, symbolized assimilation, an outcome that is hardly probable as long as African Americans maintain distinctive forms of social organization. Thus, a critical focus on the interrelationship between social organization and

culture, I believe, becomes one of the key theoretical concerns of African American studies.

SUMMARY: PARAMETERS OF AFRICAN AMERICAN STUDIES

I have argued that the problem of cultural
hegemony produced by European expansion, contact
with, and exploitation of African peoples has
posed a unique historical problem for institutional and cultural development for African
people in general and African Americans in particular. The particulars of the resulting cultural dialectic have formed the basis for a
Black intellectual tradition that spawned distinctive parameters for an evolving discipline
called Black, African American, or Africana
studies.

My discussion reveals how structure and process stimulate key epistemological issues. For
example, I have discussed the evolution of the
metaproblem of cultural hegemony and the plantation prototype, which illustrates how cultural
hegemony affects the organization of African
American life with respect to status configurations, marginality, and the process by which
leaders and values are defined for African Americans. I also noted the role of religion as an
imperial and fragmenting force (despite its cohesive and liberating potential) and its role,
along with language, in the cultural dialectic
facing African Americans. The minstrel model
points to the evolving and systemic tendency by
Euro-American culture to absorb, distort, and
redefine African American cultural forms. I have
also noted the role of social organization for
understanding cultural dislocation. I am not,
however, suggesting causal primacy for either
social organization or culture, and I am not
suggesting that they covary in some linear relationship. Studying how these phenomena are in-
terrelated is, however, important for generating
relevant cultural theory in the field.

We have been able to see how the dialectics
of cultural hegemony spawned the rebirth of an
African-centered intellectual tradition. I have
endeavored to show how the birth of this tradition transcends nomenclature and is linked to

relevant conditions of survival and development; related values, ideals, and ethical discourse; perspective (historiography and location); and historical imperatives associated with culture building. I noted that particular care is needed to guard against the problem of metaphysical dualism and to strive for a more holistic, contextual analysis. Also, the imperatives of cultural hegemony have produced variegated expressions of African-centered or Afrocentric theorizing. Cultural and artistic movements, efforts to reform the social sciences and humanities, and efforts to build Black universities are examples. Variations in Afrocentric forms have included the prototypical vindicationist tradition, the Kemetic focus, the world presence focus, the West African focus, the reconstructivist focus, the bicultural focus, and the White supremacy and comparative societies focus.

NOTES

1. See for example, E. Franklin Frazier, *Race and Culture Contacts in the Modern World* (Boston: Beacon Press, 1957); Vincent Bakpetu Thompson, *The Making of the African Diaspora in the Americas 1441-1900* (New York: Longman, 1987).

2. Detailed discussions of racism and White supremacy are given in St. Clair Drake, *Black Folk Here and There: An Essay in History and Anthropology,* 2 vols. (Los Angeles: University of California, Center for Afro-American Studies, 1987-1990); George M. Frederickson, *White Supremacy: A Comparative Study in American and South African History* (New York: Oxford University Press, 1981); Frances Cress Welsing, *The Isis Papers: The Keys to the Colors* (Chicago: Third World Press, 1991); Robert Staples, *The Urban Plantation: Racism and Colonialism in the Post Civil Rights Era* (Oakland, Calif.: Black Scholar Press, 1987).

3. Economic and cultural underdevelopment are addressed in Walter Rodney, *How Europe Underdeveloped Africa* (Dar-es-Salaam, Tanzania: Tanzania Publishing House, 1972); Harold Cruse, *Crisis of the Negro Intellectual* (New York:

William Morrow, 1967); Eric Williams, *Capitalism and Slavery* (New York: Capricorn, 1966).

4. See Lerone Bennett, Jr., *Confrontation Black and White* (Baltimore: Penguin, 1966).

5. Franz Fanon, *Toward the African Revolution* (New York: Grove Press, 1967), pp. 31–44.

6. E. Franklin Frazier, *The Negro Family in the United States* (Chicago: University of Chicago Press, 1939), and *Black Bourgeoisie: The Rise of a New Middle Class* (New York: The Free Press, 1957).

7. Ibid.

8. John W. Blassingame, *The Slave Community*, rev. edn. (New York: Oxford University Press, 1979).

9. Nathan Hare and Julia Hare, eds., *Crisis in Black Sexual Politics* (San Francisco: Black Think Tank, 1989).

10. A discussion of religion and the issue of African cultural survivals is found in E. Franklin Frazier, *The Negro Church in America*, new edition bound with the *Black Church Since Frazier* (New York: Schocken Books, 1974); Albert J. Raboteau, *Slave Religion* (New York: Oxford University Press, 1978); Joseph E. Holloway, ed., *Africanisms in American Culture* (Bloomington, Ind.: Indiana University Press); Blassingame, *The Slave Community*.

11. Frazier, *The Negro Church in America,* p. 14.

12. LeRoi Jones (Amiri Baraka), *Blues People* (New York: William Morrow, 1963), p. 39.

13. Blassingame, *The Slave Community*, p. xiii.

14. Raboteau, *Slave Religion*, p. 96.

15. Sterling Stuckey, *Slave Culture: Nationalist Theory and Foundations of Black America* (New York: Oxford University Press, 1987).

16. Drake, *Black Folk Here and There*; Frederickson, *White Supremacy*.

17. Ibid.

18. The phenomenon by which oppressed groups take on the values and beliefs of their oppressors is widely known. In the most prominent cases, the oppressed espouse belief in myths regarding their own inferiority or actively seek to preserve the privileged position of their oppressors. However, this phenomenon is much more

complex and subtle. It is critical to determine the ways in which an oppressed group sustains its own oppression by accepting aspects of the social reality constructed by the dominant group. See, for example, Bennett, *Confrontation Black and White*, pp. 86-93; Franz Fanon, *Black Skin White Mask* (New York: Grove Press, 1967).

19. Characteristics of African American speech patterns are described in Geneva Smitherman, *Talkin' and Testifyin': The Language of Black America* (Detroit: Wayne State University Press, 1977); Ronald Jemal Stevens, "What the Rap is About: Some Historical Notes on the Development of Rap Music and the Hip-Hop Movement," *Word: A Black Culture Journal* 1 (Spring 1991):53-83.

20. Jannette L. Dates and William Barlow, eds., *Split Image: African Americans in the Mass Media* (Washington, D.C.: Howard University Press, 1990), p. 80.

21. See Nathan Huggins, *The Harlem Renaissance* (New York: Oxford University Press, 1971).

22. Drake, *Black Folk Here and There,* vol. 1, p. xv.

23. Rodney, *How Europe Underdeveloped Africa;* Williams, *Capitalism and Slavery.*

24. Blassingame, *Slave Community;* Raboteau, *Slave Religion.*

25. A notable response to intellectual racism is Cheikh Anta Diop, *The African Origins of Civilization: Myth or Reality,* translated and edited by Mercer Cook (Westport, Conn.: Lawrence Hill, 1974). Also see, Chukwuemeka Onwubu, "The Intellectual Foundations of Racism," in Talmadge Anderson, ed., *Black Studies: Theory, Method, and Cultural Perspective* (Pullman, Wash.: Washington State University Press, 1990), pp. 77-88.

26. Clovis E. Semmes (Jabulani K. Makalani), "Foundations of an Afrocentric Social Science: Implications for Curriculum Building, Theory, and Research in Black Studies," *Journal of Black Studies* 12 (September 1981):3-17.

27. Raboteau, *Slave Religion,* p. 149.

28. Ibid., p. 96; Blassingame, *Slave Community,* p. 71.

29. Raboteau, *Slave Religion,* p. 152.

30. Blassingame, *Slave Community,* pp. 71-72.

31. Ibid.; Raboteau, *Slave Religion*; Frazier, *The Negro Church in America*.

32. Ibid.

33. Blassingame, *Slave Community*, pp. 98, 100.

34. See St. Clair Drake, *The Redemption of Africa and Black Religion* (Chicago: Third World Press, 1970).

35. Ibid.

36. George Washington Williams, *History of the Negro Race in America: From 1619 to 1880,* vol. 1 (New York: G.P. Putnam's Son, 1883; reprint ed., New York: Bergman Publishers, 1968).

37. See John H. Bracey, Jr., August Meier, and Elliott Rudwick, eds., *Black Nationalism in America* (New York: Bobbs-Merrill, 1970), p. 119.

38. Drake, *The Redemption of Africa*, p. 11.

39. Drake, *Black Folk Here and There,* vol. 1, p. 32.

40. See, for example, Ernest Kaiser, "The History of Negro History," *Negro Digest* 17 (February 1968):10-15.

41. Alain Locke, ed., *The New Negro* (New York: Atheneum, 1974), p. 4.

42. Ibid., p. 10.

43. Ibid., p. 4; W. E. B. DuBois, *The Souls of Black Folk* (Greenwich, Conn.: Fawcett Publications, 1961), pp. 16-17.

44. Joyce A. Ladner, ed., *The Death of White Sociology* (New York: Vintage, 1973), p. xix.

45. Robert Staples, *Introduction to Black Sociology* (New York: McGraw-Hill, 1976).

46. Ibid. Also see, Edward G. Armstrong, "Black Sociology and Phenomenological Sociology," *Sociological Quarterly* 20 (Summer 1979):387-97.

47. Reginald L. Jones, ed., *Black Psychology* (New York: Harper & Row, 1972); Addison Gayle, Jr., ed., *The Black Aesthetic* (Garden City, N.Y.: Doubleday, 1971).

48. Harold Cruse, "Black Studies: Interpretation, Methodology, and the Relationship to Social Movements," *Afro-American Studies: An Interdisciplinary Journal* 2 (June 1971):15-51.

49. Maulana Karenga, "Black Studies and the Problematic of Paradigm: The Philosophical Di-

mension," *Journal of Black Studies* 18 (June 1988):395-414.

50. *Negro Digest, Special Issue: The Black University,* part 3, vol. 19 (March 1970).

51. Semmes, "Foundations of an Afrocentric Social Science."

52. John Henrik Clarke, "The Fight to Reclaim African History," *Negro Digest* 19 (February 1970):10-15, 59-64.

53. Molefi Kete Asante, *The Afrocentric Idea* (Philadelphia: Temple University Press, 1987).

54. Erskine Peters has posited a similar approach to distinguishing trends in Afrocentric theorizing. He argues that in one sense, Afrocentricity focuses on how the status of African Americans has been affected by American slavery and Euro-American racism, and in another, it espouses adoption of ancient and traditional African values. Peters sees both as essential but, at times, not mutually exclusive. He proposes that the word "Afrocentric" be applied to the former (conditions affecting development and survival) and that "Africentric" be applied to the latter (ideals for behavior). Peters also recognizes a tendency for some Afrocentric theorizing to flow from an oppositional stance to "White culture" rather than from an accurate affirmation of African ideals and values. I define one aspect of this tendency as the problem of metaphysical dualism. See Erskine Peters, "Afrocentricity: Problems of Method and Nomenclature," *Working Papers in African American Studies*, University of Notre Dame, series 1, no. 3, 15 (April 1991).

55. Cf. Asante, *Afrocentric Idea*, p. 124; Stuckey, *Slave Culture*; DuBois, *Souls of Black Folk*, pp. 16-17.

56. The following works address these various debates: Talmadge Anderson, "Black Studies: Overview and Theoretical Perspectives," in Anderson, ed., *Black Studies*, pp. 1-10; Amiri Baraka, "`Why I Changed My Ideology': Black Nationalism and Socialist Revolution," *Black World* 24 (July 1975):30-42; Nathan Hare, "What Black Intellectuals Misunderstand About the Black Family," *Black World* 25 (March 1976):4-14; Harold Cruse, *Rebellion or Revolution* (New York: William Morrow, 1968); Holloway, *Africanisms in*

American Culture; William J. Wilson, *The Declining Significance of Race: Blacks and Changing American Institutions* (Chicago: University of Chicago Press, 1978).

57. Cf. Janice E. Hale-Benson, *Black Children: Their Roots, Culture, and Learning Styles* (Baltimore: Johns Hopkins Press, 1986).

58. Robert Park, "The Conflict and Fusion of Cultures with Special Reference to the Negro," *Journal of Negro History* 4 (April 1919):111-33.

59. Welsing, *Isis Papers*; Joseph Baldwin, "Notes on an Africentric Theory of Black Personality" in Anderson, ed., *Black Studies*, pp. 133-41; Daudi Ajani ya Azibo, "Advances in African Personality Theory," *Imhotep: An Afrocentric Review* 2 (January 1990):22-47.

60. Naim Akbar, "Africentric Social Sciences for Human Liberation," *Journal of Black Studies* 14 (June 1984):395-414.

61. Welsing, *Isis Papers* (emphasis in the original), p. 132.

62. Semmes, "Foundations of an Afrocentric Social Science."

63. Drake, *Black Folk Here and There,* vol. 1.

64. Frank Martin, "The Egyptian Ethnicity Controversy and the Sociology of Knowledge," *Journal of Black Studies* 14 (March 1984):295-325.

65. Diop, *African Origins of Civilization.*

66. See, for example, Ivan Van Sertima, ed., *Egypt Revisited,* 2nd ed. (New Brunswick, N.J.: Transaction Publishers, 1989); Yosef ben-Jochannan, *African Origins of the Major "Western Religions"* (New York: Alkebu-lan Books, 1970), and *Black Man of the Nile and His Family* (New York: Alkebu-lan Books, 1972); Martin Bernal, *Black Athena: Afroasiatic Roots of Classical Civilization.* Vol. 1: *The Fabrication of Greece 1785-1985* (New Brunswick, N.J.: Rutgers University Press, 1987); Chancellor Williams, *The Destruction of Black Civilization* (Chicago: Third World Press, 1974).

67. See Ivan Van Sertima, *They Came Before Columbus* (New York: Random House, 1976); Floyd W. Hayes III, "A Bibliographical Essay: African Presence in America Before Columbus," *Black World* 22 (July 1973):4-22.

68. Ibid.; Ivan Van Sertima, ed., *African Presence in Early Europe* (New Brunswick, N.J.: Transaction Publishers, 1985); Ivan Van Sertima and Runoko Rashidi, eds., *African Presence in Early Asia,* rev. edn. (New Brunswick, N.J.: Transaction Books, 1988); John G. Jackson, *Man, God and Civilization* (New Hyde Park, N.Y.: University Books, 1972); J.A. Rogers, *World's Great Men of Color,* rev. edn., 2 vols. (New York: Collier, 1972).

69. Drake, *Black Folk Here and There,* 2 vols.

70. See, for example, Holloway, *Africanisms in American Culture*; Smitherman, *Talkin' and Testifyin'*; Blassingame, *Slave Community*; Stuckey, *Slave Culture.*

71. Wade W. Nobles, "African Philosophy: Foundations for Black Psychology," in Jones, ed., *Black Psychology*, pp. 18–32.

72. See Jerome H. Schiele, "Organizational Theory from an Afrocentric Perspective," *Journal of Black Studies* 21 (December 1990):145–61; Akbar, "Africentric Social Sciences."

73. Examples are found in Bracey et al., eds., *Black Nationalism in America.*

74. See Maulana Karenga, "Kawaida and Its Critics: A Sociohistorical Analysis," *Journal of Black Studies* 8 (December 1977):125–48.

75. Karenga, "Black Studies and the Problematic of Paradigm."

76. An excellent discussion is provided by Amuzie Chimezie, *Black Culture: Theory and Practice* (Shaker Heights, Ohio: Keeble Press, 1984).

77. Blassingame, *Slave Community*; John Edward Philips, "The African Heritage of White America," in Holloway, ed., *Africanisms in American Culture*, pp. 225–39.

78. Cruse, *Crisis of the Negro Intellectual* and *Rebellion or Revolution.*

79. See Clovis E. Semmes (Jabulani K. Makalani), "Black Studies and the Symbolic Structure of Domination," *Western Journal of Black Studies* 6 (Summer 1982):116–22.

80. Cedric Clark (Sayed Malik Khatib), "The Concept of Legitimacy in Black Psychology," in Edgar G. Epps, ed., *Race Relations: Current Perspectives* (Cambridge, Mass.: Winthrop, 1973), pp. 332–54.

81. Welsing, *Isis Papers.*

82. See for example, Frazier, *Race and Culture Contacts in the Modern World*; Thompson, *The Making of the African Diaspora*; Staples, *The Urban Plantation*.

83. Walter L. Wallace, "Some Elements of Sociological Theory in Studies of Black Americans," in James E. Blackwell and Morris Janowitz, eds., *Black Sociologists: Historical and Contemporary Perspectives* (Chicago: University of Chicago Press, 1974), pp. 299-321.

84. Ibid., pp. 311-12.

2

The Frazerian Paradigm

E. Franklin Frazier was one of the great sociologists of our time and has made enormous contributions to sociological theory, the study of African Americans, and race relations theory in general. It is rare that any study of African American culture and institutional life occurs without reference to Frazier's work. Frazier's prominence and accomplishments as a sociologist, at a time of intense, legally sanctioned racial segregation and bigotry, attested to his brilliance and skill in conveying his ideas to peers, to students, and to a diverse public. Further, Frazier maintained an unwavering commitment to African American liberation and equality, despite the rigors and realities of Black life that discouraged such stances.[1]

The corpus of Frazier's work makes broad and significant contributions to the foundations of the intellectual tradition called African American studies and captures the essential problems driving the discipline. Because of Frazier's concern for African American institutional development and the problem of assimilation, his works have become epistemologically linked to the metaproblem of cultural hegemony. Assimilation as a social problem involves the problem of cultural negation. The study of institutional development provides the focus to discern the degree and direction of cultural negation and addresses the issue of becoming. What will be the character and identity of racial/cultural groups as they encounter one another? How does structured inequality or hegemony affect these encounters and their outcomes? To what degree will a subordinate group be able to reconstruct or preserve its institutional viability and direct the formation of its identity? These are the issues to which Frazier has shed significant light.[2]

Ironically, Frazier has been both celebrated and maligned. For example, Frazier's critique of the Black bourgeoisie and the Black intellectual, no doubt, contributed to the seminal work by Harold Cruse, *The Crisis of the Negro Intellectual*, which literally ushered in the self-conscious Black Studies movement of the 1960s.[3] At the same time that this movement deeply benefited from Frazier's efforts, many movement proponents attacked him on two fronts. First, some African Americans who embraced the importance of African culture and values did not take kindly to Frazier's argument that African culture in North America had been destroyed.[4] Second, responding to the report on the African American family in 1965 by White sociologist (later Senator) Daniel Patrick Moynihan, which was interpreted by some to blame the plight of the Black community on disorganized families, Black and White scholars launched a counteroffensive to demonstrate the strengths of Black families. Moynihan claimed to be embracing a Frazerian interpretation, and by association, Frazier's work fell into disfavor. It did not matter that many scholars had failed to read Frazier or to examine his insights as much as they did his limitations and shortcomings. Of course, Frazier had already died by the time of the Moynihan report and could not respond to those who failed to read, who misread, or who misquoted his work.[5]

Nevertheless, Frazier's analytical and theoretical efforts were simply too important to be ignored, as they made profound contributions to understanding the Black experience. With regard to the foundations of African American studies, Frazier's contributions are most prominent in five areas. The first is Frazier's focus on the family and its relationship to the assimilation problem. The second contribution is his work on middle-class formations in order to assess mobility, leadership potential, and economic development. The third is Frazier's analysis of the relationship between religious values and social organization. The fourth is his study of the personality development and consciousness of Black youth, an important barometer of an African American future. The fifth area of focus is Frazier's comparative work. Here he directs his various empirical and theoretical interests globally in order to advance a more general understanding of race and culture contacts and the specific impact of European expansion on African and African diasporic development. Despite their categorical distinctiveness, these five research areas are empirically and theoretically linked, and the study of each one informs our understanding of the other. Thus, my own view is that Frazier was profoundly aware of the interrelationship of multiple layers of social phenomena affecting African Americans and made great effort to reveal these interrelationships in diverse and subtle ways.[6]

FAMILY AND THE ASSIMILATION PROBLEM

E. Franklin Frazier was best known for his work on the African American family, and this was also the area where he was most criticized. As I stated previously, Frazier became associated with perspectives that blamed family disorganization for Black impoverishment. Female-headed households and so-called matriarchal family structures became part of this "blame-the-victim" scenario. Also, Frazier's assertion that African culture was destroyed in the New World sparked the so-called Frazier-Herskovits debate. Melville Herskovits was a White anthropologist who argued strongly for the presence of surviving African culture in the New World. However, both men admitted that surviving African culture was strongest in the Caribbean and South American context and weakest in the North American context.[7]

These conceptualizations and debates have been to some degree dysfunctional and nonproductive. They have obscured the logic and theoretical insight of Frazier's work. As a consequence, my intent is not to rehash these spurious dialogues but to focus on Frazier's logic and insight. Who is to blame for continued African American inequality is an important question, but Frazier was more concerned with process; that is, how does structured inequality actually manifest itself within the institutional workings of the African American community? Furthermore, whether or not African culture survived is one question, but revealing how values and institutional structures adapt, interact, and are reproduced is another. Therefore, because of the failure to deeply penetrate Frazier's theoretical conceptualizations, many of the observations for which Frazier was criticized have been ignored for their sociological acumen and explanatory power.

As we shall see, Frazier raised the issue of surviving African culture as a part of his concern for analyzing African American family development and not as an effort to prove that African people had a viable culture deserving of respect. From a Black perspective, the need to prove that one has a valued culture is unnecessary. It is only when others are able to project and sustain the myth of Black cultural or biological inferiority that proving the contrary becomes an epistemological concern. Furthermore, there is no question that various factors have continued to distort African American life. The objective is for African American scholars to understand these factors. Thus, one must guard against reacting to a normative Eurocentric propensity to blame the victims of White supremacy.

The Negro Family in the United States gives us a comprehensive and valuable look at Frazier's theoretical and conceptual approach to analyzing assimilation as a social problem. A cursory observation of the organization of this work reveals that Frazier divides his study into five parts. They are: "In the House of the Master," "In the House of the Mother," "In the House of the Father," "In the City of Destruc-

tion," and "In the City of Rebirth." What is
most significant about these divisions is that
they represent variations in the type of social
organization under which the African/African
American family had to adjust. Frazier examined
these variations in social organization in terms
of their natural history and their implications
for institutional viability. He revealed how socio-historical phenomena provide disorganizing
influences to the African family and then identified conditions that tended to restructure or
reorganize the family. Thus, Frazier's objective
was not to characterize the African family as
either organized or disorganized but to discover
the conditions under which one or the other took
place.[8]

Frazier's first chapter, "Forgotten Memories"
under Part One, "In the House of the Master," is
intriguing and gives some insight into how he
wanted to develop his analysis. The idea of forgotten memories is somewhat enigmatic. How can a
memory at the same time be forgotten? Frazier
soundly hypothesized that an African cultural
heritage could not be sustained because of the
way in which Africans were enslaved. For example, slave traders had little regard for family
bonds and ethnic distinctions. Seasoning, the
process of breaking Africans into slavery, and
the scattering of Africans among the smaller
plantations in the North American South tended
to erode African culture. In other words, Frazier recognized that a profound disruption of
African social organization tended to efface
cultural memory. Also, if there was a surviving
African culture, it was inclined to be meaning-
less in the context of the new conditions of enslavement. Thus, in this first chapter, Frazier
gave numerous examples of memories of a surviving African culture, but his fundamental argument was that these were the exceptions and that
they had little to do with how slave culture and
therefore family life were to be restructured in
the New World, particularly in the North American South. Furthermore, the notion of forgotten
memories pointed to the submergence of an
African consciousness.

Frazier's argument and underlying theory were
quite powerful and have sustained their validity

despite some limitation, but we need also to understand the context of Frazier's argument as well as its implications and shortcomings. In Frazier's theoretical approach the status of the family was critical to analyzing the question of African assimilation. But why was assimilation such an issue? White sociologist Robert Park, Frazier's mentor at the University of Chicago, where Frazier received his doctorate in sociology, was a leading theorist on race relations and was considered by some to be an expert on Black Americans. Park had been a secretary for Booker T. Washington and president of the Chicago Urban League. Park theorized that contact between Africans and Europeans proceeded through a cycle that resulted in conflict, accommodation, and assimilation. Thus, for Park, African culture automatically gave way to European culture. Also, Park believed that Africans brought little culture with them to the New World and had produced no culture of their own.

Park explained that the cultural distinctiveness that he observed among African Americans was a consequence of their "racial temperament." This temperament, according to Park, was characterized by a "genial, sunny and social disposition, in an interest and attachment to external, physical things rather than to subjective states and objects of introspection, in a disposition for expression rather than enterprise and action." Also, reflecting the sexist views of the time, Park referred to African people as the "lady of the races," since they presumably lacked the intellectual and pioneering characteristics of White men. Park theorized that through this racial temperament, African Americans selected aspects of White culture to which they had the greatest biological affinity. This theory was rather benign in light of other racist theories concerning African biological and cultural inferiority that were extant.[9]

Frazier, of course, rejected Park's notion of racial temperament in favor of a more environmentally and socially based argument. A distinctive African American culture was a function of the persistence of a distinctive social organization. Furthermore, Frazier noted that assim-

ilation also involved identification, a step beyond acculturation, the simple process of acquiring the cultural traits of another group.
Thus, assimilation meant that one group would no
longer see itself as distinct from another. For
Frazier, the end result of contact between
Whites and Blacks was not automatically Black
assimilation, the effacement of Black culture
and identity. The inevitability of assimilation
was an empirical question whose answer was to be
found in an analysis of the specific configurations of social life. As a consequence,
Frazier's study of the African American family
became a test of the assimilation question.
Thus, the relevance of Frazier's work for analyzing the metaproblem of cultural hegemony, the
systemic negation of one culture by another for
the purpose of manipulation and control,
emerges.[10]

Regarding the concept of forgotten memories,
Frazier understood that African social organization no longer applied in North America and concluded that African values, beliefs, and behaviors also no longer applied. This was not completely true, but most scholars recognize that
African culture was radically altered by New
World experiences. Frazier concluded that an
African social heritage was not sufficient to
shape or to explain the basis of African family
life in the New World. For Frazier, what were
the conditions that shaped the Black family? The
answer existed in five areas. First was the
organization of the plantation that produced a
distinctive division of labor. Second was the
variety of natural relationships that grew up as
men and women sought to fulfill their sexual de-
sires. This included the sexual domination and
exploitation of the African women by the White
male. Third was the imposition of a European
American social heritage (in the presumed absence of an African heritage) through European
Christianity, and fourth, there were the implications of the natural bonds that grew up between mother and child. The fifth was the system
of domination itself that promoted White supremacy and the intrusion into Black family life by
White oppressors.

The intersection of these diverse social relationships produced complex variations in social organization that shaped the character of the African family in North America. Since the elements of personality and culture were transmitted through the family, an understanding of the dynamics of this institution and the various factors affecting its viability was central to an analysis of the assimilation question. If social forces existed that moved African Americans toward assimilation (cultural negation), it is the family that would impede or facilitate this process. For example, Frazier identified two family forms, the natural family and the institutional family. The natural family usually consisted of a single-parent, mother-child household, which was held together by parental affection and sympathetic ties. It should be noted that the concept of natural family was not posed as a definition of female roles but as a description of the structures that evolved as women gave birth and cared for their children. The institutional family was two-parent, based on formal marriage, and possessed greater stability and continuity. Frazier saw the institutional family as more capable of preserving and transmitting a social heritage and more capable of integrating African Americans into the organized life of the broader community. In other words, the institutional family could better serve as a sponsor for its members and could better preserve a social heritage. Frazier understood that there were variations on these family forms that could make them more or less effective in carrying out family functions.

Throughout the various phases of the African American experience, which included slavery, emancipation, postslavery rural life, migration, and urbanization, Frazier was interested in the conditions that offered family stability and continuity as well as those conditions that were disorganizing. Environments that offered an organized life, an adequate economic foundation, and a social heritage provided fertile ground for the family to flourish. However, out of disorganizing influences could come stabilizing factors. Unfettered sexual hedonism could spawn caring and sympathetic relationships. Despite the fact of slavery as an economic institution, the plantation system took on an institutional character in which some elements of family life could be achieved. Emancipation was another disorganizing experience because it removed the economic foundation for survival in light of the reality of a high number of widows and fatherless children. Social relations were torn asunder as former slaves moved about on a mass scale to test their new freedom, find new methods to survive, and to reconstruct their families. Nevertheless, there were female-headed family forms, particularly those headed by elderly Black women, that kept the generations together, took in orphaned children, and provided the characteristics of an institutional family.

By comparison, Frazier analyzed the variations in family forms following emancipation in which the Black male could assert authority in the family and provide an economic role. Frazier's chapter titles pointed to the fact that under the plantation system, Black men, women, and children were "In the House of the Master." But following emancipation, women and children were either "In the House of the Mother" or "In the House of the Father." The reintroduction of male authority and a male economic role was central to greater family stability. In the context of American society, the male role facilitated the economic stability and protection of the family, which gave strength to the affective and socializing components of the family. However, because Frazier had already looked at stabilizing factors among the "Matriarchate," it is clear that there was no inherent instability in a female-headed household. What is important is that wherever social and historical conditions provided for the characteristics of an institutional family, there was greater stability, sponsorship, and continuity for family members. Thus, as Frazier identified broad family types, and levels and conditions of social organization, he used a historical and contextual analysis to explain situational and conditional factors that strengthened or weakened these social forms. Most importantly, institutional family forms that provided material support and a social heritage, that is, traditions that gave direction and coherence to family activity, were better able to sustain themselves in the midst of disorganizing and disruptive social change. The conditions under which the family was strongest and the kinds of families that were most likely to survive and thrive were central concerns of Frazier's work.

Urbanization, which, like the process of enslavement and the experience of emancipation, posed new questions for survival, was profoundly disruptive to Black family life. Part Four of Frazier's study of the Black family, "In the City of Destruction," addressed new challenges to the rural and folk culture of southern Blacks. Frazier concluded that natural family forms were least able to withstand the disorganizing influences of urbanization. We should remember that urbanization refers to a dynamic process of change in which massive groups of migrating rural people are becoming urbanized. These disorganizing influences included separation from familial and communal supports and controls, disruptions to identity due to the quest for status in a new environment, increasing social differences due to rapid social mobility generated by growing occupational differentiation, the separation of sexual gratification from human feelings and commitment, the imposition of poverty and racial segregation, the encounter with more individualistic and hedonistic values, and the like. Frazier, again, developed a natural history approach to explicating these conditions and relationships. Thus, he was always cognizant of historical origins and social contexts. Despite his own prudishness and personal biases, Frazier identified important social factors affecting family life and clearly established environmental and societal conditions as causes for family dysfunction.

Consistent with his previous analyses, Frazier went on to describe the seeds of organization within the disorganizing influences of urban life in Part Five, "In the City of Rebirth," the final section of his study. Frazier emphasized that African Americans who were able to sustain a strong social heritage that gave direction to the family were better able to cope with urban life. This fact also led Frazier to look very closely at stratification. Stratification helped to determine privilege, which in turn helped to define a family's relative ability to establish economic stability. This usually meant a male presence, an institutional family, and quite possibly, home ownership. Frazier observed that the emergence of a new Black middle class and an urban proletariat presented new opportunities for males to gain authority in the family and to contribute economically to their families. A critical component of family stability, along with the maintenance of a social heritage, was the degree to which racial barriers would fall and Blacks could achieve economic integration in American society. Furthermore, as a Black middle class expanded, this group would cease to look at itself as a privileged and wealthy upper class in the Black community. It is the character and evolution of this group for which Frazier developed a more detailed and critical assessment.

MIDDLE-CLASS FORMATIONS

Frazier's analysis of a Black bourgeoisie grew out of his analysis of Black family life.[11] It was connected to his examination of an African American division of labor and the sources of a social heritage that could provide direction to family functioning. Frazier concluded that family functioning was facilitated by material wealth but also required values that could give direction to family life. Because Frazier believed that an African social heritage had dissipated in the North American context, he looked to other sources for values that could direct behavior. The institutional family--for Frazier, the most stable family form--emerged from a certain strata of African Americans based upon specific historical circumstances. The most stable families could be found among Blacks who were free prior to the Civil War, who disproportionately were the offspring of White fathers and Black mothers, and freed Blacks who had been domestic servants or skilled artisans on the plantation. These groups, free Blacks, skilled artisans, and domestics, when compared with the masses of Blacks who had been field slaves, had been in closest proximity to aristocratic White culture and had derived much of their social heritage from this group. Thus, the origins of an elite stratum among African Americans were disproportionately of mixed parentage, distinguished by their behavior and social conventions, and more privileged materially, socially, and educationally in terms of the criteria for status in a White-dominated society.

In contrast to an elite stratum, Frazier observed that the masses of Blacks developed a folk culture based upon the fact that this group was most isolated from White culture and social organization. Nevertheless, we should not assume that there was not interaction and cultural sharing among various Black strata, but Frazier frequently identified modal types of social organization in order to emphasize dominant trends. Also, it is probably the case that Frazier was most in error in failing to recognize the significance of surviving African culture among the Black masses, and, probably to some degree, among the Black elite stratum. What is most significant is that Frazier showed how the division of labor intersected with White supremacy and sexual exploitation to produce variations in social life that could affect the relative stability of family life. A Black folk culture emerged as most vulnerable to racial oppression and later, urbanization.

Frazier's study of African American elites revealed that racial oppression stimulated Western capitalist expansion but eclipsed the emergence of a true bourgeoisie, that is, a business or capital-owning class among African Americans. This fact had implications for the overall development of the African American community. The status and potential of this stratum suggested the direction of African Americans as they emerged from a rigidly segregated society. The viability of this group would mean a lot to the leadership development, political and economic empowerment, institutional development, and cultural outlook of the African American community in general.

Consistent with his earlier methodological orientation, Frazier studied the Black bourgeoisie by way of a natural history approach. He traced their origins from the forms of stratification that grew up on the plantation as it took on the characteristics of a social institution. This social institution provided the vehicle and context by which Africans absorbed various aspects of European culture. As indicated previously, the organization of work resulted in a system of stratification that helped to determine levels of acculturation. This factor and the variations in the imposition of European religious instruction, a principal carrier of European culture; miscegenation and its role in affecting the self-image and consciousness of African Americans within the context of a White supremacy system; and the status of being slave or free all contributed to the way in which an elite stratum grew up among African Americans. Frazier also pointed to the role of language in the deculturation process.

Frazier's fundamental finding was that there was an old elite and a new bourgeoisie. The former was defined by convention and skin color. Its members were disproportionately of mixed parentage (White slave-owning father and African mother), more likely to have been free prior to the Civil War, and more likely to have internalized the aristocratic and puritannical religious ideals of upper-class, slave-owning Whites. This old elite was relatively stable institutionally because of its economic and social privilege and organized social heritage relative to other African Americans. There was significant variation within this class, however, which Frazier does not overlook.

The new bourgeoisie emerged as a consequence of a new division of labor spawned by urbanization and industrialization. As African Americans were attracted from the land into the urban and industrial North, they experienced greater occupational differentiation. As a consequence, a new elite stratum emerged that was based upon income and occupation and not convention, skin color, and family background. This new bourgeoisie replaced the old elite as the dominant elite stratum. Nevertheless, the persistence of skin color and convention as characteristics of upper-class status continued in the African American community. Frazier argued persuasively that the new bourgeoisie was superficially cloaked in White aristocratic culture. In fact, this new stratum was culturally alienated. Because of the stigma that White supremacy attached to Black culture, the new bourgeoisie rejected the folk culture of the masses of Blacks and were not of the culture of the old elite. As a result, the new bourgeoisie expressed its status through imitating the White upper classes, conspicuous consumption, and an inordinate focus on play and leisure activity.

It is because of these social circumstances that Frazier wanted to make a clear distinction between the objective conditions of the new bourgeoisie and the social image they attempted to create in their quest for status. He divided his study into two parts, "The World of Reality" and "The World of Make-Believe." In Part One, Frazier identified the historical roots of the bourgeoisie that led to its social formation, and he systematically examined the opportunities for and constraints on Black capital accumulation. These included opportunities to own land, banking activities, small business development, and the roles of religious and fraternal organizations in generating economic enterprises. Frazier paid attention to self-help efforts and to governmental and philanthropic influences. He also made clear the limitations of these efforts within the context of a White supremacy and racially segregated system. The emerging Black bourgeoisie would derive its income from white-collar jobs and not from business enterprises, and the few small businesses that did develop served the needs of a segregated community.

Frazier always emphasized the interrelationship between the organization of a social phenomenon and its ideological or value component. Thus, his theoretical approach systematically embraced a focus on social organization and culture. In this regard, Frazier looked very carefully at those social formations that affected the outlook, values, and social heritage of the old elite and new bourgeoisie. Again, the religious values of a White aristocracy, in their most rigid forms, were imposed on this stratum in an organized manner via the work of White northern missionaries and the directives of White industrial elites who supported and controlled "Negro" colleges. Under the autocratic control of Blacks who were controlled by White elites, Negro colleges imposed on their students a type of piety, thrift, and image of respectability that was acceptable to their northern benefactors. Frazier traced the value orientation of Negro colleges from their rigid religious instruction and rituals to a more secular and materialist outlook.

Of course, White elite control of Black thinking was not monolithic, but Frazier demonstrated the historical basis of the need for White approval and the structural basis of African American dependency. Also, the fact that a Black bourgeoisie was not a true bourgeoisie meant that this stratum essentially became a pawn of White capital-owning classes. The dependent status of this class was reflected by the fact that they had no significant power as employers or as political financiers. The Black bourgeoisie could gain concessions from White political machines based primarily on its ability to direct the masses of Blacks to serve the interests of White propertied classes. Frazier clearly described in his study the process by which White elites attempted to shape Black leadership and control the Black masses. Blacks were restricted socially to their churches, fraternal organizations, and Greek letter societies, but the influence of White supremacy could be seen in these organizations. They developed their own distinctive characteristics but imitated the worst characteristics of White elites in their quest for status in a segregated and racially stratified society. For example, according to Frazier, Greek letter societies grew up to become a main expression of social snobbishness separating the Black bourgeoisie from the masses; they espoused conspicuous consumption and diversion from serious educational pursuits. Frazier identified variations in the behaviors of a Black elite stratum, but he was very clear that historical and institutional forms of racism generated feelings of inferiority.

In Part Two, Frazier elaborated on the social and self-image created by the Black bourgeoisie. He attempted to examine the values and norms of this group and how it reproduced itself. Frazier found a contradiction in form and substance. In its imitation of White propertied classes, the Black bourgeoisie had a tendency to glorify its power and importance as a business class when in fact it had little status as a true bourgeoisie. Because of racial oppression, Blacks had not and could not become captains of industry. Frazier identified and discussed the myth of a strong Black business class. He showed how Black newspapers, magazines, and organizations perpetuated this myth, and how the creation of Black "high society" served to secure the image of a successful bourgeoisie. Again, imitation of a White high society, conspicuous consumption, and an emphasis on play (an imitation of the tradition of the "gentlemen" who engaged in no serious work) became symbols of status.

Finally, Frazier examined the stresses and strains of life as a Black bourgeoisie attempted to live up to an image that had little substance. He noted the tendency to be attracted to religious expression that claimed to bring material prosperity. Because there were so few eligible Black men in this stratum, there was the fear of White women competing for Black men. There was also the fear of a loss of status. Frazier observed the frustrations of Black men who could not play the "masculine role" as defined by White America; they were compelled to allow Black women to take the lead in demonstrations of militancy for fear of being punished. Black males gained influence through personality and not through competition for power. Frazier also observed a tendency by a Black bourgeoisie to have negative views and expectations regarding other Blacks, and saw that they would rather submit to White authority than Black authority. There was the belief that wealth, and hence conspicuous consumption, brought acceptance. Frazier felt that the frustrations of a Black bourgeoisie were not released through the delusions of wealth and power and were thus directed toward games of chance and excessive sex and alcohol. He considered the quest for the free and easy life to be a mask for an unhappy existence.

Frazier's analysis of a Black bourgeoisie was very disturbing to some African Americans, particularly those who considered themselves to be of this stratum, but Frazier clearly identified systemic characteristics of racism and oppression that affected the form and substance of a Black elite. The problems of a Black elite were a function of the racial discrimination and segregation that gave this group no true standing in American society. Also, the outlook of this group was linked to the broader changes that were occurring in an industrializing American society. Advancing capitalism was beginning to redefine status in terms of material consumption and, as a function of the need to expand markets, was beginning to make the status-infused cultural products of bourgeois and aristocratic elites available to the masses. A shortened work week increased the opportunities for leisure activity, which became a further impetus to commodity formation. Thus, conspicuous (radical) consumption as a measure of status was consistent with broader American economic and cultural trends. However, for African Americans, these trends were complicated by the problems of economic dependency, racial segregation, and White supremacy. In addition, Frazier's analysis stopped at the period of urbanization and before the pervasive removal of legalized racial segregation. He did not witness the dynamics of post-urban life or the next wave of Black middle-class development, which emerged as a consequence of the Civil Rights movement and Black matriculation at historically White colleges and universities.[12] Also, as was stated in an earlier study, Frazier expected this white-collar stratum to think of itself less as an elite as it grew in size.

RELIGIOUS VALUES AND SOCIAL ORGANIZATION

The significance of a social heritage that gave substance and direction to organized life was very important to Frazier's analysis, and he considered religious values to be at the root of this social heritage.[13] Thus, Frazier's study of African American religious values was a reflection of his concern for the way in which they affected social structure generally and their role in the social organization of Black life specifically. Because Frazier felt that there had been a complete break with African traditions, he felt that European Christian religious forms and not African religious forms provided the new basis for social cohesion among Africans in America. This was not absolutely true but, in a sociological sense, was modally true.

As the influence of African religious traditions waned, European Christian traditions took on greater social prominence, utility, and function. Frazier noted that by the closing years of the eighteenth century, there was active proselytizing among the slave population by White Baptists and Methodists. European religious forms stimulated feelings of hope and contributed to group solidarity among the slave populations, but at the same time organized religious instruction brought messages of White superiority and African inferiority. Africans, according to Frazier, developed, through this alien religious heritage, a new orientation toward existence. However, Frazier observed that Africans also interpreted the Bible to fit their own experience and embraced an other-worldly outlook that emphasized the good life that would come after death.

Eurocentric religious expression varied by social experiences that were shaped by African American stratification. Frazier identified two dominant religious social forms prior to the Civil War. The first was the "invisible institution" of the slave population, which was a mode of religious expression that developed in relative isolation from European scrutiny and influence. The second was the "institutional church," which developed among free Blacks who regularly participated in White Christian religious rituals. The former developed a mode of expression that reflected the indigenous folk culture of the African American masses. (Also, contrary to the Frazerian thesis that this folk culture was almost completely a result of an isolated social

existence, surviving African culture probably
had a significant role in shaping its character
and form.) The latter had greater kinship with
European American forms of expression. After the
Civil War, the institutional and the invisible
church merged, but the masses, with their more
emotional and ecstatic forms of worship, became
concentrated in Methodist and Baptist churches,
and Black elites became concentrated in Episcopal, Presbyterian, and Congregational churches.

Frazier saw the church as a support to family
stability, economic cultivation, and leadership
development. The church functioned as a moral
guide and gave support to patriarchal authority,
an important countervailing force to a White
supremacy system that tried to destroy Black
male authority in the family and in the society.
Because the church provided the basis for
African Americans to pool their resources, it
was a mechanism for economic cooperation, capital accumulation, and business development. Mutual aid societies grew out of the church, and
secular insurance companies grew out of these
mutual aid societies. Fraternal organizations
were strongly influenced by religion, usually
organized by preachers, and were significant aspects of elementary forms of economic development. The Black church came to represent all institutional participation denied by racial segregation. It became the incubator for Black
leadership and grew to be the most dominant organized structure in the Black community outside
of the family. Although there were some exceptions, the imposition of European religious
forms functioned to diffuse threats to White
supremacy.

Urbanization, Frazier observed, radically
transformed African American religious expression. It uprooted people from families, friends,
and neighbors. Children were less subject to
family discipline. An impersonal environment
lessened mutual aid and support. The mental outlook of urbanized African Americans changed
since now they could do many of the things that
other Whites could do, and occupational differentiation lessened the dominance of preachers
among the professional classes. Whereas the old
rural church was other-worldly, the new urban

church tended to focus on conditions of this world. Urban churches tended to become more complex. The upper-middle and upper classes continued to attend Episcopal, Presbyterian, and Congregational churches, and the lower-middle class tended to be Baptist and Methodist. Storefront churches were established by the poorer masses and recent migrants who attempted to reestablish a southern, communal environment.

Urbanization, according to Frazier, brought an abrupt rupture with traditional religious forms developed during the slavery period. Holiness and Spiritualist churches and other fundamentalist religious expressions were reactions to the stresses, strains, and temptations of urban life. Additional movements that advocated sanctified living promoted cooperative economics and a deracialized social order. One such example was the Father Divine Peace Mission movement. Some newer forms of religious expression made the image of God Black and/or recast Black people into a chosen and divine people rather than into an inferior caste as defined by White supremacy. Black Jews and the Moorish Science movement, a Black Islamic sect, were examples. What is most important is that Frazier demonstrated that religion is critical to uprooting people from old traditions and to creating new ones. Epistemologically, Frazier helped to reveal the historical and conceptual purpose behind the study of African American religious forms. They are integrally related to the assimilation question, the mechanisms of cultural hegemony, the potential for institutional and cultural development, and the substance and image of what African Americans will become.

BLACK YOUTH: PERSONALITY DEVELOPMENT AND CONSCIOUSNESS

Frazier's research on African American youth examined the personality development of Black youth in the context of a racially segregated society.[14] Frazier was concerned with the kind of person African American youth were in the process of becoming as a consequence of the limitations placed upon their participation in community life. This 1939 study focused on Black youth in the mid-state regions of Louisville, Kentucky, and Washington, D.C. The research itself was part of a series of studies on Black youth initiated by the American Youth Commission of the American Council on Education. Despite the external impetus for this work, Frazier was able to apply his extraordinarily developed conceptual and theoretical scheme to this endeavor. This study, perhaps more than any other, gives the reader a solid glimpse into Frazier's methodological approach and theoretical perspective. His masterful examination of the interaction between social organization and culture and his skillful use of phenomenological, historical, and contextual data, which also included appropriate ecological and demographic materials, should be considered a paradigm for holistic sociological study and for Afrocentric inquiry. As is the case for Frazier's work in general, this study revealed much about the context of processes related to African American development and comprehensively revealed important linkages between the pertinent dynamics within related institutional formations. Frazier's focus on the family, religion, stratification, racial segregation, and culture remained dominant. Also, Frazier rejected biological, Freudian, behaviorist, and instinctual explanations of personality development in favor of the view that personality is directed by social interaction. Further, predating the critiques of the 1960s, he rejected the false notion of a value-free social science.

Frazier's analysis of the personality development of Black youth began with a spatial (ecological) and demographic analysis of the surrounding Black community and proceeded with a type of naturalistic approach to the study of institutional interactions. Frazier began with interactions in the family, the institution in which the individual is born, and systematically proceeded to examine interaction in the neighborhoods, schools, and churches. He ended with an analysis of the interactions surrounding the process of seeking employment. Frazier scrutinized each category of interaction in terms of the class position of his respondents. He compared the interactions and consciousness of lower-, middle-, and upper-class youth. Frazier also observed that even though class structure rested upon an economic foundation, stratification also reflected certain purely cultural and social distinctions.

Frazier's findings were diverse, but he noted that a segregated society defined by White domination permeated the consciousness of all strata of Black youth in every form of interaction. Black youth, at this time, maintained no ideologies related to social movements. Most importantly, Frazier observed that the actions of the family were central to the discipline and the social control of youth and central to their conception of self as African Americans. Lower-class youth were more likely to accept views on Black inferiority and have negative feelings about being Black. Middle-class youth were more race-conscious and motivated by a determination to rise in the world, and they maintained values that were concerned with an image of respectability. Upper-class families attempted to shield their youth from racial slights; these youth tended to identify with the culture of upper-class Whites. They exhibited significant prejudice toward middle-class and lower-class Blacks, as well as poor Whites, who they falsely believed were most responsible for racism.

Other findings that related to specific institutional interactions were as follows. Lower-class youth, for example, were most vulnerable to White hostility. School interactions indicated that teachers frequently responded to Black youth based upon their skin color and social class. Lighter-skinned children who behaved in a manner consistent with upper-class culture were treated better.

Variations existed in how diverse strata of youth interpreted God. The lower class tended to see Jesus and God as the same; the upper class extended a more human personality to Jesus. Lower-class youth tended to question the value and sincerity of the church. There were also variations in the forms of worship, with the lower classes being more ecstatic and expressive. All strata saw God as White, and Frazier found that even though the church was an

institution controlled by Blacks, no values existed in church interactions that encouraged
Black youth to have greater respect for a Black
self-image. An equal chance to compete with
Whites for jobs was desired by all strata of
youth, and lighter-skinned Blacks considered
passing as White to get employment. Lower-class
youth perceived that limited job opportunities
justified illegal means for making a living. For
all strata, experiences with Whites bred distrust, and many youth were convinced that various techniques were necessary to conceal their
true feelings in order to appease Whites.

Frazier's study of Black youth proved to be a
rich complement to his works on the family, religion, and stratification. It remains important
for this fact alone, but it also validates the
substance and process of White supremacy, racial
domination, and racial segregation. This validation is needed to compare contemporary conditions with the past. Without a historical reference point, we can lose sight of the natural
history of racial domination and its variations
in form, content, and process. Also, Frazier
identified the origins and existence of social
problems that continue to plague the Black community. For example, he observed and labeled as
pathological the severe imbalance in the sex ra-
tio for African Americans. The excess of women
over men distorts male/female relationships to
the detriment of women. This is a critical problem today. Furthermore, Frazier emphasized that
the pathology of poverty greatly contributes to
family instability, a similarly pressing and
persistent contemporary problem. Frazier always
stressed, however, the pathology of racism that
stood behind other social problems affecting
African Americans.

COMPARATIVE STUDIES AND THE ASSIMILATION PROBLEM

Race and Culture Contacts in the Modern World
is perhaps Frazier's most sophisticated and
richly insightful work on assimilation as a social problem.[15] Frazier elevated his analysis of
the relationship between social organization and
culture to a global level in order to assess the

results of European contact with non-Europeans. He identified three significant areas of race and culture contact. The first area involved substantial European penetration and settlement and included the United States; Latin American, which incorporated Mexico, Central America, and South America; the West Indies and the Guianas; South Africa; Australia; and New Zealand. The second area, Frazier observed, involved less European settlement. It included the tropical areas of Africa south of the Sahara (excluding South Africa), Southeast Asia, and the Pacific Islands. The third area was the least penetrated by European contact and included China, India, and Japan. Frazier noted that these were the oldest civilizations of Asia. The constant in Frazier's analysis was the fact of European expansion in the world, but variations occurred in the degree of European penetration and settlement, and the character of the cultural transformations that took place.

Frazier's analysis tried to account for these variations and to describe the common and most salient features of culture contact. For example, climate and level of development were significant factors affecting penetration. Although Frazier used the term "culture contact," his study revealed the processes of cultural hegemony because in every case European contact resulted in the effort by Europeans to dominate a non-European group. Nowhere did Europeans seek to sustain a peaceful and an egalitarian coexistence.

Once again Frazier took a natural history approach in his analysis to show how various social relations emerged. For example, he observed that the first phase of race and culture contact was not truly social since the persons that were brought together were of different moral orders. Frazier generalized that conflict may or may not occur; if it did, the consequences were biological. European invaders, for example, changed the environments of indigenous peoples through the introduction of new plants, animals, and diseases. The European introduction of firearms made warfare more devastating, and changes in diet and clothing weakened the health of non-European peoples. Frazier observed that symbiotic

rather than social relations developed that
first consisted of a system of barter. An ecological organization emerged from this symbiotic
relationship that resulted in the racial division of labor. The motivation for this system of
control was economic but required a system of
political organization and control. Frazier revealed how a racial division of labor broke down
but economic control remained in the hands of
European invaders. This analysis is very important because it demonstrated that racism could
change its appearance but preserve itself structurally at other levels of social control. It
also showed how cultural hegemony profoundly affected nonpolitical and noneconomic institutions
like health.

Given the above dynamic, Frazier systematically examined the impact of European expansion
and hegemony on the ecological organization of
non-European groups, the economic organization
that resulted from this contact, the variations
of political organization that were used to control indigenous peoples, and the social organization that emerged as a consequence of variations in the structure of domination. The
resulting social organization, for Frazier, was
key because it was in this arena that people
from different racial and cultural backgrounds
were accommodated. A caste system, racism inter-
woven with class distinctions, cultural pluralism, and nationalistic movements were all variations in the forms of social organization
observed by Frazier. He saw nationalistic movements, for example, taking place when assimilation did not occur. Also, Frazier noted the role
of the marginal man in nationalistic movements.
The marginal man was an accident of the
acculturation that occurred in race and culture
contact. This acculturation produced a divided
self as people absorbed the elements of antagonistic cultures. Frazier did not originate this
idea, but he utilized it in a richly insightful
manner. The idea, of course, also has a kinship
with Duboisian double-consciousness, and most
significantly points to the dialectical dimensions of cultural hegemony. Cultural negation,
under certain conditions, breeds cultural revi-

talization, a critical aspect of assimilation as a social problem.

CONCLUSION

E. Franklin Frazier's corpus of work represents a central foundation for Afrocentric inquiry because it captures theoretically and substantively the key issue driving epistemological configurations in the field, that is, the metaproblem of cultural hegemony. Despite Frazier's shortcomings, his methodological approach, with its historical, contextual, phenomenological, and ecological components, is properly suited for the kind of study needed in the field. Further, Frazier's conceptual constructions appropriately direct our attention to key research questions. A careful reading of Frazier reveals numerous findings that hold true today and that provide an understanding of current social phenomena affecting African American cultural and institutional development.

Frazier also makes immense contributions to understanding sociological processes generally. His highly developed analysis of the relationship between social organization and culture and the inter-relationships between various levels of social phenomena serves as a model for future social scientists to develop their scientific eye. The role of the family in social development, the effects of sacred beliefs on social organization, the sources of social consciousness in youth, the factors affecting leadership, business and political development, and the effects of race and culture contacts on personality development are only a few of the areas where Frazier provided substantial insight. More than any other social scientist, E. Franklin Frazier created an integrated body of work, methodologically, theoretically, and empirically, upon which Afrocentric inquiry in the social sciences can rest.

NOTES

1. See, for example, John H. Bracey Jr., August Meier, and Elliot Rudwick, eds., *The Black Sociologists: The First Half Century* (Belmont, Calif.: Wadsworth, 1971); James E. Blackwell and Morris Janowitz, eds., *Black Sociologists: Historical and Contemporary Perspectives* (Chicago: University of Chicago Press, 1974); Anthony M. Platt, *E. Franklin Frazier Reconsidered* (New Brunswick, N. J.: Rutgers University Press, 1991); G. Franklin Edwards, ed., *E. Franklin Frazier on Race Relations* (Chicago: University of Chicago Press, 1968).

2. Clovis E. Semmes, "The Sociological Tradition of E. Franklin Frazier: Implications for Black Studies," *Journal of Negro Education* 55 (Fall 1986):484-94.

3. Although Carter G. Woodson's *Mis-Education of the Negro* provided an early critique of the role of mainstream education in the reproduction of African American subordination, E. Franklin Frazier made a now classic assessment of the failures of the Black intellectual. See E. Franklin Frazier, "Failure of the Negro Intellectual," in Edwards, ed., *E. Franklin Frazier on Race Relations*, pp. 267-79.

4. For a succinct and accurate discussion of this criticism, which became embodied in the classic Frazier-Herskovits debate, see Joseph E. Holloway, ed., *Africanisms in American Culture* (Bloomington, Ind.: Indiana University Press, 1990).

5. See Andrew Billingsley, *Black Families in White America* (Englewood Cliffs, N.J.: Prentice-Hall, 1968); Robert B. Hill, *The Strengths of Black Families* (New York: Emerson Hall Publishers, 1971), p. 57; Joyce A. Ladner, *Tomorrow's Tomorrow* (New York: Doubleday, Anchor Books, 1972), pp.266-68, 270; Robert Staples, ed., *The Black Family: Essays and Studies* (Belmont, Calif.: Wadsworth, 1971). Hill linked the tradition of focusing on the weaknesses of Black families to E. Franklin Frazier, but he acknowledged that Frazier had been misused to advance pejorative views. Ladner argued that classic studies on the Black family focused only on the attitudes and behaviors of Blacks and not

on the structural effects of oppression. This was partially true, and Ladner did not entirely eliminate such a focus from her own work. However, Ladner correctly observed that too much emphasis was placed on conforming to the status quo. She helped to clarify the adaptive and cultural dimensions of Black behaviors by rejecting White middle-class values as a model for analysis.

Ladner also argued for the persistence of surviving African culture in African American family forms. The "strength-of-Black-family" school made important contributions to stimulating new directions in Black family research, but Nathan Hare astutely observed that this school of thought was used by some to move away from an attack on Black suffering and the conditions that stifled the economic position of the male as a provider in the African America family. See Nathan Hare, "What Black Intellectuals Misunderstand About the Black Family," *Black World* 25 (March 1976):4-14. Semmes, "The Sociological Tradition of E. Franklin Frazier" and Platt, *E. Franklin Frazier Reconsidered*, applied correctives to the interpretation of Frazier's work. John Scanzoni, *The Black Family in Modern Society: Patterns of Stability and Security* (Chicago: University of Chicago Press, Phoenix Edition, 1977), p. 1, argued that Moynihan never intended to fix blame on the Black family. Other scholars used what they considered to be Moynihan's continuation of Frazier's negative characterization of the Black family as a stimulus for their own work. These scholars generally made important contributions to the study of the African American family, but a careful reading of these works and Frazier clearly indicates a gross misinterpretation of Frazier. See, for example, Herbert G. Gutman, *The Black Family in Slavery and Freedom, 1750-1925* (New York: Pantheon, 1976); Elmer P. Martin and Joanne Mitchell Martin, *The Black Extended Family* (Chicago: University of Chicago Press, 1978); Carol B. Stack, *All Our Kin* (New York: Harper & Row, Harper Colophon Edition, 1975); Jualyne Dodson, "Conceptualizations of Black Families," in Harriette Pipes McAdoo, ed., *Black Families* (Beverly Hills, Calif.: Sage, 1981). Those who

wished to shift blame for certain social problems plaguing the African American community
from racism and White oppression to the Black
family obviously misused Frazier's work. Also, a
Black middle class (including intellectuals)
overreacted to the stigmatization of Black family life and sought to prove that positives existed in the Black family. White feminist and
Marxist scholars also transformed Frazier's
interpretations to fit their own agenda. These
various scenarios demand a more consistent and
in-depth reading and discussion of Frazier's
work.

6. The five major empirical works upon which
this analysis is based are: E. Franklin Frazier,
The Negro Family in the United States, rev. edn.
(Chicago: University of Chicago Press, 1966);
*Black Bourgeoisie: The Rise of a New Middle
Class* (New York: Free Press, 1957); *The Negro
Church in America*, new edition bound with the
Black Church Since Frazier (New York: Schocken
Books, 1974); *Negro Youth at the Crossways:
Their Personality Development in the Middle
States* (New York: Schocken, 1969); *Race and Cul-
ture Contacts in the Modern World* (Boston: Bea-
con Press, 1957).

7. Melville Herskovits, *The Myth of the Negro
Past* (Boston: Beacon Press, 1958); Frazier, *The
Negro Church*; Holloway, ed., *Africanisms in
American Culture*.

8. For more concise examples of Frazier's use
of the concepts of organization and disorganization, see "Problems and Needs of Negro
Children and Youth Resulting from Family Disorganization," and "The Negro Family in America," in G. Franklin Edwards, ed., *E. Franklin
Frazier on Race Relations*, pp. 191-209, 225-35.
Frazier was very clear that organization and
disorganization were not necessarily related to
the presence or absence of standard (two-parent)
family forms.

9. See Semmes, "The Sociological Tradition of
E. Franklin Frazier"; Robert Park, "The Conflict
and Fusion of Cultures with Special Reference to
the Negro," *Journal of Negro History* 4 (April
1919):111-33.; John H. Stanfield, *Philanthropy
and Jim Crow in American Social Science*
(Westport, Conn.: Greenwood Press, 1985), pp.

38-60. A discussion of various theories of Black culture in vogue during the time of Park and Frazier can be found in Herskovits, *Myth of the Negro Past*.

10. Semmes, "The Sociological Tradition of E. Franklin Frazier."

11. E. Franklin Frazier, *Black Bourgeoisie*.

12. For a posturban, post-Civil Rights analysis of the Black middle class, see Sidney Kronus, *The Black Middle Class* (Columbus, Ohio: Charles E. Merrill Publishing Co., 1971); Bart Landry, *The New Middle Class* (Berkeley: University of California Press, 1987).

13. E. Franklin Frazier, *The Negro Church in America*.

14. E. Franklin Frazier, *Negro Youth at the Crossways*.

15. E. Franklin Frazier, *Race and Culture Contacts in the Modern World*.

3

The Dialectics
of Harold Cruse

The critical thought of Harold Cruse became prominent at a time when various movements for social justice were gaining strength in American society. Beginning in 1966, African Americans entered predominantly White colleges and universities in greater numbers because Civil Rights legislation and public policy, backed by federal dollars, made it illegal to continue to exclude Blacks, and, to some degree, even rewarded the elimination of racially exclusionary policies. Whites and other non-Blacks benefited because need-based federal aid mitigated class barriers to higher education. White colleges and universities experienced increased market demand for their services. Furthermore, White, elite institutions profited significantly because they were in the strongest position to maximally use federal student grants and guaranteed student loans to subsidize their tuitions.

Greater class and racial diversity found a more politicized environment on college campuses in the context of a waning but radicalizing Civil Rights movement, a rising Black Consciousness movement, massive protest against the Vietnam War, and a general questioning of capitalist culture. This questioning challenged a social system that seemed to turn its back on poverty and racism in favor of materialism and profit.

Unlike their White counterparts, Black students found mainstream higher education to be devoid of a curriculum that could address the dynamics of an African world presence and the complexities of global White supremacy. They also found that just as European forms of Christianity were the most acceptable vehicles for religious expression in the United States, Marxist thought was the most acceptable radical philosophy in the mainstream academy.

The direct encounter by increasing numbers of African Americans with Eurocentric intellectual traditions in higher education, including Marxist theories, dramatically raised the question: Where is the social philosophy, the social, political and economic theory that could change the condition of African Americans? In his 1967 book, *Crisis of the Negro Intellectual*, Harold Cruse contributed significantly to this dialogue when he attempted to analyze cyclical pluralistic impulses by African Americans to collectively advance their status in American society. Problems of identity and group status seemed to be of continuing importance for African Americans.[1] However, returning to our previous metaphor, as European Christianity presented itself as the only true path to spiritual salvation, European radical theory presented itself as the only true path to social, political, and economic salvation. Thus, for African Americans, a common experience in both the religious realm and the social, political, and economic realm was that theology and social theory that addressed African American group realities and goals were superfluous. The implicit message was that theologizing and theorizing were better left to Eurocentric conceptualizations. Cruse observed that African American intellectuals routinely failed to construct relevant social theory and proclaimed this habitual failing a cultural crisis.[2]

Cruse maintained that the organization of American society, which he said was fundamentally structured by the racial and cultural orientation of its elites, served to block an ethnic consciousness and cultural particularism among African Americans. Thus, Cruse recognized the cultural realm as the critical arena for

Black social transformation. Furthermore, he
linked the failures of the cultural arena to the
fundamental class question raised by E. Franklin
Frazier.[3] Social class is a type of social organization whose function for African Americans is
to roughly determine their proximity and relationship to White ruling elites. Given the problem of African American economic dependency, the
relationship between a Black bourgeoisie and
White elites constitutes a coercive force that
tends toward Black conformity and subservience.
That is, when groups are economically, politically, and culturally dependent, they are co-
erced to move away from their own collective
goals in order to achieve functional goals defined by more powerful others. These functional
goals relate more to individual survival and
status needs. Frazier described this dilemma in
his empirical works, but Cruse extended it
through his critique of Black intellectuals and
creative artists.[4]

Cruse utilized case studies and historical
and critical analyses to identify a culturally
negating dialectic. This dialectic for Cruse was
the systemic tendency to translate African American group problems into individual and class
problems. The effect of this systemic process
was to obscure the essential plural reality of
American society. Thus, Crusian dialectics contributes to illuminating an important dimension
of the pervasive existence of the metaproblem of
cultural hegemony. Cruse also linked his dialectic with a broader intellectual tradition that
we may immediately recognize as Frazerian but
that we may also recognize as an essential feature of a distinctive African American epistemological tradition.

Harold Cruse has referred to himself as a social and cultural critic, but he is very much a
theoretician. While Cruse has asserted that
there is a void in social theory when it comes
to transforming American society into a socially
just society, his work takes important steps toward providing such theory. Cruse contributes
the methodological approach, critical analysis,
prescriptions for change, and categories of inquiry that are relevant for further study and
analysis. These ideas can be classified into

four areas: his analysis of an integrationist ethic, his analysis of the crisis of Black intellectuals and creative artists, his assessment of the crisis of Black leadership in a plural society, and his outline for developing a theory of the cities.

INTEGRATIONIST ETHIC

By 1968, African American students had begun to confront the limitations, omissions, and distortions of Eurocentric and White supremacist curriculums on college and university campuses. Building take-overs and other forms of protest by African American students called for the development of African American studies. University administrators responded to these demands, usually in a convoluted and piecemeal fashion, but dialogue did emerge regarding the substance and form of African American studies. For example, Black students at Yale University were successful in coordinating a symposium on Black studies in the spring of 1968. Black and White scholars who had some interest in African American issues and related subjects came together to discuss the pros and cons of formally recognizing a discipline or field of study on the Black experience.

Generally speaking, conservative scholars tended to practice the politics of exclusion and liberal scholars tended to practice the politics of inclusion. In other words, the liberal position seemed to acknowledge that information and materials on Africa, the African diaspora, and African Americans should be more visible and inclusive within the mainstream academy. However, it took a third-stream position advanced by Black scholars like Harold Cruse to argue that much more was involved. Social and historical conditions had set in motion the emergence of a corpus of knowledge that embodied a tradition, a method, a set of theoretical concerns, and a way of looking at and interpreting phenomena. At the Yale symposium, Harold Cruse put forth a brief but powerful set of ideas that helped to form the parameters of this emerging field of study. He presented these ideas under the title, "The

Integrationist Ethic as a Basis for Scholarly Endeavors."[5]

Cruse described an important cultural dialectic related to the metaproblem of cultural hegemony. He stated: "It is my belief that the integrationist ethic has subverted and blocked America's underlying tendency toward what I would call a democratic ethnic pluralism in our society."[6] Cruse observed a matrix of ideas that tended to diffuse pluralistic social organization among African Americans by obscuring the essential plural character of American society. But who and what is behind this subversion, and why is it so significant? To answer these questions, Cruse looked to the cultural particularism of Anglo-Saxon elites that espoused the integrationist ethic. The effect was to establish one's own culture as the ideal for others and to negate competing subcultures indigenous to North America. Cruse observed that the consensual support for this ethic was based on the belief that an Anglo-American tradition could bring about the promise of equality. The ethic has failed, but no viable alternative philosophy exists. The implication for African Americans is a systemic nullification of their development.[7]

There have been periodic plural impulses (nationalistic movements) among African Americans, but an integrationist ethic has served to block the potential of these movements. Cruse also observed that the call for Black Studies is a form of cultural nationalism and a response to a blocked cultural pluralism. Cruse, in his neo-Frazierian way, has restated Frazier's analysis that "nationalistic movements represent in some cases the failure of people with different racial and cultural backgrounds to achieve a single social organization."[8] On a global level, Frazier looked at this issue in terms of the trend toward federated cultures (coexisting plural cultures) versus the trend toward cosmopolitan cultures (fused cultures). He concluded that cosmopolitanism will increase but will be limited by continued federated cultures. Frazier argued that the key to positive relationships between these cultures will lie in the elimination of colonialism and imperialism and notions of superiority and inferiority.[9]

Cruse's observation of a specific cultural dialectic also raised certain types of empirical questions, and the integrationist ethic emerged as both a cultural problem driving the plural impulses of African American studies and the basis upon which to identify critical parameters shaping Afrocentric inquiry. Cruse recommended that pluralistic (or nationalistic) impulses among African Americans become an object of study on all levels: political, economical, and social.[10] He stressed that methodologically, the cultural problem under study required a historical approach and should focus on middle-class formations from generation to generation, beginning after the Civil War.[11] The middle class is a key group that determines the character of subsequent leadership and intellectual strata. Cruse also argued that emphasis should be placed on assessing whether a Protestant ethic (the basis of Anglo-Saxon cultural particularism) had achieved the American creed of democratic inclusion of African Americans, and how this ethic has affected Black middle-class development.[12] Specifically, Cruse argued that a central issue is how the retardation of the middle class has affected the point of view of the intellectual class.[13] Thus, while Cruse has identified important areas of study, he has also offered a critique of specific African American social formations.

Harold Cruse implied that the field of African American studies is distinguished by the legitimacy that it extends to the study of plural impulses among African Americans. By comparison, he noted that mainstream scholarship generally responds to this phenomenon by either encouraging that integration be speeded up or by questioning the legitimacy of plural impulses by African Americans. Thus, there seems to be an inherent cultural tendency by mainstream intellectuals, probably due to the pervasive and submerged (unconscious) characteristics of White supremacy, to delegitimate the presence and significance of ethnicity among people of African descent.

CRISIS IN BLACK INTELLECTUAL THOUGHT

In *Crisis of the Negro Intellectual*, Harold Cruse developed his ideas on the effects of an integrationist ethic on Black intellectual thought. He conceived of this problem in terms of the failures of certain strata, specifically, intellectuals and creative artists and a Black bourgeois or middle class. Overall, the problem is a cultural one because it results in a lack of theory that can give direction to the group. Among African Americans there has been a wavering, a shifting back and forth between an integrationist ethic and plural or nationalistic strivings without achieving a synthesis, that is, a philosophy that can progressively interpret these impulses on a higher level.[14]

Cruse identified the competing philosophies of Frederick Douglass (integrationist) and Martin Delaney (nationalist) as symptomatic of a cyclical dichotomy. Later, the integrationist philosophy became embodied in the civil rightism of organizations like the NAACP and the Urban League. Nationalist impulses were exemplified by the economic programs of Booker T. Washington, Marcus Garvey, and the Nation of Islam. Cruse criticized the "back to Africa" components of nationalist tendencies as escapist and nihilistic. He also looked negatively on the glorification and idealization of ancient and traditional African society through dress and philosophy as practiced by some cultural nationalists because, for him, the substance of the cultural dialectic under study is distinctly American. Nevertheless, Cruse saw cultural nationalism, the promulgation of a group philosophy, as the historically determined vehicle for social change as it relates to transforming the American social order and improving the status of African Americans.

For Cruse, given the cultural character of the metaproblem facing African Americans, it was the intellectuals and the creative artists who must productively respond to this challenge. As it stands, Cruse concluded in *Crisis* that Black intellectuals and creative artists on the whole had failed to measure up as spokespersons and theoreticians for the group. Cruse asserted: "In

advanced societies it is not the race politi-
cians or the `rights' leaders who create new
ideas and the new images of life and man. That
belongs to the artists and the intellectuals of
each generation."[15] Cruse also argued that a
Black intelligentsia had adopted the illusory
ideal of integration, the ideology that individuals could enter America as an open society. For
Cruse, integrationism as a philosophy of social
action is dysfunctional because it ignores the
fact of group or ethnic struggle and competition
in American society. White Anglo-Saxon Protestants, the dominant political, economic, and
cultural group in the United States, compete
culturally with other White Catholic and Jewish
ethnic groups. Thus, on the surface, America
projects a creed of individualism and integrationism when in fact it is a nation of unassimi-
lated ethnic groups competing for power. Cultural ascendancy is effectively maintained by
the WASP group over other White (European)
groups that collectively function within a system of White supremacy in relationship to
non-White groups. For these reasons, cultural
democracy has radical implications when applied
to the American social order.

Cruse further argued that a Black middle
class had equally failed in its role. Because a
Black intelligentsia had not recognized the illusion of an integrated world, this group was
not capable of functioning effectively within
the cultural apparatus of American society. But
most importantly, this stratum could not give
direction to a bourgeoisie that was culturally
retarded and thus unable to carry out its re-
sponsibilities to the Black community on an organizational, financial, and political level. In
short, the Black bourgeoisie lacked a cultural
philosophy that could help it overcome the subversion and manipulation of a White power structure, that is, the relationship of dependency
described by E. Franklin Frazier in his *Black
Bourgeoisie*. Furthermore, Cruse observed that
the failures of these strata were reciprocal.
Because of its cultural retardation, the Black
bourgeoisie or middle class did not recognize
the need to provide financial support and sponsorship for its intellectuals and creative

artists. Cruse asserted: "The problem of cultural leadership, then, is not only a problem of the faulty orientation of the Negro creative intellectuals; it is also a problem of the reeducation of the black bourgeoisie, especially its new, younger strata."[16]

Although Harold Cruse addressed the problem of cultural negation in terms of the failure of various strata within the Black community, he clearly identified social organizational and structural dimensions of the problem that serve as subverting forces. These forces operate with varied strengths and effects in diverse social and historical contexts, and at differing levels of social phenomena. For example, a key point of subversion is in the area of sponsorship. Cruse's analysis of the Harlem Renaissance illustrated that Harlem's creative intellectuals and artists had no economic control over the cultural modes of production. The lack of Black sponsorship, including the lack of a middle-class market, contributed to the subversion, diffusion, and de-institutionalization of radical Black ideas and cultural forms. Because a plural economic philosophy did not become fused with a plural cultural philosophy, the Harlem Renaissance failed to reach its radical potential. Moreover, not only did institutionalization not occur, but a generational break developed between the cultural lessons of the 1920s and the social strivings of the 1960s.[17]

For Harold Cruse, Harlem, the largest Black community in America, was strategically significant because of its location in America's cultural capital (New York City) and because Harlem also served as the cultural capital of Black America. What is most critically advanced in Cruse's analysis is that an integrationist social philosophy can only think in terms of breaking up Black communities like Harlem and destroying the intrinsic cultural strength that flows from their distinctive form of social organization. This fact is of special significance because of the key role that African Americans have in shaping the popular culture of American society. An integrationist ethic applied to African Americans but not to White ethnic groups destroys not only the basis for group power among African Americans but also the basis for the distinctive cultural commodities that African Americans bring to the American, popular culture marketplace.[18]

Cruse saw another aspect of the culturally subverting influences of American society in the contradictory relationships between White radical elements in American society, Jewish nationalism, and Black intellectuals. He based this assessment on his personal experiences with a Jewish-dominated Left. The Communist Party and other Marxist-inspired groups were among the few organized White enclaves that supported justice and equality for African Americans during the first half of the twentieth century. However, Cruse argued that Marxism had lost its radical potential. Cruse observed that White labor would not become anti-capitalist, form alliances with African American labor, or become sympathetic as a whole to African American emancipation.[19] Nevertheless, Marxists found the Black movement becoming the most important radical force for social justice in American society and altered their tactics to incorporate the strengths of this movement. Nevertheless, they did not change their fundamental belief in a class-based, worker-led revolution. In other words, Marxists became opportunistic in relationship to the Black struggle and found it necessary to dominate, where possible, African American social thought and strategies for social change. In addition, Marxism ignored the reality of competing ethnic groups, worker collaboration with capitalist owners, and the societal changes brought on by the mass communications media that made it easier to negate and absorb anti-capitalist sentiment.[20]

Cruse addressed other contradictions in Marxist-inspired social theory. He identified the contradictions represented by radical Jews who espoused the class-based philosophy of Marxism but who also supported their own cultural particularism. In other words, Black intellectuals inside the Left were expected to ignore African American cultural and group needs while Jewish radicals actively practiced nationalism, preserved their cultural/religious base, and worked to maintain in-group cohesion. Cruse argued that despite Jewish victimization by other Whites, it was Jewish cohesion as an ethnic group that gave European Jews in America the ability to gain power and wealth in disproportion to their numbers in American society. Inside left-wing politics, Cruse argued that Jews could play a three-way game. They could behave as Americanized Jews, Jewish Jews, and pro-Zionist, nationalistic Jews despite the rhetoric of class and the left-wing view that nationalism was a retrograde, retarded, and reactionary philosophy that only obscured the true class struggle. Thus, Cruse argued that, historically and systemically, cultural nationalism was as much subverted by the illusory ideology of Marxist/radical integrationism as it was by liberal integrationism.[21]

In short, by looking at liberal and radical sponsorship of Black intellectuals and creative artists during the Harlem Renaissance and during other key historical periods (for example, the 1930s), Cruse made the point that independence and control of the cultural mode of production is key to the success of Black intellectuals and creative artists in fulfilling their historical role. In addition, Cruse examined events surrounding the ownership of theaters in the African American community and the politics surrounding the substance and content of the performances at these theaters. For Cruse, the community theater constituted a primary unit of analysis and the prototypical arena for cultural politics in American society. In advanced capitalist society, however, the arena of cultural politics is elevated from the community theater to the mass communications media, which further necessitates the need to gain greater control over all levels of the means of cultural production and distribution. Without this control, and strong reciprocal linkages between a bourgeois or middle class and intellectuals and creative artists, the socially transformative dimensions of African American culture will be blocked.[22]

BLACK LEADERSHIP IN A PLURAL SOCIETY

True to his prescriptions for research in African American studies, Harold Cruse continued his critique of the relationship between an integrationist ethic and Black middle-class development. This time, with the publication of *Plural But Equal*, twenty years after the publication of *Crisis*, Cruse analyzed the leadership dimensions of a newer Black middle class rather than the intellectual and creative arts dimensions of an older middle class. Also, rather than emphasizing the control of the mode of cultural production as a key variable in producing viable cultural theory, he focused on the relationship between the legal structure and leadership strategies for social change. In both studies the integrationist ethic functioned as a kind of lens through which an intelligentsia and a leadership class interpreted the specific oppressive social forces that confronted them. The first instance involved the structure of cultural production; the second involved the structure of law, particularly the constitutional possibilities for addressing the specific historical oppression of African American people. The problem of leadership and the problem of the crisis of the intellectual, of course, remain connected because they both are plagued by an ethic that obscures appropriate strategies for change. Thus, as Cruse has argued consistently, the cultural arena is most important since it must give direction to political and economic activities.[23]

Harold Cruse raised an important issue that has crossed the minds of numerous African Americans: What is so inherently liberating about integration? The fundamental mode of the oppression of Black people was not the fact of being separate but the fact of being made unequal. Segregation was a tool of White supremacy to maintain economic inequality. Political inequality helped to preserve this subordinate relationship, but economic inequality based on race was at the foundation of segregation. Thus, subordinating and segregating relationships were created to preserve racial economic dependency. But what if African Americans had been allowed to develop equally? As Cruse demonstrated in *Plural But Equal*, nineteenth-century, post-Civil War legislation that could have brought about some semblance of equal educational opportunities for Blacks and significant aid to poor Whites was stopped by White elites because Black development was unacceptable. He observed that de facto segregation in education still exists, and integration has succeeded in eliminating many Black teachers and administrators. Thus, even though legal precedent has defined integration as a necessary component of equality, integration would be superfluous if the issue of African American equality was really addressed.[24]

The critical components of Cruse's analysis are the ambiguity in constitutional law as it relates to African American political, economic, and cultural rights; the inability of a Black leadership class to recognize this ambiguity in the context of the plural nature of American society; and the poor response strategically of this leadership class to address these ambiguities. Cruse argued that the Supreme Court decisions involving Plessy in 1896, Brown in 1954, and Bakke in 1978 attest to the ambiguities of the Fourteenth Amendment and its equal protection clause. Further, the Slaughter House case pointed to the debate over whether the Fourteenth Amendment was meant to preserve Black rights or was not confined to any class of people. Additionally, Cruse observed that the redefining of Black/White issues into minority and women's issues has further complicated interpretation of the Fourteenth Amendment's equal protection clause beyond the original intent of its framers in 1868.[25]

These ambiguities were less significant in the context of previous Civil Rights strategies directed at securing voting rights and equal access to public facilities. Complications arose, however, when it became apparent that White elites had restricted Black leadership ideals to what Cruse identified as noneconomic liberalism, a philosophy that ignored the necessity of economic parity based upon group principles. Cruse asserted:

The guiding white philosophy of noneconomic liberalism was an insidiously debilitating leadership ideal to have been
imposed on a nonwhite minority group seeking parity under American capitalism.
Worse than that, noneconomic liberalism
was a seductive entrapment into a fixed
psychology of dependency, underdevelopment
of social intelligence, and intellectual
subservience. At best, the free market of
capitalist activity was free for whites
only.[26]

The Black-White liberal coalition embodied in
the NAACP was to become the model for noneconomic liberalistic strategies that would become
prevalent throughout the twentieth century, a
strategy engineered and institutionalized by the
NAACP's White leadership. This approach meant
that economic strategies would take a back seat
to Civil Rights protest. Economic parity for
African Americans required plural solutions,
whether they were self-help, governmental, or
private. In some cases this requirement could
take on the appearance of economic segregation,
but it spoke to the reality of historical and
structured inequalities in the distribution of
wealth and power. The liberal focus on reforms
in civil liberties and race relations would not
be enough. Cruse argued that the Depression
years first brought to light the inadequacy of
noneconomic liberalism, but the current era,
which marks the end of the cycle of Civil Rights
advocacy, glaringly reveals the necessity for
economic parity. Thus, Cruse chides Black leadership in the traditional Civil Rights, integrationist mode for not realizing this dilemma and
for not responding appropriately. The result has
been bankrupt leadership strategies and a Black
middle class that, by default, has failed to
help a Black underclass.[27]
Once again, Cruse argued that there must be
total recognition of the plurality by Black
leadership. African American life must be re-
organized if Blacks are to survive into the
twenty-first century. First, Blacks must organize into a political bloc and then a cultural
bloc and then into as many internal economic or-

ganizations as is feasible within a capitalist, free-market system. For Cruse, a Black independent political party is the first step. He observed that Jesse Jackson's Rainbow Coalition reflected the essential plural character of American society. However, Jackson could not or would not break with the tradition that tied the Black vote to the Democratic Party. Cruse also noted that eventual ratification of the Equal Rights Amendment could submerge Black concerns by legitimating the need to supersede the equal protection clause of the Fourteenth Amendment in order to ensure protection against sex discrimination directed at a particular class. However, he argued that passage of such an amendment could also justify an equal rights amendment that would bar economic, political, and cultural discrimination based on race. Cruse expressed that this strategy could become one of the planks for an independent Black political party and could reopen debate on the ambiguities of the equal protection clause. Most importantly, however, is that a new leadership strategy is needed because the Constitution cannot offer additional protections for African Americans without being amended. The ambiguities of the Fourteenth Amendment do not serve to address the specific problems of structured economic inequality facing African Americans.[28]

THEORY OF THE CITIES

In 1971 Harold Cruse published an important article that summarized many of his ideas on formulating African American studies as a serious academic enterprise. "Black Studies: Interpretation, Methodology, and the Relationship to Social Movements" appeared in the short-lived *Afro-American Studies: An Interdisciplinary Journal*. This article also appeared under the title, "Black and White: Outlines of the Next Stage," in the now defunct publication, *Black World*, as a serialization of what was believed to be a portion of Cruse's next book. The article is rich with theoretical insight and speaks very well to Cruse's stated purpose. In the *Afro-American Studies* version he asserted, "The purpose of this paper is to aid in the establishment of a definite `Position' in the approach to Black studies in economics, sociology, political science, literature, music, art, religion, labor, the family, etc." The insights of this work should not go unnoticed because they provide important parameters for theory building and research in African American studies. Cruse's dialectical approach to historical and social analysis using a Black perspective is further revealed.[29]

The first issue that Cruse addressed was one of interpretation. How do we interpret history as it relates to African Americans? First, it should be noted that Cruse consistently draws from a scholarly tradition of Black intellectuals, historians, and social scientists. Cruse speaks to this point by example. I highlight this fact because building a body of knowledge requires recognition and broad-based study of its major contributors and ideas. The sense of perspective, the theoretical stimulation, and the understanding of context that derive from careful study of classic works in the field cannot be overemphasized. Mainstream graduate programs in the social sciences and the humanities generally ignore classic historical and social scientific works by Black scholars. African American studies, in order to be viable, must fill this void.[30]

Cruse observed that Black historical studies implied a specific interpretation. They revealed contradictions inherent in the fact that African people have been an integral part of an American cultural, economic, political, and social dynamic since before the founding of this land as a united nation and the fact that the founding fathers envisioned a nation of Whites of English heritage. To ignore this reality is to obscure and muddle understanding of subsequent historical events. For example, although economically important, Blacks were not legally part of the nation, and White elites consistently tried to get rid of free Blacks. Furthermore, the Civil War resulted in the resolution of a serious sectional conflict and the solidification of the Union. Cruse argued that the concept of nation as we know it grew out of this period and repre-

sented a new quality of social development involving a multiracial nation that was Black,
Red, and White. Thus, Cruse concluded that it is
necessary to look at Blacks in the context of a
"progressively changing quality of `nation-
hood.'"[31]

Cruse de-emphasized slavery in his analysis
and saw the current evolution of African Americans through three phases of social development
from the end of the Civil War to the economic
depression of the 1930s. He observed that these
three phases of group development were political, economic, and cultural and were a consequence of the Emancipation and the migrations to
the West and to the North that culminated in
African American urbanization. Thus, the process
of urbanization became the principal socializing
feature of Black life and is relevant to understanding current African American development.
However, Cruse wanted to make it clear that all
groups or races in the United States entered
their most important stage of progression in the
context of national development after the Civil
War.[32]

Cruse described the logical and empirical relationship between the three historical phases.
The first phase in African American group development was political and took place in the context of Reconstruction. This was a period of
limited Black empowerment and then disenfran-
chisement. Subsequent to Reconstruction, Blacks
responded to conscious attacks on their collective political strength by migrating to escape
White terrorism and by accelerating self-help
efforts to build economic enterprises in order
to mitigate White oppression.[33] As a consequence, the second or economic phase became
prominent. Migration to the cities and urbanization transformed the social outlook of African
Americans and contributed to conditions that
ushered in the cultural phase of group development. This third phase was symbolized by the period of heightened cultural creativity and cultural awareness called the Harlem Renaissance
and embodied prominent elements of group identity formation.[34]

According to Cruse, all three historical
phases, the political, the economic, and the

cultural, point to the fact that migration, the
conditions that caused migration, and urbanization were the most important socializing
events for African Americans as they acted to
improve their group status in American society.
As a consequence, Cruse hypothesized that future
social movements would be urban-based; thus a
theory of the cities was required. He also
stressed that each Black population in a given
city had a peculiar history that needed to be
studied. Thus, the urban socialization experiences of Blacks need to be differentiated from
one another in order to discern their disparities and similarities and potential for African
American development.[35]

Cruse identified a number of factors differentiating the socialization experiences of
Black populations in several cities, but he
quickly shifted to a discussion of Harlem. Because of Harlem's role as the cultural capital
of Black America, and because, for Cruse, the
cultural component--which involves the ideological, conceptual, theoretical, and even theological dimensions of group identity for-
mation--is the most critical element of the
three phases of Black social development, Harlem
occupies a special importance as an object of
intellectual inquiry and scrutiny in African
American studies. In addition, Cruse observed
that the heightened social and cultural awareness during the 1960s was simply a replay of the
three phases of development from the Civil War
through the Harlem Renaissance. The 1960s generation did not understand this fact because the
Depression years seduced Black intellectuals
away from the issues of the Harlem Renaissance
and produced a generational gap that affected
the historical consciousness of their generation. As a consequence, the Harlem community was
not prepared to understand and seize its historical role in an emerging cultural revolution.
According to Cruse, Harlem's strategic importance in the cultural realm required that
self-determination (or community control) efforts be geared toward capturing ownership of
various modes of cultural production and toward
institutionalizing Black cultural forms. This
agenda was necessary for African Americans to

compete in America's rapidly growing mass communications media, and to push the implied goal of
the Harlem Renaissance, the fulfillment of the
radical potential of cultural democracy. Such a
goal, Cruse observed, required a decentralization of the ownership of the mass communications media.[36]

Cruse identified a perspective, purpose, and
direction for African American studies through
revealing a central dialectic that involved the
interplay between the ownership and organization
of cultural production and distribution and the
spiritual strivings of a people. He pointed to
the need for a school of urbanology in African
American studies that could specifically advance
our understanding of the differentiated roles of
cities in African American group development.[37]

CONCLUSION

Cruse makes a significant contribution toward
identifying critical categories of analysis that
are theoretically rich and logically consistent.
Among these categories are the study of the cultural ideals of White elites and the role of
culture in political and economic domination.
For example, Cruse revealed the tendency of
American society to rob African American culture
of its radical and socially progressive aspects.
Cruse also stressed the importance of studying
middle-class or bourgeois formations among
Blacks over each generation with specific focus
on their status, outlook, and relationship to an
intellectual and creative arts stratum and to a
leadership stratum. Cruse also punctuated the
importance of studying the relationship between
culture and social organization when he identified the effects of an integrationist ethic and
noneconomic liberalism on Black political organizational goals and activities. In a similar
manner, he highlighted the importance of studying the effects of the relationship between social organization and culture by revealing key
socio-historical phases affecting group development and outlook. Furthermore, Cruse brought to
light the problem of historical and cultural
continuity when he made some effort to identify

generational discontinuities between the 1920s and the 1960s.

Cruse's interpretive frame, his work outlining a theory of the cities, and his focus on the important role of the organization, production, and control of culture in an advanced capitalist society are useful for future theoretical and empirical work in African American studies. In sum, Cruse's work is instructive by its methodological example and by its theoretical substance. It extends a Black intellectual tradition, and it affirms the metaproblem of cultural hegemony as a significant socio-cultural dialectic driving intellectual inquiry in African American studies. Harold Cruse has given scholars a vision through which to coherently and logically recognize the key parameters and essential elements of Black, African American, or Africana studies.

NOTES

1. See Harold Cruse, *Crisis of the Negro Intellectual* (New York: William Morrow, 1967).

2. Ibid.

3. Ibid.; cf. E. Franklin Frazier, *Black Bourgeoisie: The Rise of a New Middle Class* (New York: Free Press, 1957), and "Failure of the Negro Intellectual," in G. Franklin Edwards, ed., *E. Franklin Frazier on Race Relations* (Chicago: University of Chicago Press, 1968), pp. 267-79.

4. Ibid.

5. See Harold Cruse, "The Integrationist Ethic as a Basis of Scholarly Endeavors," in Armstead L. Robinson, Craig C. Foster, and Donald H. Ogilvie, eds., *Black Studies in the University: A Symposium* (New Haven, Conn.: Yale University Press, 1969), pp. 4-12.

6. Ibid., p. 4.

7. Ibid.

8. Cf. E. Franklin Frazier, *Race and Culture Contacts in the Modern World* (Boston: Beacon Press, 1957), p. 35.

9. Ibid., pp. 327-38.

10. Cruse, "The Integrationist Ethic," p. 7.

11. Ibid., p. 5.

12. Ibid., p. 6.

13. Ibid.

14. Cruse, *Crisis of the Negro Intellectual*, pp. 3-10.

15. Ibid., p. 96.

16. Ibid., p. 111.

17. See, for example, Part One in Cruse, *Crisis of the Negro Intellectual*, pp. 3-111.

18. Ibid.

19. A more concise discussion of this view can be found in Harold Cruse, *Rebellion or Revolution* (William Morrow, 1968), p. 140. This collection of essays, although published at a later date, predated Cruse's *Crisis of the Negro Intellectual* and contains many of the ideas that led to this later work.

20. Ibid., pp. 140-41.

21. Cruse, *Crisis of the Negro Intellectual*, pp. 57, 168.

22. Ibid., Part One, pp. 3-111.

23. Harold Cruse, *Plural But Equal: A Critical Study of Blacks and Minorities and America's Plural Society* (New York: William Morrow, 1987).

24. Ibid., pp. 15, 22. A similar critique was developed by the Black American and Harvard legal scholar, Derrick Bell. See Derrick Bell, "The Curse of Brown on Black," *First World* 2 (Spring 1978):14-18.

25. Ibid., pp. 32, 53.

26. Ibid., p. 79.

27. Ibid., pp. 74-79.

28. Ibid., pp. 376-81. See Harold Cruse, "Part I: `Black Politics Series'--The Little Rock National Black Politcal Convention," *Black World* 23 (October 1974):10-17, 82-88; and "The National Black Political Convention," *Black World* 24 (November 1974):4-21. Cruse emphasized the need for a Black political and independent party movement tailored to American political realities. He was most critical of pan-Africanist and internationalist rhetoric that obscured the domestic needs of African Americans.

29. See Harold Cruse, "Black Studies: Interpretation, Methodology, and the Relationship to Social Movements," *Afro-American Studies: An Interdisciplinary Journal* 2 (June 1971):15. Also see Harold Cruse, "Black and White: Outlines of

the Next Stage, Part One," *Black World* 20 (January 1971):19–41, 66–71; "Black and White: Outlines of the Next Stage, Part Two," *Black World* 20 (March 1971):4–31; "Black and White: Outlines of the Next Stage, Part Three," *Black World* 20 (May 1971):9–40.

30. Ibid.

31. Cruse, "Black and White, Part Two," pp. 6–9.

32. Ibid., p. 14.

33. Ibid., p. 17.

34. Ibid., pp. 25–29.

35. Ibid., pp. 30–31.

36. Cruse, "Black and White, Part Three," pp. 27–33.

37. Ibid., p. 40.

4

The Problem of Legitimacy

An important dimension of the metaproblem of cultural hegemony is the issue of legitimacy. Legitimacy involves gaining recognition and respect for one's perspectives, beliefs, and actions. It is a necessary component of all behavioral systems.[1] Because cultural hegemony tends to negate self-conscious and self-defined institution building among African Americans, legitimacy, as a mediating process, becomes problematic.

Psychologist Cedric Clark (now Sayed Malik Khatib) has analyzed the concept of legitimacy in light of perennial problems characteristic of the African American experience. He noted that this experience is plagued by chronic feelings of not being recognized and of not being respected. These feelings are byproducts of White supremacy and oppression and the resulting African American subordination. In other words, as a consequence of structured inequality, elements of African American behavioral systems are systemically denied legitimacy. Even though Khatib's analysis focuses on denial, denial is not the total problem. The dominant society may also extend legitimacy to social forms among African Americans, which can originate inside or outside of the Black community, that may not be in their interest as a group. Thus, the problem of legitimacy becomes focused in two additional areas: the selective extension of legitimacy and control over the legitimation process.

African American status and self-concept, through primary socialization, are generally tied, as one would expect, to Black reference groups. However, African Americans must eventually accommodate White secondary reference groups, which have inordinate power and control to decide what should be recognized and what should be respected in society. This discontinuity and gross imbalance in power creates complex problems that are manifested in every aspect of Black life.[2]

As African Americans interact in the broader society, they encounter structured power differentials that tend to force a shift in the sources of legitimacy and the significance of those sources. Status or social worth and the self-concept may become subject to a more intense reward system determined by dominant society reference groups and needs. A range of Black behavioral responses to this reward system is possible. These responses may include rejecting the system, chronic conflict with the system, some form of accommodation to the system, or an abnormal desire to be accepted by the system. The last response could be called "the need for White approval" and reflects a pathological rejection of Black reference groups. These range of responses can, and in fact, do in some instances, become so incorporated into Black social forms that dominant culture norms, values, and perspectives become infused in Black cultural patterns even when these social forms are antagonistic to African American group norms.

Let's consider, for example, how a dominant culture reward system that is connected to legitimacy may force a radical shift in reference groups. I will offer the hypothetical but true-to-life case of a Black male whom we shall call Andrew. Andrew grew up in a Black community where he learned the values of hard work and perseverance, and the importance of education. The presence of wise and supportive African American elders and a loving extended family provided this individual with a strong belief in his abilities and a solid achievement orientation. His family was able to shield him from the numerous social problems in his poverty-stricken community. Andrew's success in school was partially based on the encouragement of his family, church, and community. However, he had also internalized some dominant culture values that caused him to see African Americans as a group who did not want to achieve as he did. Also, through maladaptive values extant in the Black community, he placed a higher value on Blacks who physically approached White somatic norms. He did not fit these norms personally, but somehow Andrew felt more comfortable when he was around those who did.

As Andrew went through college, he realized that being around certain Whites helped him to gain access to useful information, resources, and opportunities. Access to these resources, opportunities, and information was only available through informal cliques, and most African Americans that Andrew knew did not have such access. Andrew also noticed that his White friends felt more comfortable and seemed to trust him more when he did not associate with other Blacks. So as not to threaten his White friends, Andrew began on his own to alter everything about himself that he thought was offensive or alienating to Whites. Eventually, Andrew pledged a White fraternity and severed most of his relationships with Black students. He did, however, continue his relationship with a Black woman that he viewed as being very close to the White somatic norms that he had come to prefer.

Andrew was a good student and was able to gain acceptance to a highly respected graduate program at another university. Andrew continued to avoid too much contact with other Blacks and learned how to make himself appealing to the "right" people. Andrew worked hard and gained the sponsorship of a powerful White professor who saw to it that he received his first job at a highly rated university and his first publications in well-respected, mainstream journals. Andrew married his college sweetheart and took a job in which he was the only Black in his department. He worked hard for acceptance, and grants and opportunities seemed to come more easily as powerful Whites began to seek his rather conservative views on social issues affecting the status of African Americans. Ironically, Andrew had paid little attention to this group in recent years. He had been careful not to address any controversial or racial issues in his dissertation or previous publications. Andrew soon became, however, a prominent expert on African American issues and race relations.

As Andrew gained prominence, the possibility of government appointments, a more prestigious university appointment, lucrative consulting contracts, and the like became possible. He noticed, however, that his White sponsors did not care to give him entree into all the circles that he desired. Andrew knew, nevertheless, that the inner circles of power were also associated with family connections. He had already limited his interactions to powerful Whites, who were very careful to extend their support to people whom they could trust. As it turns out, things came together for Andrew after he divorced his first wife. His associations took him into social settings that led him to marry a prominent and well-connected White woman. For those well-to-do Whites for whom Andrew's loyalty was in doubt, this move brought Andrew into the inner circle. Over time, Andrew had completely shifted reference groups. Through his new marriage and his careful career choices, Andrew had achieved psychic harmony by withdrawing legitimacy from Black reference groups and seeking to realize the rewards available from gaining the legitimacy of White reference groups.

The control of legitimacy constitutes a significant aspect of the social forces tending toward African American cultural negation. Issues involving intra-racial color stratification are chronic problems for African Americans. Also, rejection of one's collective identity as an African American and conflict with the dominant society over aesthetic interpretations are equally salient. Furthermore, what should be recognized, valued, and made normative among African American cultural forms or selected from non-African American cultural forms are key areas in which the issue of legitimacy comes into play. These areas include the acceptability and use of various communication styles, and validation of the themes, images, standards, and values projected in mass forms of communication. A metaquestion that looms large in the background of the African American experience is: How would African Americans conceive of themselves and relate to one another and others if they had not experienced European domination and exploitation?

Following Khatib's analysis, legitimacy is transmitted through the processes of communications, the sending and receiving of symbols, which make possible cultural learning or socialization. Recognition, one aspect of legitimacy, is important for the development of a strong self-concept. People need to have their existence, self-image, and definitions of reality validated. Recognition, however, extends beyond the simple state of being aware and involves the conscious act of paying attention to someone or something. Recognition can be either personal (people to people) or impersonal. Thus, it can be reflected through the symbolic structures of the environment. In this society, the symbolic environment includes books, television, radio, films, newspapers, magazines, greeting cards, billboards, toys, games, and the like. Nonrecognition leads to delegitimation or a devaluation of a given cultural or social form or group. Whether or not recognition is given seems to depend upon the uniqueness of the activity for the observer and the relevance of the activity to the values and goals of the observer.

Khatib further explained that recognition or paying attention to something is necessary for legitimacy but that recognition is not sufficient; you also need respect. Respect requires mutual identification. It is communicated by messages that reflect a shared definition of a given behavior. This is important to provide harmony, consistency, and structure in patterns of interaction. In interpersonal communication both parties must enjoy an understanding and a similar interpretation of what a particular style of communication means. For example, some Whites may view the demonstrative, colorful, and metaphorical speech styles of some Black men as threatening. However, these men are simply speaking in a manner that they know is expected, understandable, entertaining, and engrossing to a Black audience.

One White scholar of African American and dominant culture linguistic patterns has noted that Black communication styles are often mis-interpreted by Whites. This researcher also ob-served that "the issue of cultural subordination has always been a powerful one for blacks."[3] His empirical findings suggest that much of the in-ter-racial conflict that arises in school and at work is based on the fact that Whites attempt to control Black behavior based on the idea that only White-defined cultural patterns should be used. He also presented evidence to show that punishment against Blacks for violating White norms is much greater than that against Whites for violating White norms.[4]

Respect takes the form of labeling, catego-rizing, and defining. It most often results in assignment of some negative or positive quality (value). Knowledge of a person's definitional universe, social reality, or culture is also im-portant to communicate respect. Without such knowledge, disrespect can be communicated uncon-sciously.

Khatib also observed that respect is commu-nicated through messages of assessment and eval-uation. People want to be supported in their as-sessment of reality and in their assessment of their own behavior. Such support is important to maintain self-respect. Similarly, assessment can be transmitted personally or impersonally, and positive or negative value is assigned to such assessments. Assessment is determined by certain criteria that the observer possesses. They are the uniqueness of the occurrence and the rele-vance of the occurrence to the observer. One may not have the proper criteria or standards for judgment within one's culture to evaluate events within another culture. Given the uniqueness of an event, one cannot assess behavior that ap-pears too unusual, and the relevance of the ac-tion is always determined by the question: Is it important to me?

Finally, Khatib related that respect is com-municated through messages of behavioral ac-countability, or the attribution of blame or credit for the occurrence of an individual's actions. Behavioral accountability is important for the maintenance of self-respect since it assigns causality or responsibility for an act to oneself (internal) or to others (external). The form of accountability depends upon the exact structuring of causality and can communicate respect (legitimacy) or disrespect (delegitimacy). The determinants of accountability are consistent with a person's goals in maintaining a satisfactory self-concept. Internal accountability will occur when a person likes his or her actions or considers them successful, and external accountability will occur when a person dislikes his or her actions or considers them unsuccessful. To the extent that individual A respects individual B, individual A will account for B's behavior in the same way that B would account for her or his own behavior. Legitimacy is always a problem in human relationships in which a gross imbalance in power favors a group that seeks to dominate and control another.

THE PLANTATION PROTOTYPE

African American conflict and ambivalence regarding self-concept, self-image, and conformity to White social and cultural needs at the expense of Black institutional development requirements can be traced to social organization on the plantation under the institution of slavery. Legitimacy, or recognition and respect, is required for status (assessment of one's relative social worth), and the status of the slave became partially but substantially tied to the system of stratification on the plantation. A type of color ranking emerged based on several factors. One factor was miscegenation in which White male slave owners had primary access to African women to fulfill their sexual appetites. The offspring from these unions acquired different color and physical gradations that later took on social significance. Another factor was the ideology of White supremacy, which glorified White "blood" or genetic traits and White somatic norms. This ideology, which existed among a White elite or powerful and thus high-status reference group, was absorbed by some African slaves but had implications for all of them.

There was both an ideological and a structural dimension to the absorption of White supremacist values by Blacks. The offspring of White and African slave unions sometimes gained more privileged positions as domestics or as skilled artisans on the plantation. This process also involved slave masters who decided to free, bequeath property to, or educate their African progeny. Thus, when chattel slavery ended, a more privileged upper class was disproportionately of mixed racial heritage. Also, irrespective of color or physical characteristics, slaves who were domestics and skilled artisans were required through the organization of work to gain greater facility with White elite culture. For example, domestic slaves had to raise the slave owner's children and provide for the slave-owning family's most intimate needs. Lighter-skinned Blacks were not always of the upper classes, but the conditions of White supremacy created a color stratification system that roughly followed the ranking of work, until urbanization, with its increased occupational differentiation, radically altered this pattern.[5] The critical point is that any sensitivity, conflict, or psychological maladjustment regarding color or other elements of the physiognomy of African Americans, among African Americans, was and continues to be a consequence of the inordinate control of legitimacy by a culturally hegemonic system of White supremacy.[6]

Along with a caste-like system based on color, a system of racial etiquette that was designed to establish deferential and obsequious relationships between African slaves and Europeans was established. This system of racial etiquette emerged not only as a form of social control but also as a method of moral sanction. African people were required to accept an inferior status and to act as though they believed in it.[7] Of course, Africans were able to develop counter values, and they adopted varying degrees and forms of resistance. However, there were many psychological casualties, and the imposition of White supremacist values on African norms became a persistent social problem for

African Americans.[8] Intra-racial conflict based
on color stratification and conformity to the
needs of White elites at the expense of African
American freedoms became a consequence of a reward system that structured legitimacy and status around White somatic norms and economic and
cultural aspirations. Political and economic
privilege and the power over life and death
stood behind the ability to extend legitimacy to
a normative order of White supremacy.

RACIAL ETIQUETTE: POSTSLAVERY DIMENSIONS

A classic study of racial etiquette, which
includes an important discussion of postslavery
conditions, was published by sociologist Bertram
Doyle in 1937. It helps to document the context
for African American personality development
under a White supremacist system. It furnishes a
vivid description for understanding the basis
for intra-psychic and intra-racial conflict
among African American precipitated by oppression. Doyle demonstrated that the entire
symbolic world of African Americans was altered
to promote a process of inferiorization. Besides
the ubiquitous use of the pejorative term
"nigger," writings would refer to White women
and Negro females. "Lady" also was a term re-
served for White women. The use of "Mr." or
"Mrs." as titles of respect were taboo when it
came to greeting African Americans. "Boy" was
used by Whites to address Black men of all ages,
and, regardless of their name, Jack or George
was considered adequate to acknowledge a Black
man's existence. References to gentleman, lady,
or American were understood never to be African
Americans. Speeches by Whites greeted the audience with, "Fellow citizens and Negroes." Signs
could say: "Negroes and dogs not allowed." They
could also refer to White "people" but the colored "race."
The securing of basic services was dehumanizing on a daily basis. Black men had to remove
their hats in all White establishments and public places and in conversing with Whites. The
reverse was not true for White men. White insurance collectors were called "muddy foots" be-

cause they typically would not wipe their feet when they entered African American homes. Black women could not try on hats or gloves, and White sales staff did this for them--if, of course, Blacks were served at all. Banks accepted deposits from African Americans but from a separate window and teller. Seriously injured African Americans could not get to a hospital, if medical care was available to them, unless a Black-owned ambulance was accessible. Blacks who purchased food from White restaurants had to wait for their food to be handed to them in a paper bag; they took it outside to eat. Soft drinks were placed in tin pails and taken outside. African Americans had to enter movie theaters by the side or rear door, and employees guided Black patrons to the balcony for segregated seating, pejoratively referred to as "nigger heaven" or "buzzard roost." Blacks who needed to purchase tickets of any sort typically had to wait until all Whites were served. Sleeping accommodations could not be secured on trains unless Blacks had sufficient funds to reserve an entire sleeping car. Sometimes African Americans could enter the dining car after all Whites had been served.

Segregation to enforce White supremacy was complete and pervasive. Separation was comprehensive in public schools, public places, railroads, streetcars, theaters, parks, and other places of amusement. Black teachers could never teach White children or receive equal pay. Public hospitals had separate wards, and Black dead bodies were separated from White dead bodies. Also, the dead could not occupy the same hearses or cemeteries. In court, Black and White witnesses were seated on opposite sides of the courtroom and separate Bibles were used. Blacks were rarely allowed to serve on juries and usually could not testify against a White person. There were separate chain gangs, jails, reformatories, and penitentiaries. Black and White workers could not perform the same task, and no Black could have authority over any White. Paved streets stopped at Black neighborhoods. Under vagrancy laws, Black women were arrested for being in front of their homes. They were not supposed to have the privilege of remaining home

while their husbands worked. Black health professionals could only work with Black patients
unless this service took jobs away from Whites.
    The daily slights and dehumanizing experi-
ences were endless for African Americans. Segregation was intended to subordinate Blacks and
to keep them powerless. Furthermore, Whites
could always move across the color line if it
was to their advantage. They could frequent
Black establishments when Blacks could not gain
access to White establishments. Similarly, White
men typically sought sexual unions with African
American women while using the law and violence
to restrict Black male and White female unions.
Open sexual exploitation of Black women by White
males was not punished. Typically, African Americans needed White sponsorship to gain services,
jobs, education, or to negotiate the criminal
justice system. This sponsorship functioned as a
more benign method of White domination and control. The entire system of segregation and
racial etiquette was supported by coercion. The
threats of lynching or of losing one's job were
central features of this system, and the legal
structure sanctioned pervasive segregation in
order to promote inequality and unequal development.[9]
    Personality and inter-personal disruptions
due to the system of White supremacy became
widespread and were particularly reflected in a
heightened color and somatic consciousness surrounding intra-racial conflict, rejection of
self, internally directed violence, and a beauty
culture that emerged as an accommodation to
White supremacist values. In the 1930s and
1940s, a substantial number of intensive,
multi-city, multi-regional studies that used
large samples documented these general maladaptations to White supremacy.[10]
    According to extensive research, inter-per-
sonal conflict could revolve around the rejection of darker-skinned people. Dark-skinned
Black women were believed to have a particular
problem securing a mate. Successful Black men
were known to seek lighter-skinned women. Black
churches and social clubs sometimes used skin
color as a criteria for membership. Black businesses sometimes sought lighter-skinned employ-

ees. The very dark and the very light were particularly made to feel ashamed of their color. Brown-skinned people seemed to have a healthier attitude about their color and expressed the ability to get along with lighter-skinned and darker-skinned people. Family conflict could result from favoritism given to lighter-skinned members. Epithets used in arguments typically denigrated skin color, hair length, and hair texture. Color was not the only criterion for aesthetic judgment; the texture of the hair was frequently of greater importance. The notion of "good" hair (long and straight hair) and "bad" hair (short coarse hair) was pervasive. Folk knowledge included numerous ways to make the lips smaller, the nose more pointed, the hair straighter and longer, and the skin lighter. Black children were found to associate being ugly with dark skin. Also, because color could block access to opportunity and status, it contributed to extreme sensitivity and proneness to fighting.[11]

Despite the internalization of White supremacist values in Black culture, what is most significant is that African Americans were able to sustain the high level of mental health that they did. Families that had significant levels of solidarity were able to mitigate negative social definitions of color and African physiognomy. Also, many African Americans were able to identify the societal source of African American self-hatred and intra-racial conflict and self-consciously strive to transcend their effects. Nevertheless, African American culture has had to devote significant amounts of psychic energy to reduce the effects of White supremacy norms. The family seems to be a key institution in this struggle, and Black children typically must mature in a society that does not automatically legitimize their somatic existence.[12] White supremacy norms are still reproduced in the Black community through both internal and external cultural processes related to cultural hegemony and the problem of legitimacy. The struggle to constructively alter an anti-African American symbolic world continues.

LEGITIMACY, INTEGRATION, AND NEW FORMS OF DOMINATION

Legitimacy is the mechanism by which a given social reality tends to be supported or tends to be negated. Cultural hegemony withholds or extends legitimacy based upon a propensity to preserve dominant group power and privilege. The legitimation of a system of racial etiquette that was most virulent in the South but that also existed throughout the United States, in varying degrees and in varying manifestations, was an expression of a socially constructed reality designed to validate the subordination of African Americans by affirming African inferiority, genetically and culturally. Other non-White and non-European groups were similarly affected but with results distinctive to their numbers in the population, their culture, their phenotype, and their relationship to European economic needs.

Over time, dominant society elites have changed the meaning of segregation for African Americans to fit their political needs. Initially, segregation was a strategy to isolate and inferiorize African people. It was used as a method to facilitate economic exploitation and to maintain political subordination. Through segregation it was easier, under certain conditions, to inequitably distribute the goods and resources of society. Ghettoization, for example, was a type of segregation that isolated Black people so that resources could be withdrawn from African American populations without hurting more privileged groups. Legal segregation also was used to maintain the system of racial etiquette that served to control and subordinate African Americans politically and economically. Today, however, the label "segregation" is incorrectly applied to any group-focused effort by African Americans and others to meet the social and cultural needs that are not automatically provided to African Americans, as they are to European Americans, or to rectify the past and current effects of White supremacist oppression and structured inequality.

Forms of integration and segregation (as in the case of group-directed strategies to elim-

inate socially produced inequality) can be positive or negative given their definition, social
context, and social function. When we do not
consider these conditional components of segregation and integration, one can inappropriately
use the ideology of integration to diffuse the
legitimate group needs and aspirations of African Americans that are intended to dismantle
structured inequality. These group-based activities clearly have nothing to do with subordinating others but have everything to do with transcending the effects of institutionalized disadvantage. Some will label any form of group
solidarity or group-directed action by African
Americans as segregation (in its traditional and
negative sense) and therefore inappropriate behavior. On predominantly White college campuses,
for example, African American students are typically criticized for eating together, for socializing together, and for creating various
groups and organizations to meet their social,
cultural, educational, and political needs. Even
in their small numbers, even in the context of
an environment that does not automatically address African American cultural needs, and even
in the circumstances of White hostility, Black
students are expected to distribute themselves
among White students to give the appearance of
integration.

Without careful scrutiny and flexible strategies for constructive change, integration can
have numerous counterproductive effects on
African American development. For example, when
African Americans attend predominantly White,
elementary, middle and secondary public schools,
but are tracked into inferior and less promising
curricula, the negative results are ignored in
favor of the appearance of integration. Other
counterproductive trends result when integration
requires shifting high-achieving Black students,
top teachers, and scarce resources from Black
neighborhood schools to a few regional magnet
schools. The purpose is to attract what usually
turns out to be a small number of White students
in order to create the image of integration.
These specialized and resource-packed schools
may even exist in poor Black communities where
the disadvantaged children of the neighborhood

cannot attend them, while White children are bused in. Also, integration may result in the removal of Black teachers, mentors, role models, and administrators from the daily lives of Black children, and it can deprive Black children of a caring and supportive educational environment.

Unfortunately, segregation has been misapplied to progressive group action, and it has taken on a singularly pejorative meaning. Integration has taken on a singularly positive meaning. Nevertheless, de facto segregation still exists wherever it is expedient to do so, and integration is absent in situations where it can be most effective in bringing about equality, for example, in the economic realm.

These trends in the definition and validation of integration and segregation are consistent with the problem of cultural hegemony. This problem has never been successfully remedied by the "segregation is bad, integration is good" conceptualization of inequality, or the mislabeling of human rights-oriented, group-directed behavior as segregation. The persistent social trend, regardless of the social form, is to serve the cultural interest of White elites at the expense of African American development.

Independent, group-based activities and institutions that are intended to meet human needs not addressed by the broader society and that are designed to remedy the effects of White domination and oppression are not the same as the segregation associated with White supremacy. To delegitimize group-empowering activities, integration is offered up as the only morally and socially correct behavior. The result is to make integration the new tool of White supremacy.

As we move beyond the memory of the Civil Rights movement and the system of legalized segregation, students and the general public forget the nature of the type of segregation practiced to support White supremacy. In addition, popular culture forms, the dominant vehicle for reality construction in society, tend not to conceptualize the oppression of African Americans as being tied to White supremacy. Therefore, segregation and integration are not understood as possible tools of oppression, given their definition, context, and social function, but as morally antagonistic ideals. Furthermore, the social forces of ideation obscure sight of the depth, pervasiveness, and virulence of the effects of the system of racial etiquette that was created in this country. As a consequence, we tend to forget what produced the complexity of intra-racial problems in the African American community. We also fail to consider how these maladaptations to White supremacy are reproduced and sustained. The problem of legitimacy is an important mechanism of cultural negation challenging African American institutional and cultural development because it distorts the ability of African Americans to define strategies for change in a way consistent with historical and social conditions leading to and supporting their subordination.

NOTES

1. Cedric Clark (Sayed Malik Khatib), "The Concept of Legitimacy in Black Psychology," in Edgar G. Epps, ed., *Race Relationships: Current Perspectives* (Cambridge, Mass.: Winthrop, 1973), pp. 332-54.

2. Ibid. My discussion of legitimacy is based on Khatib's initial formulation.

3. Thomas Kochman, *Black and White Styles in Conflict* (Chicago: University of Chicago Press, 1981), p. 159.

4. Ibid.

5. E. Franklin Frazier, *Black Bourgeoisie: The Rise of a New Middle Class* (New York: Free Press, 1957).

6. Ibid.; Bertram W. Doyle, *The Etiquette of Race Relations in the South: A Study in Social Control* (New York: Schocken Books, 1971), p. 175, 181; Lloyd W. Warner, Buford H. Junker, and Walter A. Adams, *Color and Human Nature: Negro Personality Development in a Northern City* (Westport, Conn.: Negro Universities Press, 1970); Charles S. Johnson, *Patterns of Negro Segregation* (New York: Harper & Brothers, 1943).

7. Doyle, *Etiquette of Race Relations*, p. xiii.

8. See John W. Blassingame, *The Slave Community*, rev. edn. (New York: Oxford University Press, 1979).

9. The discussion of racial etiquette is primarily from Doyle, *Etiquette of Race Relations*, pp. 136–59. Also see Hortense Powdermaker, *After Freedom: A Cultural Study in the Deep South* (New York: Russell & Russell, 1968); Hylan Lewis, *Blackways of Kent* (New Haven, Conn.: College & University Press, 1964); Charles S. Johnson, *Growing Up in the Black Belt: Negro Youth in the Rural South* (New York: Schocken Books, 1967); Johnson, *Patterns of Negro Segregation*.

10. Warner, Junker and Adams, *Color and Human Nature*; Powdermaker, *After Freedom*; Lewis, *Blackways of Kent*; Johnson, *Growing Up in the Black Belt*; Allison Davis, Burleigh B. Gardner, and Mary R. Gardner, *Deep South: A Social Anthropological Study of Caste and Class* (Chicago: University of Chicago Press, 1959); Allison Davis and John Dollard, *Children of Bondage: The Personality Development of Negro Youth in the Urban South* (New York: Harper & Row, 1964); Robert Lee Sutherland, *Color, Class, and Personality* (Washington, D.C.: American Council on Education, 1942); E. Franklin Frazier, *Negro Youth at the Crossways: Their Personality Development in the Middle States* (New York: Schocken, 1967); St. Clair Drake and Horace R. Cayton, *Black Metropolis: A Study of Negro Life in a Northern City,* vols. 1–2, rev. edn. (New York: Harcourt, Brace & World, 1970).

11. Ibid. A recent work by Cross tries to debunk the self-hate thesis ascribed to African American personality development. He blames the canonization of this thesis on the doll studies used to justify the 1954 Supreme Court decision outlawing segregated schools. Cross critiques a number of psychological studies and assumes there are no important studies that could cast light on his subject between 1939 and 1960. The studies cited in this chapter do not support this assertion. The notion that levels of self-hate among African Americans have always been insignificant and have not changed over time is untenable and is not supported by a wide range of multidisciplinary research as well as

the experiences of most Blacks who have grown up in a Black community.

The assertion by Cross that rejecting one's reference group has nothing to do with mental health indicates some confusion regarding the social and cultural basis of mental health norms. Cross also ignores the problem of double-consciousness in his discussion of biracial preferences and biculturalism. Many fine points are made in this work, but it suffers from faulty conceptualization, the lack of an analysis of racism as a social system, and a certain myopia when it comes to examining relevant studies. It is simply not normal for a people to learn to devalue reference groups that look like them and that share a common social, cultural, and historical experience.

It is unlikely that changes in social structure related to the socialization of the self, that is, the removal of legally sanctioned segregation and the decline in a pervasive system of racial etiquette, had no effect on personality development of African Americans. Further, variations in the indicators of Black self-hatred are not only a function of the virulence of racism, but also a function of the strength of the family and other institutions that can help to mitigate the effects of racism. Today, racism has taken a more sophisticated form, and the Black family is in a more weakened state. Cross is correct, however, and this is validated by the studies he ignores, when he states that other factors related to mental health can function independently of race and become much more salient issues for certain aspects of personality development. See William E. Cross, Jr., *Shades of Black: Diversity in African American Identity* (Philadelphia: Temple University Press, 1991).

12. See Frazier, *Negro Youth at the Crossways*; Johnson, *Growing Up in the Black Belt*; Sutherland, *Color, Class, and Personality*; Drake and Cayton, *Black Metropolis*; Cross, *Shades of Black*.

5

Culture, Economics, and the Mass Media

For African Americans, unique political and economic circumstances have taken place within a distinctive cultural dynamic that restricts significant portions of Black economic activity to brokering Black markets and that promotes the expropriation of African American cultural products for the purpose of stimulating capitalist expansion. These structural relationships contribute to a tendency toward African American cultural negation. However, culture is at the foundation of collective power in American society and the potential for economic development, social mobility, and progressive social transformation. Cultural negation limits group advancement and mobility because the acquisition of political and economic power requires a collective consciousness, collective action, group sponsorship, and shared goals.

WHITE SUPREMACY AND BLACK IMAGES

Media images of African Americans have been shaped by a normative order of White supremacy that distorted the cultural and human appearance of African Americans, limited their images to certain roles, and established their relationship to Whites as subordinate. The reification

of this normative order is found in the antebellum period, in which the blackface minstrel mode
of entertainment, which evolved from the 1820s,
established a comedic and buffoon-like image of
African Americans as it became America's first
form of popular culture. Negative perceptions of
African Americans were also institutionalized in
everyday life as White America displayed or constructed grotesque images of Blacks through such
objects as lawn ornaments, dolls, games, sheet
music, advertisements, postcards, eating uten-
sils, milk jugs, ash trays, and the like. Although fearful of slave revolts and fully cognizant of African American resistance to
bondage, Whites painted the psychologically
soothing image of the contented, happy-go-lucky
slave and the image of the devoted, fearful, and
childlike slave in their literary and theatrical
portrayals of Blacks. Other images denigrated
free Blacks and made them appear incapable of
grasping "White civilization." There was also
the image of the tragic mulatto, who presumably
had a genetic edge over other Blacks because of
"White blood," but who was disastrously blocked
from the full humanity of being White because of
"Black blood."[1]

Technological change provided for the emergence of motion pictures, radio broadcasting,
and television, and negative and distorted images of African Americans persisted. Radio maintained the denigrating traditions of blackface
minstrelsy as it continued the restricted and
distorted images of Black life through the commercially successful characters of "Amos 'n'
Andy." Visual mass media forms perpetuated the
ideal of the harmless and devoted Black through
the image of the sexless, obese Black mammy who
was always more dedicated to the White family
for whom she worked than she was to her own family. The ideal of the devoted and nonthreatening
Black was also continued through the sidekick
image, which paired a Black character with a
White one who was visually dominant, more cerebral, or more courageous. Typically, the White
character had a love interest while the Black
character looked on vicariously. A further dominant theme was that White women were always good
enough to be rescued and loved, but Black women

were more often sexless servants or prostitutes. As an aside, my own African American students have commented on the fact that movies normally show Blacks having sex while depicting Whites as making love. In a more general sense, White-controlled motion picture and television productions rarely show Blacks in loving relationships with one another, overly confine them to comedic and criminal roles, deny Blacks an accurate historical presence, virtually eliminate Blacks from science fiction and futuristic themes, and restrict African Americans to racial issues rather than the full range of human experiences. What is even more distressing is that Blacks have had to portray the same distortions on stage and screen if they wanted employment as actors and actresses.

Changes in the way in which the mass media portray African Americans have come about through protracted struggle and point to the significance of group power. The Civil Rights and Black Consciousness movements helped to soften grotesque stereotypes and to broaden the range of roles that African Americans could portray. Throughout the history of American media, independent African American media have been instrumental in providing an alternative to distorted White images of Blacks. A Black press, Black filmmakers, Black theater, Black television productions, and the like have helped to expand the human image of African Americans. Also, the individual efforts of African American writers, directors, actors, and actresses have brought greater substance, dignity, innovation, and artistry to Black characterizations in the media, despite limitations on the range of these characterizations. Clearly, media content is a function of racial and ethnic control. How then are the cultural and ethnic needs of groups to be handled in a mass media environment that is not culturally or ethnically diverse in terms of ownership and control? To explore this question adequately, we must briefly consider the cultural and group realities of American society.

GROUP POWER VERSUS BLACK CULTURAL FRAGMENTATION

The United States of America was founded with the idea of creating a society ruled and dominated by White, European, English-speaking, male Protestants. Aboriginal peoples were forcibly removed from their lands and relegated to the periphery of American political, economic, and cultural development. Despite the possibility for peaceful coexistence, Anglo-Saxon invaders engaged in extended genocidal warfare against Native peoples. In the broader context of the Americas, other invaders included Spanish-, Dutch-, French-, and Portuguese-speaking Whites who fought each other for control of New World riches but who collectively enslaved or exterminated Aboriginals and participated in the expropriation of African labor.[2] English-speaking, Protestant male elites achieved dominance in North America, but this group has had to reluctantly make room for other European ethnic groups of Catholic and Jewish backgrounds. Despite the presence of a collective consciousness, the White racial stratum is characterized by religious, ethnic, and class divisions that compete not only on a political and economic level, but also on a cultural level.

Thus, as observed by social critic Harold Cruse, an ideology of individualism in American society conflicts with the reality of group power.[3] For example, even though the Constitution seems to address individual rights, it in fact preserves group rights and power for some. White, Anglo-Saxon, Protestant elites preserved ethnic pluralism for themselves by espousing and institutionalizing in the Constitution the doctrine of religious freedom. In other words, ethnic and national identity for White colonizers could be subsumed within their religions.[4] Despite periodic conflict between White religious and ethnic groups, these groups have remained loosely cohesive under their Judeo-Christian traditions and maintained a collective racial consciousness in their relationships with non-Whites. Furthermore, they have responded as ethnic enclaves in their pursuit of economic and political power. African Americans, on the other hand, did not benefit from the doctrine of reli-

gious freedom because White America systematically suppressed and destroyed African religions. As a consequence, African Americans have
had to respond to a pluralistic American cultural dynamic as a religiously and culturally
fragmented group.[5]

The fact of cultural competition in the context of White Anglo-Saxon cultural dominance is
further complicated by a growing non-White
(non-African American) presence in America. As
the global satellites that serve capitalist centers in the United States are transformed economically and culturally, immigration or flight
to the capitalist centers occurs. In some instances, this flight involves workers whose native lands have been ravaged by capitalist exploitation and who now seek economic refuge. In
other instances, an indigenous petty bourgeoisie
flees from the periphery to seek better opportunities. Since in the present era many of these
workers and small entrepreneurs are non-European
and non-White, the religious, ethnic and racial
diversity of the country is increasing in
complexity. This means that the importance of
culture and group power becomes even more
intensified.[6] A critical question then becomes:
To what extent will African Americans be in a
position to compete economically and politically
within this new cultural arena?

CHALLENGES TO AFRICAN AMERICAN GROUP POWER

In light of the importance of culture and
group power in American society, there are three
additional structural relationships that critically affect African American cultural viability. First, racial oppression has up to this
point denied African Americans a foothold in the
American economy as owners or producers and has
eclipsed development of a significant entrepreneurial class. As a result, African Americans
are almost completely consumers.[7]

Second, ruling White elites no longer need
Black labor, a situation that has been evolving
since the end of chattel slavery, even though
there have been periodic stimuli to expand the
need for labor generally (e.g., wars and in-

creased industrialization). Nevertheless, there is no longer a strong collective orientation among any ruling elite stratum that looks upon African Americans as an indispensable source of labor. Surplus Black labor is absorbed by the prison system, the welfare system, and the military, and Black communities are plagued by violence stemming from economic competition associated with the emergence of alternative, illegal drug economies that are not regulated by legitimate state power.[8]

Third, African Americans have become significant primary providers but not controllers of popular (mass) culture in American society. This fact has broad implications because the extension of global economic dominance also involves the extension of national culture. As we shall see, African Americans provide a commodity that is essential to the stimulation and expansion of American capitalism but do not as a group control the structures that govern the packaging, use, and distribution of that commodity.[9]

CONTRADICTIONS OF CAPITALISM

Cultural and group power issues, however, are taking place within the context of broader capitalist transformations characterized by periodic crises. Capitalism is a dynamic system that must expand in order to maintain stable profits, and it must expand even more to increase those profits. As markets become saturated, new ones must be found or created. Globally, political and military struggles are waged to remove constraints to market penetration. Previously, the imperialist forces of colonialism and neocolonialism ensured Western capitalists continued access to raw materials and cheap labor. However, the expansionist imperatives of capitalism also breed cultural imperialism. Domestically, market stimulation is intensely cultural since the struggle is to direct consumption.[10]

For advanced capitalism the problem is not one of scarcity but of overproduction. The ability to produce is forever stifled by the limitations of consumption. This fact gives the mass media their critical importance. Through the media, limits on consumption are attacked. As a consequence, the self-image and the ego come under siege. The objective is to fuse commodity consumption with self-worth. The self feels devalued if it cannot secure status-producing objects. Moreover, the self becomes less stable. There must be change, fads, new fashions, and new lifestyles. Tradition and routine must be transformed because every shift in taste, perception and preference represents a new market.

New needs, for example, are created as the commodities of specialized, elite groups are made available to the masses. These commodities are attractive in part because of the social status enjoyed by the elite groups who use them. For example, "designer" clothes, which were initially produced for a small wealthy stratum, are now available to the masses but retain their image of social exclusivity. In fact, the display of brand names has become so status-producing that people willingly become walking advertisements. Some African American youth, for example, have made it fashionable to leave the tags that display price and brand on their newly purchased clothing. In a similar display of identification with status-producing objects, people commonly wear the paraphernalia of professional athletes but engage in no athletics. The fact that consumers purchase an increasing variety of athletic shoes for an increasing number of socially defined occasions is a further example of the union between the need to expand markets and the corresponding need to expand human wants.

Ironically, Western capitalism was stimulated by cultural values that encouraged the production of wealth but discouraged consumption; however, mature capitalism requires radical consumption.[11] Similarly, sexual repression (Freud's discontented civilization), particularly the displacement of coitus, lies at the root of the Western work ethic that stimulated capitalist formation. Nevertheless, mature capitalism has seized upon the release of sexuality into commodity formation in order to address the problem of overproduction.[12] Making commodities "sexy" helps to heighten their ability to seduce the buying potential of the consumer. Prudishness may have stimulated Western capitalism, but it is now a fetter to capitalist expansion. But what does the problem of overproduction mean for African American cultural viability?

THE GROWTH OF A BLACK CONSUMER MARKET

The answer is partially found in the growing significance of an African American consumer market. While the demand for Black labor has declined, the demand for Black dollars has increased. After chattel slavery ended, White America created a segregated society to protect White privilege. Segregation prohibited African Americans from competing on an equal footing politically, economically, and culturally. Substantial sectors of White elites and White nonelites alike sought to regulate Black-White social intercourse by law, by custom, and by violence in order to maintain Black subordination. At this point, segregation to preserve White supremacy presented a peculiar dilemma for an expanding competitive capitalism in the North that was rapidly replacing the hereditary capitalism of the South. Blacks could not fully consume and reach their full potential as a market in a rigidly segregated society. As a consequence, an industrializing society would at some point begin to look at unexploited markets. This meant African Americans.[13]

Therefore, the Civil Rights movement may have provided African Americans with equal access to public facilities, but it also facilitated White corporate access to Black markets. Increased Black participation in the political process also meant increased Black consumption in the White-controlled marketplace. Individual and political freedom became the freedom to consume. Blacks could now spend, without constraint, in the same marketplace as Whites. White business, as a consequence, no longer had to duplicate facilities, even inferior ones, for Blacks, and, of course, could avoid serious impediments to profits.

RESTRICTED ECONOMIC DEVELOPMENT AND THE ROLE OF BROKERS

Maturing capitalism cannot afford to ignore the profit-making potential of a Black market, but White supremacy has already stacked the economic deck against African Americans. Subsequent to the chattel slavery experience, the failure of land reform (no forty acres and a mule) kept former slaves dependent, landless, and without a vehicle to gain serious entree into the American economy as owners and producers. Blacks were also systematically displaced from nonagricultural economic activity that could have made them serious contenders as entrepreneurs and business persons. When American capitalism was at its most fluid stage of development, Blacks were permitted only to provide a few services to other Blacks. From the mid-nineteenth century onward, European immigrants could enrich themselves from a nascent industrial economy that was beginning to exhibit what must have seemed like unlimited unmet needs and opportunities.[14]

At the crucial stage of competitive capitalist formation, White America eclipsed development of a Black bourgeois stratum or ownership class. Thus, racism stifled Blacks' capital accumulation. Similarly, it limited the economic potential of a growing Black industrial working class through job discrimination, closed access to whole industries, and established constraints on union membership. European immigrants, because of White privilege, gained control over urban centers at a time when political machines and political patronage gave European ethnic groups political and economic leverage in an expanding industrial economy. Also, White ethnic control of city governments facilitated the use of organized crime as a vehicle for economic mobility.[15]

Beginning about 1916, the great migration of African Americans to the urban North marked their transformation into a consumer class. However, it wasn't until much later that the consumer power of African Americans began to be translated into jobs. E. Franklin Frazier, for example, observed in his post-World War II study of Black middle-class formations that "White

firms have found it extremely profitable to employ Negroes in advertising products for Negro
consumers, in establishing public relations with
the Negro community, and as salesmen." Frazier
also noted corporate interest in the Black consumer market in liquor, beer, nonalcoholic beverages, cigarettes, gasoline, and automobiles.
Further, the income received by Blacks who
worked for large corporations that sought to exploit a Black consumer market overshadowed independent Black business achievements.[16]

As a consequence of these kinds of racial and
economic realities, social conditions became
ripe for Black brokers who could deliver the
Black market to White business. Nowhere is this
reality symbolized more strongly than in the financial success of Johnson Publications. John H.
Johnson, publisher of *Ebony* magazine and other
commercial periodicals, found a lucrative niche
by providing giant White-owned corporations access to an increasingly affluent and expanding
Black middle class via the advertising pages of
his magazines, particularly *Ebony*. The fortieth
anniversary issue of *Ebony*, in November 1985,
for example, contained 162 pages of advertising
worth $6.2 million. With a monthly circulation
of 1.75 million, *Ebony* was one of the few mass
market magazines in 1985 that showed an increase
in its advertising pages.[17] *Ebony*, founded in
1945, took advantage of a Black consumer class
that had its roots in the rapid urbanization of
Black Americans surrounding the two World Wars.
In 1970, the emergence of other Black-owned magazines like *Essence*, a women's magazine, and
Black Enterprise, a business and economic-ori-
ented monthly, symbolized the expansion and
diversification of Black consumer markets.[18]
These markets were different in that they included the first post-Civil Rights wave of college-trained Blacks who had had access to predominantly White, and in some cases, elite
schools of higher education and professional
training.

In the context of maturing capitalism and a
racially stratified society, the phenomenon of
the Black broker came into its own and presented
a new and different dilemma for African American
economic and cultural development. Initially,

Black business development was a function of segregated Black markets that were ignored and underserved by White business. A small Black professional class and a few small business owners could find a successful economic niche by serving these segregated markets. Nevertheless, White businesses controlled essential goods and services like food, clothing, and housing. For the most part, Blacks were kept out of manufacturing but found their most successful niche in the production and sale of hair care products and cosmetics. However, increased competition for profit margins meant that White corporations would no longer ignore consumer markets previously controlled by Blacks.

Racial privilege contributed to White corporations gaining a competitive edge in the marketplace. Superior size, greater access to capital, larger and more sophisticated manufacturing capabilities, the control of raw materials, distribution networks and retail outlets, extensive advertising budgets, and the like have helped to place limits on how well Black businesses could compete for Black markets. At the same time, Black businesses have not enjoyed access to White markets. Therefore, an important historically and situationally defined growth area for African American entrepreneurs has been as brokers to deliver Black markets to White corporations. African American-owned media and advertising firms are therefore faced with the dilemma of negating their own markets in order to secure a position in the marketplace. Similarly, such entrepreneurial options as franchising are additional methods by which White corporations expand into Black consumer markets, further negating competition from independent Black businesses.

The long-term implications of unequal access to White markets and shrinking access to Black markets for Black business is not clear. Product diversification, innovative marketing, and so on may improve the ability of some Black businesses to compete with their White-owned counterparts. Mergers, acquisitions, and leveraged buy-outs present potential vehicles for Black business expansion. For example, the largest Black-owned business in 1990 was TLC Beatrice International, which was acquired by Reginald F. Lewis through a leveraged buy-out in 1987. In 1990, this business had gross sales of $1.496 billion. However, in comparison, the second-highest grossing Black-owned business was the family-controlled Johnson Publications, with $252.187 million in sales. The *Black Enterprise* list of the top-grossing Black-owned firms in the United States includes the 100 top service and industrial firms and the 100 top automobile dealerships. These 200 Black-owned firms collectively had $7.169 billion in gross sales in 1990. This figure can be compared with the fact that in 1988, eight White-owned corporations collectively spent $10.882 billion on advertising alone, 52 percent more than these top 200 Black-owned businesses were able to generate in total gross annual sales for 1990.[19] Mature capitalism simply does not present many opportunities to allow growing businesses to compete with established corporations. Newer and smaller businesses will either be absorbed by larger ones or they must be satisfied with limited market share.

Nevertheless, because of the scale of the economy, this limited market share may represent millions of dollars. Top Black-owned advertising firms exemplify this subordinate economic position when we note the disparity between their billings, which may number in the millions of dollars, and the billings of top White firms, which number in the billions of dollars. Indeed, the largest White-owned corporations probably offer Black professionals more lucrative salaries than they could achieve as independent business persons, and the sheer size of White-owned corporations means that Black professionals can achieve significant vertical mobility without threatening the power, positions, and salaries of top White executives. As a corollary, White corporate America has spawned a class of Black professionals who have decided to leave private industry because of the stresses of institutionalized racism and the limits that racism places on corporate advancement.

Black brokers who link Black markets with White corporate needs are manifestations of an American racial and economic dynamic that has constrained and shaped Black economic opportunity and development. Sometimes mainstream corporate goals are compatible with Black market needs, but a serious problem arises when they are not. What are the products and messages that these brokers are bringing into the Black community? To what degree is the Black community able to discriminate and select among various products and messages in a way that will promote its well-being? No doubt, some brokers are aware of this dilemma and try to balance negative images with positive ones, realizing that "whoever pays the piper calls the tune." Calling the tune includes encouraging negative consumption patterns, exploiting weaknesses in Black institutions, like the family, and capitalizing on dysfunctional values and insecurities that are linked to centuries of economic disadvantage and racial oppression.[20] One Black advertising firm has responded by producing commercials that show positive images of Black families, and at least one Black mass-market magazine actively seeks advertisers that sell products that encourage positive lifestyles for African Americans.

However, as previously observed by Frazier, liquor, beer, cigarette, and soft drink companies aggressively market to Black consumers. In fact, it is not uncommon to see soft drink, liquor, beer, and cigarette companies underwrite a very large number of the activities of Black philanthropic, cultural, educational, professional, and Civil Rights organizations.[21] These companies gain valuable name recognition in a Black market that disproportionately consumes health-destroying and socially debilitating commodities. Financial support for Black organizations is traded for access to Black minds weakened by oppression.

The relationship between market expansion and consumption brings into sharper focus the relationship between economic activity and culture. Every cultural trait becomes an economic need, and market transformations are cultural transformations. It is because of this relationship that unrestrained capitalist exploitation threatens African American cultural viability. This problem, although a source of concern for postindustrial society in general, presents a

special challenge to African Americans, whose
institutional viability has been made tenuous by
historical and societal conditions. Countervailing constraints to market-generated cultural
hegemony are minimal.

In contrast, the Nation of Islam under Elijah
Muhammad showed potential as a countervailing
force to market-driven cultural hegemony. The
Nation established an impressive self-help economic program that was driven by a highly developed religious ethic. This religious ethic provided rules for dress, social intercourse,
health care, diet, childbirth, child rearing,
and so on. Thus, the religious ethic provided
rules for consumption but at the same time generated economic needs that members of the group
sought to fulfill through their own business activities. Therefore, the religious order became
its own primary market. Elements of the religious culture were attractive and useful to
other segments of the non-Muslim African American community who in fact became a secondary
market for Muslim businesses.

Concomitantly, the Muslim community existed
within the broader context of the American economic system. However, it was in a stronger position to mediate external values that were intended to influence African American patterns of
consumption. This community could offer re-
straints on an unrestrained system of commodifi-
cation through its organized way of life and
through a countervailing religious ethic. In a
more general sense, we might expect that any
ethical system that contributes to hu-
man-directed economic activity while con-
straining dysfunctional consumption should enhance cultural viability and stifle cultural
negation.

Moreover, the tools of market-driven cultural
hegemony and cultural negation are concentrated
on certain sectors of the African American community. Black women as a class, for example, are
an important object of media messages because of
the traditional role of women as managers of domestic consumption. What this means is that
there$mthere a systemic propensity by White
male-dominated media to penetrate Black markets,
which disproportionately translates into the

control and manipulation of Black female patterns of consumption. This fact probably height-
ens conflict between Black men and women because
Black male legitimacy is structurally diminished
in the society.

Freedom and status, if they are to be in harmony with market forces, must be translated as
the "independent" power to consume. The contradiction, however, is that a postindustrial society is radically interdependent. Even though individuals have less actual independence--that
is, the ability to meet human material needs
without the help of others--the ideological reduction of independence to buying power gives
the illusion of self-sufficiency. Consumption
becomes the measure of success and self-worth.
Family and interpersonal dependence is replaced
by corporate dependence. Market forces tend toward reducing the internal necessity of the family. Family members contribute less and less to
socialization, food production and preparation,
health care, education, entertainment, and so on
as family needs and functions are achieved outside of the home and through the mass media.
Family life, stripped of its instrumental inter-
dependence, is held together with fragile emotional bonds.

The distorted and deformed values of radical
consumption become more problematic as they are
received and absorbed by African American youth.
Because they are a remaining frontier of un-
tapped market potential, the fight to stimulate,
create, and find new markets shifts to young
people as a class. Most importantly, this group
can be shaped as a future cohort for consumption. At this early stage of human development,
lifestyles and tastes are fluid and changing.
The herd instinct under the guise of individualism abounds, and peer pressure and youthful
insecurities make consumption a vehicle for status and acceptance.

Again, African American communities with
fragile primary institutions become ripe for
marketing hype. Egos are invested in designer
clothes, top-of-the-line gym shoes, gold chains,
and any material fad that delivers recognition.
Economic disadvantage adds fuel to the quest for
status because a materialistic society ties

self-worth to image-enhancing consumption. Thus, hidden corporate entrepreneurs utilize the mass media to expand markets by exploiting the institutional weaknesses of the Black community, and they convey a cultural agenda that conflicts with African American group needs. However, these structural features of African American cultural negation do not stop here but are combined most virulently with tendencies toward the expropriation of African American culture.

BLACK CULTURE AND ATTRACTING MARKETS

American culture grew up on African culture, but White America has had a love/hate relationship with African people. African peoples (ethnic groups) have contributed in a significant way to the formation of American culture since before America's founding as a nation. The fusion of an African cultural ethos into the American milieu could not go unnoticed by European colonizers. On the plantations, Africans raised and socialized White children; changed the speech patterns of English-speaking Europeans in the South; affected dietary practices and food preparation; introduced new agricultural techniques and methods to organize work; helped to shape the architectural image of the South; introduced a distinctive religious culture that affected the belief systems and religious expression of some Whites; and were the entertainers, creative artists, dancers, singers, and musicians on the plantation. Despite European chattel slavery's assault on traditional African cultures, Africans in America constructed a distinctive way of life from African aesthetic and expressive sensibilities, beliefs, values, and norms that survived in the New World and from the emergence of a separate form of social organization.[22]

Even though White supremacy became a tool of oppression, Whites were always drawn to and fascinated by the creative ethos of African peoples. As a servant class, African Americans injected their creative expression directly into the consciousness of White ruling elites. The minstrel tradition, with its pejorative and grotesque images, was both an attempt by Whites to copy Black creative expression and to preserve White supremacy. The so-called "coon" songs of the late nineteenth century achieved commercial success. "Coon," a shortened form of "raccoon," was meant to denigrate Black men, but it was clear that Black-inspired musical forms could capture White markets. Ragtime was a profound stimulus to the commercial sales of sheet music, and later, blues and jazz had a similar effect on the sales of phonograph records. Talented Black performers were associated with recorded music from the inception of the industry, but Whites gained greater success through performing Black music. The fascination for Black life continued, but the formula by which White audiences could experience their version of Black culture through White performers became a lucrative one.[23]

Several landmarks in the development of the mass media reflected this fascination by White Americans with Black images, even though the images were distorted to reflect how Whites wanted Blacks to appear. D.W. Griffith's silent film and technological wonder, *Birth of a Nation* (1915), passionately argued for Black inferiority and attempted to depict Blacks during Reconstruction as ignorant, lustful villains.[24]

The 1927 Warner Brothers' film, *The Jazz Singer*, launched the "talking" motion picture era and featured the popular White entertainer, Al Jolson, singing, in blackface, an emotional rendition of the song, "Mammy." This movie tugged at the heartstrings of White America and reminded them of an idyllic past. *The Jazz Singer*, a throwback to the minstrel tradition, was a great commercial success and stimulated further expansion of the movie industry.[25]

The motion picture, *Gone With the Wind* (1939), a technical, artistic, and financial landmark, perpetuated themes that captured White expectations regarding Blacks as servile and comedic characters. An important characteristic, however, was that the Black characters in this White film were played by Black actors and actresses, instead of Whites in blackface. These talented Black actresses and actors brought

great human depth to their roles despite the
limitations of the story line.[26]

Concomitantly, the early 1900s saw the growth
of phonographs and radio. Radio reached commercial maturity in 1929 when two White men, Free-
man Gosden and Charles Correll brought blackface
minstrelsy to the national airways. Their "Amos
'n' Andy" series achieved phenomenal success.
This series imitated Black comedic styles while
preserving White stereotypes of Black life and
language. "Amos 'n' Andy" received a salary of
$100,000 a year, but the toothpaste company that
sponsored them increased its business by 300
percent.[27]

Between 1900 and 1920, blues and jazz found a
mass market through phonograph records. Again,
Black artists were the creators and innovators
and the most accomplished performers. However,
White imitators of Black-inspired music found
greater commercial success since they were assured access to larger White audiences. In 1917,
Sophie Tucker, a Russian immigrant, recorded a
version of the "Saint Louis Blues" that sold
over a million copies, and five White musicians
who called themselves the Original Dixieland
Jass Band recorded two records that sold over a
million copies each.[28]

The 1920s was a critical period for African
Americans because it was at this time that Black
cultural products became fused with a nascent
mass media in the context of an expanding business, advertising, and consumer environment. For
example, in the 1920s the work week was reduced
from 60 to 48 hours; radio became a bil-
lion-dollar industry; large motion pictures
palaces came into vogue; and diverse forms of
advertising, particularly radio advertising,
proliferated. Economic growth was supreme, and
business became a way of life as business colleges became an adjunct to nearly all leading
educational institutions.[29] In this setting, the
Harlem Renaissance, a Black literary movement
stimulated by a White reading audience, achieved
prominence as Whites discovered the music and
dance of southern Black migrants who swarmed to
the urban centers of the North. Harlem, the
largest and most culturally and economically diverse Black community in America, was strategi-

cally located in the cultural and media capital of the country. White entrepreneurs took notice and freely began to expropriate Black cultural products. The problem, of course, was that oppression and White privilege eliminated Blacks from entrepreneurial entree into the broader technological revolution in mass media or from competitive control over their own cultural products.[30]

In the context of maturing capitalism, because of its tremendous power to attract audiences and to stimulate whole lifestyles, African American cultural products achieved pre-eminence as both commodities and as vehicles to sell other commodities. The roots of their attractive power were music and dance. The 1920s became known as the "Jazz Age" or, as one might interpret, the age of Black music. This was also, as I noted before, the era of the Harlem Renaissance, a period that symbolized the rapid, mass diffusion of Black culture into the White psyche. Whites flocked to Harlem to learn the latest dances and to absorb the music and creative art forms of African Americans.[31]

However, in Harlem the process of cultural diffusion had begun much earlier. For example, Harlem's Lafayette Theater attracted Whites to its highly successful Darktown Follies in 1913. White theater producer Florenz Ziegfeld was a much interested visitor and purchased the rights to the finale of the first act and to several musical numbers for his Follies.[32] In 1921, the musical comedy, *Shuffle Along*, produced and performed by African Americans F.E. Miller, Aubrey Lyles, Eubie Blake, and Noble Sissle, took New York by storm and stimulated interest in Black theater for years to come. The Miller and Lyles play, *Runnin' Wild*, introduced the "Charleston" to White America, a dance that had its roots in the African experience.[33] This phenomenon further exemplified the nascent process in which Black cultural forms in general would be absorbed by White markets, deracialized (separated from an African American context), and appropriated by Whites.[34]

Moreover, African American music and dance forms and cultural sensibilities have distinctive characteristics that seem to mesh well with the market needs of maturing capitalism and the cultural psychology of White markets. African music and dance were always both spiritual and sensual. African culture made no separation between religious and spiritual life and sexual forces. In contradistinction to European traditions, sex was not sin, and bodily movements that involved the torso and pelvis were not inherently sinful. Before African American dance developed as a secular social activity in the urban American context, it was a vehicle for spiritual elevation, emotional catharsis, inspiration, cultural cohesion, healing, communion, and the organization of work. The "ring shout" or spiritual dancing remained a significant survivor of African culture in America.[35]

African and African American dance meant something much less and very different for European America, particularly when it involved movements that might suggest the release of sexual energies. European culture did not link as one the sensuality and spirituality of certain types of bodily movements. However, African American music and dance are attractive and commercially exploited for their sensual qualities. It is quite possible that European Americans found Black culture as a way to symbolically circumvent the sexual repression, particularly the displacement of guilt associated with coitus, imposed by their own culture. Nevertheless, the juxtapositioning of Black music and dance forms with commodities has proven to be an effective method to attract non-Black markets domestically and globally.

However, as Black cultural forms become a powerful vehicle for commodity formation, two problems emerge. First, market forces tend to distill and distort the spiritual and other functional aspects of African American cultural products into a form that only serves market needs, for example, the transformation of spiritual sensuality into vulgar (hedonistic and self-centered) sexuality. Second, a process of deracialization occurs in which the cultural product is detached from a Black referent. Since fragile structures of social organization in the Black community (and this includes economic instability) fail to institutionalize processes that preserve and rejuvenate the full range of African American cultural traditions, mass media use of African American cultural products tends to alienate Blacks from the origins, deeper meanings, diverse functions, cohesive elements, and elevating aspects of their own culture.[36]

Moreover, African Americans do not benefit fully as creators and innovators from the commercial potency of their culture. White performers who can imitate Black cultural forms have greater access to commercial markets than do Black performers. These African American artists must displace certain aspects of their cultural image in order to gain access to White markets on a consistent basis. However, cultural effacement does not ensure White market exposure or White market acceptance because access to markets is not purely a function of talent and public demand but of racial and ethnic power and control. Thus, White-controlled market forces select trends, images, and messages based upon racial, cultural, and economic criteria that have little to do with the collective human needs of African Americans.[37]

Another aspect of African American aesthetic sensibilities that powerfully attracts markets and dominates the transformation of American popular culture is the characteristic of style. Style in African American culture refers to the tradition of artfully embellishing movement, speech, and appearance. This means that, culturally, technical proficiency and competency is not sufficient; one must inject beauty, heightened emotion or feeling, and idiosyncratic expression into a product or action.

The characteristic of style is exemplified by African traditions in the sport of basketball. Every African American knows that learning the fundamentals of shooting, dribbling, and passing is not sufficient. These skills must be done in an interesting and artful manner. Thus, the traditions of dribbling between the legs and behind the back, doing 360-degree turns, and learning to rapidly change hands and directions are common. Also, deep attention to all manner of putting the ball in the basket, including stress on jumping, "hang time," "double and triple pumping," fading away," shooting with either

hand, and various styles of "dunking" the basketball, is a must. Similar respect is given to
long-distance shooting; young people can be
found practicing half-court and full-court
shots. Injecting style into basketball has permeated the sport professionally and has significantly increased its value as an entertainment
commodity. Even more importantly, African American style effectively attracts broad and diverse
audiences through which to sell other commodities. The promotional power of the accomplished
professional athlete who combines African American style with a personality that a White public
can accept goes without saying.

Moreover, the element of style permeates every aspect of Black life and, over time, is absorbed into American popular culture as Whites
and others are attracted to its innovative and
artful quality and commercial potential. We
should also remember that African American creative traditions are viewed as American culture
by those outside this country. Because these
traditions prove attractive to foreign coun-
tries, American capitalism is able to shape foreign patterns of consumption and extend American
consumer markets. It is interesting to note that
the style of shaking hands that became popular
among African Americans in the 1960s as a symbol
of Black solidarity and of the Black liberation
struggle is now practiced all over the world as
an "American" greeting.

In a more general sense, African American music and dance forms and creative artists have
become the standard for a global, market-based,
popular culture. The curious figure of Japanese
youth imitating rap musicians, tanning their
skin to look Black, forcing their hair into
Black hairstyles, wearing red, black, and green
images of Africa engraved with the words, "Fight
the power," is a case in point. The improvisational and cryptic speech patterns of African
Americans, with their rhythmic and antiphonal
character, colorful and penetrating metaphors,
and other innovative figures of speech, are
rapidly absorbed by non-Black Americans, usually
through mass media exposure to elements of a
Black music and dance culture. White youths and
others attempt to emulate African American hair

styles, walks, greetings, speech patterns, and colorful dress. In commercials, of course, Black entertainers and sports figures like Michael Jackson, Bo Jackson, Hammer, Ray Charles, and Bill Cosby have become cultural icons. Also, it is common to hear Black music as a background for commercials in which there are no Black images and as background for television shows that have no Black characters. The problem, of course, is that organic cultural expression is transformed into superficial fads and styles.

CONCLUSION

The spiritual, humanistic, and commercial power of African American cultural forms has evolved in American society within the context of a shifting racial arena and changing market forces. Black creative artists have gained greater creative options in the broader society, and mass media images of African Americans have expanded in substance and scope. However, African Americans are overly restricted to fulfilling the cultural and economic needs of other groups. Their individual economic success depends almost exclusively upon linking White products to Black markets. As a consequence, there is a tendency to cultivate and select Black creative products that serve only the market and cultural goals of White owners and producers. In addition, as African American creative products are expropriated via their consumption by the dominant market, Blacks retain less and less control over what they have produced. The Black community becomes separated from its cultural traditions, and African Americans lose the human, spiritual, and commercial utility of their creative heritage.

Recognition of the above dilemma should motivate Black entrepreneurs who benefit from existing avenues of Black economic activity to direct their energies toward expanding the boundaries of African American economic endeavors while paying attention to the preservation and cultivation of positive cultural and institutional development in the Black community. Thus, becoming owners and producers, gaining greater control over Black cultural products, and aspiring to greater input, control, and direction over the dominant mass media apparatus are important goals. A Black business stratum must pay attention to how cultural development and economic advancement go hand in hand, and it must understand that the distinctiveness, attractiveness, and potency of African American cultural products are what provide the Black business stratum with the basis to compete in the general marketplace. Moreover, strong, positive cultural traditions provide the basis for restraining negative and dysfunctional economic exploitation of the Black community. The values of radical consumption must not go unmonitored and unfettered in African American communities, lest human and communal relationships turn purely hedonistic, individualistic, and destructively competitive.

NOTES

1. A number of excellent studies exist that analyze the images of African Americans in the mass media. Most describe the evolution of these images from the rise of nineteenth-century blackface minstrelsy. My discussion of white supremacy and Black images has been informed by the following: Nathan Huggins, *Harlem Renaissance* (New York: Oxford University Press, 1971); Edward Mapp, *Blacks in American Films: Today and Yesterday* (Metuchen, N.J.: Scarecrow, 1972); Thomas Cripps, *Slow Fade to Black: The Negro in American Film, 1900–1942* (New York: Oxford University Press, 1977); Donald Bogle, *Toms, Coons, Mulattoes, Mammies, and Bucks: An Interpretive History of Blacks in American Films* (New York: Continuum, 1973; 1989); Jannette L. Dates and William Barlow, eds., *Split Image: African Americans in the Mass Media* (Washington, D.C.: Howard University Press, 1990); Dorothy Porter Wesley, "Black Antiquarians and Bibliophiles Revisited, with a Glance at Today's Lovers of Books and Memorabilia," in Elinor Des Verney Sinnette, W. Paul Coates, and Thomas C. Battle, eds., *Black Bibliophiles and Collectors: Pre-*

servers of Black History (Washington, D.C.: Howard University Press, 1990), pp. 3-20.

2. See, for example, Vincent Bakpetu Thompson, *The Making of the African Diaspora in the Americas, 1441-1900* (New York: Longman, 1987).

3. Harold Cruse, *Crisis of the Negro Intellectual* (New York: William Morrow, 1967).

4. See Charles H. Anderson, *White Protestant Americans: From National Origins to Religious Group* (Englewood Cliffs, N.J.: Prentice-Hall, 1970). This work specifically illustrates how nationality is subsumed within religion. Thus, religious freedom preserves nationality, and the Constitution, which preserves religious freedom, sustains collective power under the protection of individual freedom. Within American society, White Anglo-Saxon Protestant ethnicity becomes less obvious as this group is able to convince others that it represents the "American" culture.

5. Despite frequent discussion regarding the importance of the church as an African American institution, religious confusion and fragmentation remain characteristic of the African American experience. All efforts to reconstruct an African American culture and identity have involved the quest for religious expression that transcends European (White) domination. African Americans, because of racial and cultural oppression, do not possess an allegiance to a religious heritage in the same way that European Americans do. African Americans frequently change denominations and can shift between Protestantism, Catholicism, Islam, Judaism, and the like. Through discussions of the African American religious experience, I have, for nearly two decades, found many Black students, for example, who may identify their religious affiliation as Baptist but who fail to realize that they are also Protestant. The cultural, historical, and ethnic significance of this label is not known, or, if it is, has very little significance.

6. The growing presence of Arab and Korean merchants in Black communities is a case in point. Increasing Hispanic, Asian, and Middle Eastern populations represent new and important elements in the equation of American cultural

pluralism. Native American interests are also becoming more prominent.

7. E. Franklin Frazier, *Black Bourgeoisie: The Rise of a New Middle Class* (New York: The Free Press, 1957).

8. For a discussion of trends in employment, crime, social welfare, and military participation since 1940, see National Research Council Committee on the Status of Black Americans, *A Common Destiny: Blacks and American Society* (Washington, D.C.: National Academy Press, 1989).

9. See, for example, Cruse, *Crisis of the Negro Intellectual*; Dates and Barlow, eds., *Split Image*; Nelson George, *The Death of Rhythm and Blues* (New York: E.P. Dutton, 1989); Ortiz Walton, *Music: Black White and Blue, A Sociological Survey of the Use and Misuse of Afro-American Music* (New York: William Morrow, 1972); Mark Neuman, *Entrepreneurs of Profit: From Black-Appeal to Radio Soul* (New York: Praeger, 1988).

10. See Stuart Ewen, *Captains of Consciousness: Advertising and the Social Roots of the Consumer Culture* (New York: McGraw-Hill, 1976).

11. Max Weber, *The Protestant Ethic and the Spirit of Capitalism*, translated by Talcott Parsons (New York: Charles Scribner's Sons, 1958).

12. Marcuse's discussion of repressive desublimation is useful here. See Herbert Marcuse, *One Dimensional Man* (Boston: Beacon, 1964).

13. For example, Frazier, *Black Bourgeoisie*; Neuman, *Entrepreneurs of Profit*; MacDonald, *Blacks and White TV*.

14. Frazier, *Black Bourgeoisie*; Lerone Bennett Jr., *Confrontation Black and White* (Baltimore, Md.: Penguin Books, 1966).

15. The effects of Jim Crow on Black economic activity is illustrated in Allan H. Spear, *Black Chicago: The Making of a Negro Ghetto, 1890-1920* (Chicago: University of Chicago Press, 1967), pp. 29–59. The role of crime in White ethnic social mobility is illustrated in Daniel Bell, *The End of Ideology: On the Exhaustion of Political Ideas in the Fifties* (New York: Free Press, 1962), pp. 127–50.

16. Frazier, *Black Bourgeoisie*, p. 171.

17. George Lazarous, *Chicago Tribune*, 11 November 1985, section 4, p. 8.

18. Dates and Barlow, *Split Image*, pp. 372-76.

19. See *Black Enterprise*, June 1991, pp. 92, 94, 107; data on White corporate advertising expenditures can be found in the *The Guinness Book of World Records 1991 Edition*, edited by Donald McFarlan (New York: Bantam Books, 1991), p. 390.

20. This dilemma is noted in Dates and Barlow, *Split Image*, pp. 436-37; also, see Djata, "The Marketing of Vices to Black Consumers," *Business and Society Review* 62 (Summer 1987):47-49.

21. For example, there is the perennial sponsorship of the United Negro College Fund telethon by Budweiser Beer. Miller Brewing Company sponsors the Thurgood Marshall Scholarship Fund. Brown and Williamson Tobacco Company has underwritten a national conference on the Black family, and R.J. Reynolds Tobacco Company was a major contributor to a recent national Black theater festival.

22. Sterling Stuckey, *Slave Culture: Nationalist Theory and Foundations of Black America* (New York: Oxford University Press, 1987); Joseph Holloway, ed., *Africanism in American Culture* (Bloomington, Ind.: Indiana University Press, 1990); John W. Blassingame, *The Slave Community*, rev. edn. (New York: Oxford University Press, 1979); Lawrence W. Levine, *Black Culture and Black Consciousness: Afro-American Folk Thought from Slavery to Freedom* (New York: Oxford University Press, 1977).

23. Dates and Barlow, *Split Image*, pp. 25-121; George, *Death of Rhythm and Blues*; Walton, *Black Music*.

24. Mapp, *Blacks in American Films*, p. 19.

25. Bogle, *Toms, Coons, Mulattoes, Mammies, and Bucks*, p. 26.

26. Ibid., pp. 86-92; Mapp, *Blacks in American Films*, pp. 27-28.

27. George E. Mowry, ed., *The Twenties: Fords, Flappers and Fanatics* (Englewood Cliffs, N.J.: Prentice-Hall, 1963), p. 65.

28. Dates and Barlow, *Split Image*, pp. 29-30.

29. Mowry, *The Twenties*, pp. 3-17, 43.

30. Cruse, *Crisis of the Negro Intellectual*; Huggins, *Harlem Renaissance*.

31. See, for example, James Weldon Johnson, *Black Manhattan* (New York: Atheneum, 1930; 1972); Emory Lynne Fauley, *Black Dance in the United States From 1619 to 1970* (Palo Alto, Calif.: National Press, 1972); Katrina Hazzard-Gordon, *Jookin': The Rise of Social Dance Formation in African-American Culture* (Philadelphia: Temple University Press, 1990).

32. Johnson, *Black Manhattan*, p. 174.

33. Ibid., pp. 186–89.

34. See, for example, Cruse, *Crisis of the Negro Intellectual*; Walton, *Music: Black White and Blue*; George, *Death of Rhythm and Blues*; Hazzard-Gordon, *Jookin'*; LeRoi Jones, *Blues People* (New York: William Morrow, 1963).

35. Stuckey, *Slave Culture*; Fauley, *Black Dance*; Hazzard-Gordon, *Jookin'*.

36. George, *Death of Rhythm and Blues*; Hazzard-Gordon, *Jookin'*; Jones, *Blues People*; Walton, *Music: Black, White and Blue*.

37. Ibid.

6

Religious Fragmentation and Social Cohesion

Religious beliefs are powerful determinants of the character of social organization. Just as people are faced with the inevitable need to generate social activity to solve basic material needs, they inevitably face questions of existence, life, death, and human meaning and purpose. Beliefs about identity and group origins and boundaries also flow from existential questions. Reflections on the nature of things produce cosmological or theological assumptions that function as lens through which to view and elucidate other phenomena. Religious thinking emerges as a higher-order interpretive tool, guiding our perception of whether or not phenomena are compatible with what we consider to be the natural order of things. It gives us the feeling that a social reality is desirable and should be preserved. We gain a similar sense of whether a social reality should be transformed. As a consequence, religious beliefs become powerful motive forces, shaping such things as economic activity, family life, and social movements. Thus, the religious dialectic, which contains the seeds for social transformation and for social conservatism, is critical.

THE RELIGIOUS DIALECTIC AND CULTURAL HEGEMONY

Social scientists have generally recognized that no single institution has played a more important role in the social cohesion of African American communities than the church.[1] Chattel slavery created a severe disruption to the institutional life of African peoples who were brought to the Americas. European Christianity provided a new social ethic through which to reconstruct these institutional forms.[2] This fact had both positive and negative effects on African American development, and it continues to shape current possibilities for group advancement. Religion has been a force for change and human transcendence, and it has also been a force for oppression and human degradation. The latter characteristics of religion are frequently difficult to grasp by believers who have become steeped in the mythological constructs of a particular religious world view.

An important aspect of religion is how it defines people outside of its belief structure. Historically, European Christianity divided the world into those who believed and those who did not. Because Christianity emerged as an imperial force, it viewed those who were not Christians as having no God and no religion. As a consequence, the racism and cultural imperialism of Christianity were obscured. Believers became oblivious to the fundamental hegemonic and oppressive qualities of their sacred beliefs. Today, Black theologians inside the tradition lament its hypocrisy and struggle to find a way to "fix" Christianity, but they do not question its fundamental imperialism. The stated universality of the religion hides its parochialism and its hegemonic qualities. In Africa, Asia, North and South America, and elsewhere, Christian domination meant Western political and economic exploitation and cultural genocide. Even zealous adherents inside the imperial religion found it necessary to break away and start new churches, denominations, sects and cults--all within the boundaries of the ethic, and all intolerant with respect to non-Christian religions. Expressions of human compassion and love, as sincere as they might have been, had to take place within predefined theological boundaries and the context of cultural imperialism in order to be justifiable and legitimate. This circumstance brings us to additional characteristics shaping the religious context of the African American and diasporic struggle for existence and transcendence.

The United States of America was founded on principles of religious tolerance and religious freedom. The separation of church and state was paramount. However, religious tolerance and freedom were intended to apply only to variations in Christian theology and ethics. Also, as it was conceived by European invaders (settlers), Christian also meant White.[3] It was only after intense confrontation with the contradictions between the stated universality of the religion, the goal of White supremacy, and the functional need to redefine the cultural world of non-Whites that Europeans decided that Christians could also be non-White.[4] More extreme groups totally denied the possibilities of a Christian identity to non-Whites. Non-Christian religious forms were not envisioned as legitimate candidates for religious tolerance. Catholicism and Protestantism could look askance at Judaism, for example, but they had to acknowledge its fundamental role in their tradition. However, in America, Aboriginal peoples and Africans stood outside humanity unless transformed by the White Christian God. For European (Christian) invaders and slave traders, non-White, non-Western religions were not religions at all. White supremacy, directed through Christian hegemony, defined other religions as inadequate to guide human culture and to direct human ethical discourse.

African slaves born into slavery were permitted no religious traditions other than that provided by the slave master. Even though elements of African expressive culture survived, African beliefs were replaced by Old Testament imagery and myth, and later by evangelical language. Black persons born into White supremacy sometimes believed that God intended the White man to be the master and the Black man to be a slave, but, at the very least, all Black people were conditioned to feel that embracing Christianity gave them status and a place in human existence. If Christianity makes the White man human, then the Black Christian is human too.

By appealing to a "common" religious heritage, Black ministers and preachers sought to gain legitimacy and protection from the extremes of White supremacy while they ministered to the spiritual needs of Black people. The Black leader, in pursuit of legitimacy in a White-controlled world, learned to ask: "How can you make me a slave and deny me human dignity when I am a Christian just like you?" Some Whites accepted this logic; many did not. Both categories of White believers saw humanity attached only to a Christian identity. Also, for Whites, the respectable Black leader was to be steeped in Christian piety and idealism far beyond that of his White counterpart.[5] Furthermore, even though the message of Christian brotherhood implied movement toward human equality and the negation of White supremacy, the structure of Christianity, both theologically and organizationally, repelled Blacks from shared power and legitimacy.

Because of the psychological circumstances of slavery, Black Christians were forced to exist with their feet in two worlds. Religious indoctrination was intended to make African Americans supportive of their own subordination. This is difficult to accept because many African Americans now believe that certain universal, human, and spiritual truths have legitimate expression only within Christian religious forms. Again, historical facts reveal the fundamentally political, imperialist, and racialist nature of Western Christianity. Christianity's European proponents stamped out competing beliefs through brutal force and transformed the good/evil dialectic into the social dialectic of White over Black and Western over non-Western. Liberal and conservative religious adherents may have differed in their methods of proselytizing, but cultural domination was the result and their common goal. These basic relationships must be understood if we are to understand the character of the Black religious experience in America, and, for that matter, throughout the African diaspora. If we ignore the significance, degree, and character of a shared but politically and culturally asymmetrical religion, then we cannot analyze or accurately interpret the Black religious experience in modern times.

RESPONSES AND TENDENCIES

The African American experience has to be understood as a process of fusion and differentiation. Africans enslaved by Europeans were of diverse ethnic and religious origins. Many practiced what are called traditional African religions. Although they share common characteristics, these traditional religions varied considerably in their specific theological content. Other enslaved Africans were Muslims and Jews.[6] The slave experience in the New World fused African ethnic groups into a more singular culture. Europeans who had the power of life and death over Black people in the New World did not respond to Africans with respect or regard for their ethnic differences. They responded purely on a racial basis. In fact, Christian imperialism became the vehicle by which Europeans denied respect to the diverse cultures and religions of Africans. The self-image of racial superiority for Europeans was embodied in their religious identity as Christians. This social context contributed to the systematic denigration of African ethnic variation and consciousness.

Over time, the surviving features of African cultures became fused with cultural adaptations derived from contact with Europeans and from the fact that Africans, slave and free, maintained a largely separate form of social organization. This meant not only that Africans lived separately from Europeans but that every phase of social, political, economic, and cultural life was organized to subordinate the African. The organization of work on the plantation; White supremacy and miscegenation, which contributed to color stratification; slave and free status; and the type of religious orientation received from Europeans contributed to a new basis of differentiation among the captive and displaced African population.

Traditional African religions survived most under Catholic or Latin slavery and least under Protestant or English slavery. In the latter context, fragments of traditional African religions were preserved in the practices of conjuring, hoodooism, folk health beliefs and practices, various forms of expressive culture, and personal religious experiences, such as, spiritual dancing and spirit possession. Under Catholic slavery, holistic and syncretic religious forms emerged with a Christian (Catholic) veneer.[7] Under Latin and Protestant slavery, Islam was stamped out completely, or at least went underground until it was resurrected via the practice of Masonry. Little is known about African Jews until African Americans began to reclaim this heritage in the urban centers of the northern United States in the early part of the twentieth century.[8]

In the North American context, the major religious differentiation during the slave period was between what sociologist E. Franklin Frazier referred to as the "institutional church" and the "invisible institution." The former symbolized the fact that "free" Blacks in the North attended White churches but were segregated and kept in a subordinate position. In some instances, Whites built separate churches for Blacks. The latter referred to the observation that slaves practiced a form of religious worship that was less formal and sometimes hidden from the slave master and other Whites. The presumption is that slaves, through the "invisible institution," had a greater opportunity to develop and to inject a distinctive folk culture into their religious expression.[9]

Although efforts at Christian conversion corresponded with the slave trade, Europeans were always ambivalent about systematically Christianizing slaves because there was some concern that this might require manumission. This concern, however, was resolved in favor of slavery. In addition, the Great Awakening, the religious revival that took place among North American Whites in the early 1700s, created a renewed interest in the conversion of the slave population. At this time, many slaves were brought into Christianity. The second Great Awakening, which took place toward the end of the 1700s and extended into the 1800s, was stimulated by an emotional Methodism that also captured the attention of the captive African population. Extensive proselytizing among the slave population resulted in Blacks predominantly becoming Baptists and Methodists. However, these religious outlets, which became infused with the folk culture characteristic of the "invisible institution," did not become institutionalized until after the Civil War.[10]

It is important to understand that the racially oppressive world created by Whites made Christianity a primary outlet for Blacks to gain status in American society. In addition, the conditions of bondage contributed to the eventual erosion of African religious practices and the erosion of a widespread African consciousness. Furthermore, more and more Africans were being born into bondage as opposed to being taken directly from Africa. This, of course, corresponded with the eventual decline of the slave trade. As a consequence, the spiritual needs of Africans could only find expression in very specific and limited ways. Thus, we must separate African spirituality and religiosity from the modes of expression that were available to Africans in bondage. What is significant in a sociological sense is that Whites removed African outlets for religious expression and provided outlets that they could define and control. As a consequence, Africans in bondage transferred their deep spirituality and the sense of reality associated with their previous religious practices to Christianity. Thus, variations in Christian religious forms became the basis for new configurations of social differentiation among Africans in America.

Variations in religious interpretation that were somewhat independent of European constraints also emerged among Africans in bondage. African Americans developed interpretations of the Scriptures that were at variance with the slave master's use of the Bible to exhort them to be good slaves. They also produced the spirituals, a distinctive sacred music that combined African spirituality and song with biblical imagery. Christianity for slaves largely took on an other-worldly character and gave slaves hope for a better life after death. However, this conservative aspect of Christian indoctrination paralleled more radical interpretations. Nat Turner, for example, found a subversive rationale and strength through spiritual revelation that was couched in biblical imagery. God, he felt, told him to lead a revolt against the slave system. Harriet Tubman drew upon the profound spiritual strength that existed among African peoples, which was now expressed in European religious terms, to lead hundreds of slaves to freedom through the underground railroad.[11]

The tradition referred to as Ethiopianism by anthropologist St. Clair Drake emerged. In this tradition, Black people turned to the Bible and its redemptive reference to Ethiopia as a symbol of Black humanity and human worth, and of an anticipated earthly salvation. The prophetic words, "Princes shall come out of Egypt; Ethiopia shall soon stretch forth her hands unto God," found in Psalms 68:31 stimulated a radical intellectual divergence from the imperial designs of European Christianity. Many Africans in America learned that the Bible spoke of Africa and gave deference and respect to its people. Egypt was in Africa, and Ethiopia symbolized African humanity. Biblical stories at times became metaphors for Black struggle and for Black redemption.[12]

In the North, free Blacks broke away from White churches and developed separate, parallel institutions. The African Methodist Episcopal Church is an example. This separation was not motivated by a desire to change the faith but to gain a status and equality in religious worship that was denied under White domination.[13] These divergent tendencies reflect a dialectic of cultural hegemony that required the recasting of European religious imperialism.

Subsequent to the Civil War, the "invisible institution" and the "institutional church" became fused. The urbanization of the church corresponded to increasing Black urbanization by World War I. In the urban environment the church became more focused on the here and now, rather than the hereafter. It also became more complex and distant from rural folk culture. However, Spiritualist churches, Holiness (Sanctified) churches, and Pentecostalism provided new avenues for rural folk culture in the urban environment. These religious outlets were simply additional forms of White religious expression that were brought to the oppressed African American populations in the South. As one Black religious scholar has observed, "Black religion cannot be understood apart from white revivalists (Baptists and Methodists, Sanctified Holiness and Pentecostals)."[14]

Some have argued that Pentecostalism is a Black-inspired sect, but history indicates that all of the elements characteristic of this religious expression existed among White evangelicals.[15] An African American was instrumental in the popularization of Pentacostalism. This resulted in a brief period of inter-racial fellowship and then separate Black and White groups. Ultimately, White Pentecostal ministers could not accept Black direction in religious affairs. One scholar who studied Black influences in Pentecostalism commented:

> Black Pentecostals like their forefathers in slavery, witnessed once again the hypocrisy of White Christians, yet clung to the faith which they had received from them—a faith underpined by the black leitmotive yet still substantially inherited from white Americans. One of the miracles of history is that so many black people have in spite of everything, remained steadfast Christians.[16]

It is important to note that ecstatic religious worship was not exclusive to Africans in North America. Whites had a similar tradition. However, Africans maintained their distinctive expressive forms, which included personal experiences of the power of God. They altered African methods of expression to fit New World experiences and found further legitimacy for their religious expression through biblical description and such outlets as the White Holiness and Sanctification movements.[17]

Urbanization provided the context for a radical alteration of the African American religious experience. Up to this point, nearly all forms of African American religious expression had their roots in variations of White Christianity. Spiritualist, Holiness (Sanctified), and Pentecostal churches spread in the urban North as extensions of southern, rural religious expression. Variations of these religious forms produced mass cult figures like Father Divine or Daddy Grace. Some, like Father Divine, attracted a White following as well. In the urban context, Baptist and Methodist churches became larger, more complex, and more socially conscious. African American music, with its blues-based, antiphonal, and polyrhythmic structures, emerged in a sacred form as gospel music.

However, there was a conscious break with many of the ideas of a White Christianity. The Garvey movement and its African Orthodox Church was one example.[18] This was the largest social movement that ever occurred among African Americans. There was also a distinctive break with Christianity with the emergence of Moorish Science under Noble Drew Ali, a proto-Islamic movement, Black Jews, and the Nation of Islam. The redemptive message of Ethiopianism continued in the context of these movements, which were critical of Western Christianity or which broke with Western Christian symbolism altogether. Some early adherents of Ethiopianism had flirted with the doctrine of providential design. In this doctrine, Black and White Christians explained the European enslavement of Africans as God's way of converting Africans who could return to Africa and spread Christianity to the African masses.[19] This sentiment sustained little strength in Black redemptive philosophies, and urbanization saw the prominent display of widespread rejection of the stated and implied White supremacy embodied in mainstream Christianity.[20]

THE PSYCHOLOGY OF OPPRESSION AND RELIGIOUS IMAGERY

Despite the universalist claims of Christianity, it was presented to African people as a White or European religion. The dualistic imagery of the purity and goodness of whiteness and the contamination and evilness of blackness was translated into social terms via an ideology that justified the subordination and oppression of African people. Europeans created biblical interpretations that suggested that Black skin was a divine curse and that God intended African people to be slaves.[21] Scholars have examined and revealed the inconsistencies of these biblical interpretations, and they have demonstrated that biblical and Christian tradition changed from dark-skinned images to white-skinned, European-like images. Also, scholarship clearly shows that Europeans venerated sacred images of African divines in their early history. It was the African slave trade and the full-scale development of White supremacy as a stated or implied creed that contributed to the denigration, elimination, or displacement of African images as sacred symbols.[22] Most critical in these transformations was the image of the Holy family, the Madonna and child, and the racial identity of Jesus.

African Americans began to realize that Whites did not separate White supremacy from their religious beliefs. For them, God was White and Jesus was White. Also, because of the psychology of oppression, many Black people believed that Christianity affirmed a sort of "natural" relationship between Blacks and Whites, that is, that White people were racially connected to God and thus superior. Even Black people who claimed that God had no color, it seemed, could readily accept White images of Jesus but vehemently rejected Black images. Similarly, White Christians were distinguished by their overt support for a White God and Jesus or those who claimed that color (race) did not matter. However, the idea of the African origins of biblical and divine characters in Christianity is generally rejected by Whites, while European imagery is stringently maintained, even among the more liberal believers who claim that color does not matter. Race and religion are inextricably intertwined in the Western religious ethos.

There is an acknowledged psychology of oppression and domination stemming from White supremacy that lies below the conscious mind. For example, Franz Fanon, the psychiatrist, revolutionary, and student of colonial oppression, stated that in his practice he had interviewed over 500 Whites of French, German, English, and Italian nationality. After developing an air of trust and relaxation in which his clients spoke to him freely, he inserted the word "Negro" among some twenty others in the midst of associational tests. Fanon observed that nearly 60 percent of the responses to this word "brought forth biology, penis, strong, athletic, potent, boxer, Joe Louis, Jesse Owens, Senegalese troops, savage, animal, devil, sin."[23] Fanon's analysis of the phobias of his White clients led him to conclude that "the Negro symbolizes the biological danger."[24] Others have noted the sexual basis of racism, a White fear of Black sexuality.[25] For example, during slavery and in the recent past, castration was commonly used against Black males if Whites perceived them as sexually threatening. Further, sex and religion are connected in the Western mind because sex symbolizes sin and evil within the Western religious ethos.

Psychiatrist Frances Cress Welsing has always argued that White supremacy is the result of a fear of genetic annihilation. Europeans, she observed, had a phobic reaction to the reality that the normal human condition on the earth was to have color, perhaps a psychic reaction that was created or exacerbated through European exploration and imperialism. In addition, the inability to produce color stimulated a kind of alienation from ones own body. Western culture, she said, has repressed these racial and sexual fears and its sense of somatic alienation from the conscious mind. These insecurities are portrayed symbolically, and they are acted out through the oppression and subordination of non-Whites. There is both a desire to have color and a fear of domination by those who have color (with Africans having the greatest color potential). As a consequence, the Black female is particularly desirable (she can be dominated by the White male and she can, through procreation, produce offspring with color), and the Black male is particularly feared (he can produce offspring with color through procreation with the White woman when the White male cannot).[26]

European Christian symbolism, she said, is particularly significant. The symbol of the cross, Welsing argued, is a highly abstracted phallus (which includes the testicles containing the all-important genetic, color-producing material) symbolizing the castrated African male. Welsing believes that European Christian theology is unconsciously White supremacist and can be translated as:

> Jesus (a Black man) shed his Black genetic material in a crucifixion, which in reality was a castration and a killing, so that the white genetic recessive population, in fear of its genetic annihilation could be saved (genetically survive).[27]

Most White scholars and many Black ones have refused to seriously explore Welsing's thesis. However, Welsing's theorizing has more credence when one realizes that Christianity's theological particulars and religious imagery have been transformed over centuries and have taken on a distinctive Western and White supremacist form. In addition, Welsing has raised a critical question: How has Western religion perpetuated and obscured a White supremacist culture? The Black religious experience has always reflected a profound recognition, reaction, and response to this problem. Is it possible to embrace Western religious traditions without embracing, at least partially, its White supremacist assumptions? Will the West ever acknowledge the African elements of the religious tradition it reveres? Will Western culture continue in a state of denial with respect to its underlying structure of White supremacy?

The above are important empirical and theoretical questions that Black theologians inside the tradition have not adequately addressed.

Nevertheless, the Black masses have confronted these issues in various ways throughout their sojourn under Western domination. In one sense, the contradictions of a White supremacy system (which also operate at the higher-order, interpretive level of religion) have created a situation in which there is not yet a true African American religion.[28] Nevertheless, there is a profound Black spirituality and religiosity that is looking for a vehicle of expression. The diverse and fragmented nature of Black religious expression suggests a perennial problem with regard to negotiating the psychology of oppression.

Religious symbolism and a spiritual purpose were integral parts of the Garvey movement, the largest Black movement of the twentieth century. Marcus Garvey erected the philosophy of self-help and Black nationalism as a remedy for racial oppression. Most significantly, he saw the problem of the suffering of Black people as a state of mind. Of course, Africa and the African diaspora were the victims of Western imperialism, but, for Garvey, it was up to African people to first free themselves from the mental slavery that inhibited their salvation.

Garvey came into religion through Christianity. As a boy he was involved in the Methodist church to which his parents belonged. Garvey converted to Catholicism but remained independent in his religious thinking. It is not clear whether he literally accepted the sacred myths of Christianity, but he was quick to use the life of Jesus as a model to stimulate courage and conviction among his followers. In addition to his emphasis on self-help and nationalism, he advocated brotherhood and love among Blacks and with all other races. Garvey could not be categorized with the White supremacists of the period because he did not argue for the inherent inferiority of any group. Garvey envisioned a "live and let live" world that was free of racial oppression and the extremes of wealth and poverty.[29]

Most importantly, Garvey said that he and Black people believed in "the One God of all ages, . . . but we shall worship Him through the spectacles of Ethiopia."[30] He did not fault

Whites for worshiping a White God or Asians for worshiping an Asian God. Garvey acknowledged the colorlessness of his conception of God, but he also felt that it was necessary for Black people to see God in their own image, through their own spectacles. Garvey's African Orthodox Church was able to embody this image, which, by its very nature, seemed to transcend Western Christian dogma, even though Garvey continued to use the symbols of Christianity. The spiritual and messianic character of the Garvey movement appeared to heal a fractured and fragmented religious expression, and diverse Black Christian groups, Black Jews, and Black Muslims had no trouble embracing Garvey's message or joining his movement. Garvey's followers compared him to Jesus and proclaimed him a prophet.[31] Perhaps this behavior exemplifies a key aspect of African American and diasporic spirituality, religiosity, and faith. No religion, whether it was Christian, Islamic, Judaic, or the like, can place limits on how Black people will choose to experience the power of God. The time of miracles and of prophets can not be temporally or theologically limited; God can speak at any time.

After Marcus Garvey, the Nation of Islam under Elijah Muhammad became the most dominant galvanizing force in urban Black communities and spawned the charismatic and beloved Malcolm X. Like Garvey, the Nation reversed the religious imagery of a White God and of White supremacy. Black Muslims stressed that Black people were the original inhabitants of the earth and that Whites were grafted from Black people by a process of mutation. According to the group's sacred myths, Whites were genetically engineered by Yacub, a brilliant Black scientist who intended these grafted people to be the embodiment of evil. They were expelled from Paradise (Asia) but returned to wreak havoc on the world and Black people. However, God, through a divine plan, would redeem Black people and restore them to their rightful place in the world. Islam, it was taught, was the Black man's original religion. Black people, Muslims believed, were not a race but a nation waiting to be reborn.[32]

The Nation of Islam, through its redemptive philosophy, functioned as catalyst for social transformation in the Black community. It provided a model for economic and social self-help. The Nation taught that salvation for Black people was that they would be mentally born again. Upon realizing their past greatness, their connection to the will of God, and their basic goodness, it was believed that Black people could transform their lowly status in American society and on earth. Through a powerful religious ethic, the Nation of Islam attacked the crushing mentality of dependency and inferiority caused by White oppression. The Nation transformed the lowest of the oppressed (criminals, drug addicts, and prostitutes) into model citizens, and Malcolm X, its most prominent minister, was a shining example.[33]

Even though all Blacks could not accept the whole of the Black Muslim philosophy, many groups looked to the Nation as a model and tried to emulate its many positive activities. During the 1970s, the Nation grew to around one million members. It had acquired 15,000 acres of farmland in several states, poultry and dairy farms, several thousand head of cattle, warehouses and cold storage facilities, the *Muhammad Speaks* newspaper with its own printing press, aircraft, a bank, apartment complexes, a fleet of tractor-trailers, and a variety of retail businesses across the country. Muslim restaurants, bakeries, and supermarkets were known for their wholesome and high-quality goods. There were seventy-six Black Muslim mosques in the United States, Bermuda, Jamaica, Trinidad, Central America, England, Ghana, and the U.S. Virgin Islands. Muslim enterprises were worth over $85,000,000 by the late 1970s.[34] Like Garvey, the Nation proved to Black people that they could help themselves and achieve self-respect in a world that had removed their dignity as a people.

When Elijah Muhammad died in 1975, the Nation of Islam had begun to attract larger numbers of middle-class and college-educated Blacks. In addition, more and more Whites looked to the Nation as a positive force for change. The Nation had developed visible, positive relationships with Black Christians and Black Jews, and other oppressed segments of the society and abroad, including Native Americans. The death of Elijah Muhammad also contributed to a schism between those Muslims who continued to embrace a nationalistic philosophy and the Nation's original sacred lore, and those Muslims who became more orthodox in their beliefs and rituals. This former group was most prominently led by Louis Farrakhan, and the latter group was led by Wallace D. Muhammad, the seventh child of the late Elijah Muhammad.[35] However, just as Malcolm X was embraced by many Black Christians, Louis Farrakhan and his Nation of Islam developed a significant non-Muslim and Christian following.[36]

What can we learn from the Garvey movement and from the Nation of Islam? These movements were part of a continuing response to oppression that was characterized by White supremacy. They symbolized the powerful role of religion in oppression and in the struggle for liberation. These movements challenged the religion given to African slaves by their European slave masters, which was intended to induce a state of mental dependency and a radical need for White approval. Self-hatred, self-doubt, and intra-group aggression and exploitation were also characteristics. Christian symbolism was used by Black social movements to draw upon the emotional attachment that Blacks had developed for Christianity's sacred myths, but serious alterations were necessary to negate some of the religion's White-supremacist components. The Nation of Islam and other Islamic responses went a step further and eliminated the visual image of God. Islam also provided a framework through which to break with European Christendom altogether and thus its hegemonic interpretive framework.

If history is our teacher, religion is a necessary component to bring about social change in the Black community, but it is most galvanizing and progressive when it can embrace the prophetically and socially redemptive traditions of the Black experience. The dynamism of Black social movements are sustained when Black people see themselves connected as a group to God and when they are able to remove constraints to how God can speak to them. This means that prophets and messengers from God are possible for all times.

Also, regardless of the universalist conceptions of religion, that is, recognition of the brotherhood and sisterhood of humankind, there must be a powerful self-help component that speaks to the well-being of the group. Further, the religion must be able to address intra-group as well as inter-group relations. It must give direction to secular activities that will help to empower its adherents.

Nowhere was the power of religion and of the church exemplified more than in the Civil Rights movement.[37] Religious unity (Christian) was achieved under the leadership of Martin Luther King, Jr. However, the South was a much more homogeneous religious community for African Americans than the urban North. In the context of a more urbanized South, the "old-time religion" of the slaves prevailed but provided an independent financial and organizational base and an ideological justification for challenging segregation and injustice. Black ministers sought to execute the "true" principles of Christianity through social action. Nonviolent direct action was compatible with the extant interpretation of Christian principles and was sufficient to gain the civil disruption necessary for social change. However, as it would be learned later, this strategy was insufficient to bring about a total transformation of racial oppression, particularly on a cultural and economic level.

The challenge of Black Power and the militant tone of Malcolm X, particularly after his break with the Nation of Islam, no longer called for Black people to turn the other cheek. Many African Americans saw the struggle for desegregation as a necessary one, but they realized that integration that did not lead to power for Black people was an empty strategy. Similarly, nonviolent direct action became unpopular if it meant that Black people must always do nothing if attacked by White racists. Black people wanted all strategies and options for social change and self-determination available to them. After the assassinations of Malcolm X and Martin Luther King, Jr., and the exhaustion of Civil Rights protest strategies, Black people shifted to a more determined commitment to collective struggle that called for a psychological cleansing. In this circumstance Black theologians were moved to challenge traditional Christianity and the more conservative religious strains in the Black community. Black theology, or liberation theology, was born.

James Cone and others developed Black theology as a reaction to the assertion by religious scholar Joseph Washington that Black religion was only a consequence of Black exclusion from the "genuine" Christianity of White churches. They also argued that it was the Black church that was truly Christian. Black theologians exposed the hypocrisy of White churchmen, embraced the idea of Black Power, and extended greater legitimacy to the nationalism of Malcolm X. They challenged the idea that Blacks must appeal to the conscience of Whites while Whites used raw power to maintain Black oppression. These Black ministers were also seeking greater relevance in the midst of urban revolts. Albert Cleage, the Detroit minister who founded the Shrine of the Black Madonna and who was involved with the early phases of the development of Black theology, unabashedly preached that Jesus was the Black Messiah. Cleage's view that Christianity was a stolen legacy was too radical for other Black theologians and their professional body, the National Conference of Black Churchmen (NCBC). Thus, Cone and his colleagues retreated to a less provocative view on the non-White image of Christ.[38]

Black or liberation theology, although viewing itself as radical, sought to reform White Christianity rather than to make a break with it. Cone argued that because Christianity is a theology of liberation and Black theology is liberation theology, Black theology is the "true" Christian theology. Black or liberation theology has not penetrated the masses of Black people as a vanguard movement and explicitly seeks to preserve the essential, sacred myths of Western Christianity.[39] Nevertheless, Black theology is evolving and it remains to be seen how it will speak to the aspirations of African Americans and their need for religious independence and for religious unity.

Black churches around the country, however, have continued to respond to the contradictions of traditional Christianity and the needs of their communities in many ways. Some utilize images of a Black Christ and a Black Madonna and child. Others use no images at all. Some churches utilize symbols, rituals, and dress based upon traditional African culture in their religious services and ceremonies. A number of churches advocate Black solidarity and attempt to stimulate a pan-African consciousness among their congregations.

Many churches actively provide social services to uplift their communities. Affordable housing and child care, food and clothing for the needy, assistance to the elderly, economic cooperatives, tutoring for young people in school, Black history classes, classes to promote positive family living and to develop positive values among young people, political education, and the like are examples.

Nevertheless, diverse Christian or theological interpretations and attachments to Christian orthodoxy remain as barriers to African unity and thus to substantial community elevation and development. C. Eric Lincoln has observed a continued conservatism in the Black church and believes that Black churches are the institutional embodiment of the DuBoisian problem of double-consciousness.[40] Accordingly, no broad ethic of social change is evident in Black Christian institutions, and their attachment to narrow and literal theological interpretations makes religious unity problematic. A significant segment of the Black population remains alienated from organized religion, and Christian dogma provides little attraction or direction to large numbers of the Black community's dispossessed and alienated youth, particularly its male populations.

THE MYTH OF THE TRUTH AND THE TRUTH OF THE MYTH

Up to this point, we have addressed the contradictions inherent in Western Christianity as it was transmitted to African peoples by European slave owners. Historical fact revealed that while claiming a universalist philosophy, Western Christian forms were the principal vehicle for transmitting White supremacy. In addition, these forms were inherently imperialistic by virtue of their systemic denigration of all religions and cultures that were perceived as outside the tradition. These religious forms continued to exist, through sacred imagery and the weight of a socially constructed set of religious myths, as justification for White domination. The Black religious experience subsequent to European contact has responded to Western religious imperialism by assimilating European religious forms via segregated but parallel institutions; through altering European religions to justify rebellions, protests, and social reform activities; or through leaving European religions altogether. Other variations occurred within these categories of response.

Western Christian forms remain dominant in the Black community, but New World Black religious history implies that Black religiosity and spirituality transcend Western Christian doctrines. There is a certain fluidity in Black religious expression, which suggests that Black people are searching for a religious vehicle that can more fully embody their social and spiritual needs. Nevertheless, emotional and conceptual ties to Western Christian forms have produced a dilemma for African American development. African Americans cannot fully free themselves from the implicit reality that a White power structure defines their sacred beliefs, and does so completely in the interest of preserving White supremacy. For example, this power structure selectively legitimates Black leaders that show allegiance to a Western Christian ethic, regardless of its form. Such an allegiance, White elites believe, will ensure that their hegemony will not be challenged, at least beyond a certain point. Furthermore, Christian institutions in the Black community are highly fragmented and competitive. Competition for members and struggles and disagreements over theological interpretations are frequent. Substantial efforts by Black religious leaders to critique Western religious dogma or to produce a mode of religious expression that can unify the masses of Black people are nonexistent.

A fundamental issue for producing Black religious unity is to liberate the religious thinking of African Americans. The bulk of this thinking revolves around the interpretations of biblical lore. Black theologian James Cone, for example, has attacked White Christianity for using literal interpretations of the Bible as justification for Black oppression.[41] However, the unifying characteristic of Western Christianity is that all adherents accept some literal interpretation of biblical lore. A large proportion of the conflict that occurs within the tradition generally revolves around how literal biblical interpretations should be. Even if some biblical stories are viewed as allegorical, the Christ myth is not. It is this attachment to a literal historical interpretation of biblical lore that gives Western White supremacy power over the Black mind.

Some Black scholars have attempted to challenge this psychological hegemony by revealing two fundamental facts. First, Western Christianity attempts to preserve White supremacy by hiding African influences in Judeo-Christian traditions. This includes obscuring the African origins of many biblical personalities. Second, Western Christianity attempts to hide the political and syncretic dimensions of the religion that show that it has borrowed from previous religious myths and has altered these myths to accomplish political ends. Indeed, many of the pagan symbols and practices that remained under Romanized Christianity were allowed because it was impossible to completely destroy the attachment of the masses to their previous religious practices. In addition, much of the lore regarding evil spirits, devils, and witches were created to vilify religions that might compete with the state religion or challenge patriarchal authority. Unfortunately, Black theologians have not addressed these issues.

No religion springs forth anew without paying some debt to other religions. Europeans typically ignored the similarities between the more ancient traditional African religions and European Christian religious forms in order to advance the idea that Africans had no religion or had defective religions. Western Christianity

also ignores the fact that numerous other religions around the world have similar but older
myths regarding creation, a great flood, the
fall of man, and savior-gods. Scholars have
demonstrated that much of the Bible can be
traced back to the sacred writings of ancient
Egypt.[42] John Jackson has argued that the
African father of the Christian church, St. Augustine, acknowledged that the Christian religion existed among the ancients. Jackson said
that according to Augustine, there was not a
time when Christianity did not exist.[43] This
view suggests that the fundamental ethical components of the religion were of much earlier
origin.

Historical data show the existence of numerous savior-god religions before Christianity.
An examination of the possible origins of the
Christ myth provides additional food for
thought. John Jackson argued that the Christ
myth was based on the allegorical veneration of
nature, that is, the material universe and the
forces, spiritual or otherwise, that are at work
in the cosmos. Underlying the veneration of
these forces was the practical ability to harmo-
niously live with nature through an understanding of cyclical relationships. Ancient savior-gods were personifications of the sun, and
the Christ myth represented the movement, alle-
gorically, of the sun through the twelve signs
of the zodiac. Lunar, vegetative, and astral elements were also included. Jackson explained
that in ancient Egypt, the birth date of the
sun-god was the twenty-fifth of December, reflecting the first noticeable lengthening of the
day following the winter solstice (the shortest
day of the year). During this ancient period,
the sun was in the zodiacal sign of Capricorn,
and was then known as the Stable of Augeas.
Thus, the newly born sun emerged from a stable.
On the meridian was Sirius (the Eastern star);
Virgo the virgin was rising from the east. To
the right of Sirius was the constellation Orion,
the Great Hunter, who had three stars in his
belt. These stars were in a straight line and
pointed at Sirius. They were known in ancient
times as the Three Kings.[44]

Another scholar of comparative religions described the diffusion of the African image of Isis and Horus (mother and child) into European Christendom as the image of the Black Madonna and child. This image was later whitened. The cult of the African goddess Isis had widespread appeal in Europe. However, the fifth century saw the elevation of the Madonna and child image to compete with Isis and Horus. The worship of Isis was suppressed.[45]

Yosef ben-Jochannan demonstrated that the term "Western" religions is a misnomer since these religions came from Asia-Minor, Arabia, North African, West Africa, and East Africa.[46] For example, he observed that the "Negative Confession," a much larger body of ethical statements, included what have been called the Ten Commandments more than 1,300 years before the time of Moses.[47] Further, the Proverbs ascribed to King Solomon can be found in the collection of poetry and songs by an indigenous African king, Amen-em-ope, hundreds of years before Solomon's reign.[48] Also, ben-Jochannan's data suggest that the significance of the antiquity and the presence of Ethiopian or Falasha Jews is obscured and ignored in the interpretations of White-dominated religious history and theology.[49]

Other scholars pointed to indigenous Africans who made significant contributions to early Christianity. Three Popes were indigenous Africans. Years later, their images were painted by Europeans as Europeans. These artists simply used their own ethnocentric imaginations.[50] Augustine, Cyprian, and Tertullian (a contemporary of the indigenous African Roman emperor, Septimus Severus) are other examples. African scholars explained that because Rome occupied North Africa, this does not mean that the people ceased to be African. Thus, history shows that Judeo-Christian traditions are indebted to Africa and to Africans, but White supremacy has obscured and distorted this reality. In addition, traditional Eurocentric scholarship leads us to overlook African influences in Islam (note the contributions of Bilal), Buddhism, and Hinduism.[51] A more accurate assessment of the existence and historical evolution of African peoples in the ancient world would make their involvement in the formation of world religions easily comprehensible.

The above-mentioned explorations into comparative religious history serve to reveal the human constructions of religion and raise fundamental doubts concerning the literal truth of religious myth. These scholars also wished to reveal the racial hypocrisy in the way the Western world has characterized its religious traditions. White elites removed the African presence from religious history, and they altered the meaning and structure of the ancient religions traditions they embraced. These facts call for further questioning of the literal interpretations of Western sacred mythology. A more fruitful method of religious interpretation may be to look for the truth in the myth.

The truth in the myth means that one looks for the spiritual revelations, universal laws, and human understandings that can be found in religious myth. From this perspective, religions take on a more unified character, and their imperialist quality fades. Religions rise from a common source, the human experience. Realization of this underlying universal reality means that no religion is greater than another.

Black religion, for example, should speak to universal truths through the historical and social experiences of African peoples. One might argue in an allegorical sense that an oppressed people is a spiritually chosen people because oppression produces a cultural tension or a historical impetus to restore human dignity and freedom. This is, perhaps, a universal impulse. Therefore, we may view religion, in part, as an embodiment of the feelings, emotions, struggles, and types of relationships encountered through the human experience as people struggle against domination, oppression, and human degradation. Thus, an important function of religious myth is that it illustrates what some oppressed people have done to elevate their status in the world. For example, an oppressed people, in order to elevate their status, must believe that they are a chosen people. This means that they believe that God is on their side. What this also means is that the oppressed must become cohesive as a group, and they must align themselves with certain ethical principles (an empowering mode of life) in order to transcend oppression.

An oppressed people also must learn from the experience of oppression in order not to reproduce oppression. What this suggests is that no group is a chosen people forever. The concept of a chosen people simply embodies a requirement for liberation. What emerges from this conceptual metaphor is a universal truth that shows that justice is the only way to remove the potential for reproducing oppression. If there is no justice, there is the danger that an oppressed group may become oppressors at another point in time. Pain and suffering, of course, are the result of a failure to implement justice, and a world is created in which eventually even the rich and powerful cannot live.

The African American religious experience suggests that a deeper and more unifying religious vehicle must be found if African Americans are to develop and advance in American society and the world. At the very least, Black scholars and theologians must develop a sustained dialogue on these issues. Nevertheless, grassroots elements will continue to assess existing religious vehicles and move to develop meaningful alternatives of their own. Religious leaders can be impediments to human liberation, they can be followers, or they can lead the masses in their struggle for human dignity. Clearly, African spirituality is a common thread that runs through the Black experience, and in the present era, the redemptive dimension of religion is the most powerful and potentially unifying force available to African Americans. Thus, a more potent and liberating spiritual ethic is needed to give direction to African American institution building.

NOTES

1. See, for example, National Research Council Committee on the Status of Black Americans, *A Common Destiny: Blacks and American Society* (Washington, D.C.: National Academy Press, 1989), p. 173; E. Franklin Frazier, *The Negro*

Church in America, new edition bound with *The Black Church Since Frazier* (New York: Schocken Books, 1974), p. 14; John W. Blassingame, *The Slave Community*, rev. edn. (New York: Oxford University Press, 1979), p. viii.

2. Frazier, *The Negro Church*.

3. See Winthrop D. Jordan, *White Over Black: American Attitudes Toward the Negro 1550-1812* (Baltimore, Md.: Penguin Books, 1969); George M. Frederickson, *White Supremacy: A Comparative Study in American and South African History* (New York: Oxford University Press, 1981).

4. See, for example, Carter G. Woodson, *The History of the Negro Church*, second edn. (Washington, D.C.: Associated Publishers, 1945); Albert J. Raboteau, *Slave Religion* (New York: Oxford University Press, 1978); Blassingame, *Slave Community*.

5. See E. Franklin Frazier, *Black Bourgeoisie: The Rise of a New Middle Class* (New York: The Free Press, 1957).

6. See Yosef ben-Jochannan, *African Origins of the Major "Western Religions"* (New York: Alkebu-lan Books, 1970); Blassingame, *Slave Community*; Raboteau, *Slave Religion*.

7. Ibid.; Leonard E. Barrett, *Soul Force: African Heritage in Afro-American Religion* (Garden City, N.Y.: Anchor Press/Doubleday, 1974).

8. See Arthur H. Fauset, *Black Gods of the Metropolis: Negro Religious Cults in the Urban North* (Philadelphia: University of Pennsylvania Press, 1944).

9. Frazier, *Negro Church*.

10. Ibid.; Joseph Washington, *Black Sects and Cults* (Garden City, N.Y.: Anchor Books/Doubleday, 1973); Iain MacRobert, *The Black Roots and White Racism of Early Pentecostalism in the U.S.A.* (New York: St. Martin's Press, 1988).

11. Blassingame, *Slave Community*; Raboteau, *Slave Religion*; Sterling Stuckey, *Slave Culture: Nationalist Theory and Foundations of Black America* (New York: Oxford University Press, 1987).

12. St. Clair Drake, *The Redemption of Africa and Black Religion* (Chicago: Third World Press, 1970); Barrett, *Soul Force*.

13. See Washington, *Black Sects and Cults*, p. 33.

14. See Frazier, *Negro Church;* Washington, *Black Sects and Cults;* MacRobert, *The Black Roots and White Racism of Early Pentacostalism,* pp. 36–40.

15. C. Eric Lincoln and Lawrence H. Mamiya, *The Black Church in the American Experience* (Durham, N.C.: Duke University Press, 1990); Washington, *Black Sects and Cults;* Stuckey, *Slave Culture;* MacRobert, *The Black Roots and White Racism of Early Pentacostalism.*

16. MacRobert, *The Black Roots and White Racism of Early Pentacostalism,* p. 94.

17. See, for example, Stuckey, *Slave Culture;* Washington, *Black Sects and Cults;* Lincoln and Mamiya, *The Black Church;* MacRoberts, *The Black Roots and White Racism of Early Pentacostalism.*

18. Tony Martin, *Race First: The Ideological and Organizational Struggles of Marcus Garvey and the Universal Negro Improvement Association* (Westport, Conn.: Greenwood Press, 1976), pp. 67–88.

19. Drake, *The Redemption of Africa,* p. 61.

20. See, for example, Claude McKay, *Harlem: Negro Metropolis* (New York: Harcourt Brace Jovanovich, 1968); Alphonso Pinkney, *Red, Black, and Green: Black Nationalism in America* (New York: Cambridge University Press, 1976); Martin, *Race First;* Fauset, *Black Gods.*

21. See Jordan, *White Over Black;* Frederickson, *White Supremacy.*

22. See St. Clair Drake, *Black Folk Here and There: An Essay in History and Anthropology,* 2 vols. (Los Angeles: University of California Center for Afro-American Studies).

23. Franz Fanon, *Black Skin, White Mask* (New York: Grove Press, 1967), p. 166.

24. Ibid., p. 165.

25. See Calvin C. Hernton, *Sex and Racism in America* (New York: Grove Press, 1965); William H. Grier and Price M. Cobbs, *Black Rage* (New York: Bantam, 1969), p. 84; Jordan, *White Over Black,* p. 154.

26. Francis Cress Welsing, *The Isis Papers: The Keys to the Colors* (Chicago: Third World Press, 1991).

27. Ibid., p. 69.

28. Cf. Washington, *Black Sects and Cults,* p. 142.

29. See Amy Jacques-Garvey, ed., *Philosophy and Opinions of Marcus Garvey,* two vols. in one (New York: Arno Press and the New York Times, 1969); Martin, *Race First.*

30. Jacques-Garvey, ed., *Philosophy and Opinions,* vol. 1, p. 44.

31. See Martin, *Race First.*

32. See, for example, C. Eric Lincoln, *The Black Muslims in America* (Boston: Beacon Press, 1969); E. U. Essien-Udom, *Black Nationalism: A Search for Identity in America* (New York: Dell, 1964); Clifton E. Marsh, *From Black Muslims to Muslims: The Transition from Separatism to Islam, 1930-1980* (Metuchen, N.J.: Scarecrow Press, 1984).

33. Ibid.; Malcolm X, *The Autobiography of Malcolm X,* with the assistance of Alex Haley (New York: Grove Press, 1964).

34. Marsh, *From Black Muslims to Muslims*, pp. 90-91.

35. Marsh, *From Black Muslims to Muslims.*

36. During Jesse Jackson's bid for the Democratic presidential nomination in 1984, in Chicago there was an overt show of unity between Jackson (who symbolized Black Christians), Black Muslims, and Black Jews. This display of unity electrified many sectors of the Black community but was destroyed by the White-controlled media and White elites who sought to make such alliances a liability for Jackson as he attempted to gain acceptability among White voting populations and White financial supporters. Thus, this form of religious unity remained elusive to the Black community. Furthermore, it is commonly known that White elites have actively worked to destroy Black leaders who appeared to be able to galvanize a fragmented Black community. J. Edgar Hoover, for example, used the FBI that he headed to disrupt the potential for a Black "Messiah" from emerging who could unify the Black community. Marcus Garvey, Malcolm X, Martin Luther King, Jr., and others were his victims.

37. See, for example, Aldon D. Morris, *The Origins of the Civil Rights Movement: Black Communities Organizing for Change* (New York: The Free Press, 1984).

38. James H. Cone, *For My People: Black Theology and the Black Church* (Maryknoll, N.Y.: Or-

bis Books, 1984); Albert B. Cleage, Jr., *The Black Messiah* (Trenton, N.J.: African World Press, 1989).

39. Ibid.; also see James H. Cone, *A Black Theology of Liberation* (Maryknoll, N.Y.: Orbis Books, 1986); Maulana Karenga, *Introduction to Black Studies* (Inglewood, Calif.: Kawaida Publications, 1982), pp. 183-87.

40. Lincoln and Mamiya, *The Black Church in the African American Experience*, pp. 228-29.

41. Cone, *Black Theology of Liberation*, p. 36.

42. John G. Jackson, *Man, God and Civilization* (New Hyde Park, N.Y.: University Books, 1972), and *Christianity Before Christ* (Austin, Texas: American Atheist Press, 1985); Cheikh Anta Diop, *The African Origins of Civilization: Myth or Reality,* edited and translated by Mercer Cook (Westport, Conn.: Lawrence Hill, 1974); ben-Jochannan, *African Origins of the Major "Western Religions."*

43. See Jackson, *Christianity Before Christ,* p. 1.

44. Ibid., pp. 126-27; and Jackson, *Man, God and Civilization,* pp. 133-34.

45. Danita Redd, "Black Madonnas of Europe: Diffusion of the African Isis" in Ivan Van Sertima, ed., *African Presence in Early Europe* (New Brunswick, N.J.: Transaction Publishers, 1985), pp. 108-33.

46. ben-Jochannan, *African Origins of the Major "Western Religions."*

47. Ibid., p. 70; also see Maulana Karenga, "Black Religion," in Gayraud S. Wilmore, ed., *African American Religious Studies: An Interdisciplinary Anthology* (Durham, N.C.: Duke University Press, 1989), pp. 171-300.

48. ben-Jochannan, *African Origins of the Major "Western Religions,"* p. 164.

49. Ibid.

50. See Edward Scobie, "African Popes," in Ivan Van Sertima, ed., *African Presence in Early Europe,* pp. 96-107.

51. John G. Jackson, "Krishna and Buddha of India: Black Gods of Asia," in Ivan Van Sertima and Runoko Rashidi, eds., *African Presence in Early Asia,* rev. edn. (New Brunswick, N.J.: Transaction Books, 1988), pp. 106-11; J. C. de-

Graft-Johnson, *African Glory: The Story of Vanished Negro Civilizations* (Baltimore, Md.: Black Classic Press, 1986); ben-Jochannan, *African Origins of the Major "Western Religions."*

7

Toward a Theory of African American Health

The health of a people is an important measure of the viability of their culture. Health is also negatively affected by oppression and exploitation. More than this, in the struggle for liberation, a people must seize control of their health as a requisite to transforming their subordinate status in society and the world. Better health improves the quality of life and therefore helps to mitigate the terrible effects of exploitation. Most importantly, however, better health frees the potential for positive change by increasing the vitality of a people. Their mental, physical, and spiritual strength can be released and directed toward greater empowerment at all levels of life. The process of liberating health requires transformations in thinking, consciousness, and habits. Because poor health is connected to structured subordination, changes in health thinking, consciousness, and behavior challenge the very core of exploitation. Moreover, through health promotion, oppressed people actively become involved in eliminating their participation in their own exploitation. They self-consciously and enterprisingly begin to alter health-related maladaptations to oppression.

CULTURAL HEGEMONY AND INSTITUTIONAL WEAKNESS

African Americans must develop an appropriate response to the problem of cultural hegemony if they are to improve their health status in American society. Cultural hegemony consists of those social forces surrounding African American institutional development that tend to place the African American community in a state of dependency and economic dislocation. These forces contribute to chronic maladaptation and institutional weakness and therefore cultural negation. Cultural hegemony, the fundamental vehicle of systemic White supremacy, tends to deprive African Americans of a sustained capacity to develop a social and spiritual ethic that can serve their collective needs. It does this through the control and manipulation of communications that govern ideas and images, both sacred and secular. Furthermore, the dominant society automatically extends legitimacy (recognition and respect) to Eurocentric ideas and aspirations but as a reflex, systemically denies the same for African Americans. As a consequence, African American thinking and dialogue about how to live is obstructed and fails to achieve institutionalization.

Economic underdevelopment and dislocation contribute to social disorganization, particularly if there is no countervailing social ethic to guide people in progressively resisting the culturally maladaptive effects of structured inequality. A particular problem is the stability of the family. For example, when the instrumental functions of the family are disrupted, the family becomes tenuous as a force to guide the education of its youth and as a basis for social control. The key role of the family in elevating the health status of African Americans is also weakened. It is this weakening of the central role and capacity of the family in maintaining the health and well-being of the community that is most crucial.

Crime is a further problem of social disorganization, since in the Black community, criminal activity functions as an alternative economy and symbolizes the frustrations and pressures of economic underdevelopment and despair. The drug trade, for example, has injected enormous violence into this alternative economy as people compete for markets and apply their own rules of force to survive in a chaotic, alternative, free-market system. Furthermore, White elites isolate the results of extreme economic dislocation through urban ghettoization, prisons, educational tracking, and the like, and, as a consequence, have little incentive to ameliorate Black suffering or move toward economic parity. The health-negating aspects of crime, particularly through drug use, homicide, and other forms of violence, are an immense health problem for African Americans and represent a serious maladaptation to oppression.

THE NEED FOR A COUNTERVAILING HEALTH ETHIC

One tool that African Americans have to resist and perhaps to transform health-related maladaptations is to develop a social ethic that can reintroduce an appropriate and positive strategy for living. This ethic must resist the psychologically and spiritually debilitating effects of structured inequality. The struggle to create and institutionalize such an ethic challenges the tendency of mainstream society to serve the cultural aspirations of economic elites at the expense of African Americans. This problem is coextensive with White supremacy because economic and political control is also racially stratified. White elites maintain a cultural agenda and a racial consciousness that reflect an extant system of values, norms, and beliefs that they seek to reproduce. Thus, there is a systemic inclination to resist a countervailing Black social ethic that tends to negate African American dependency and White supremacy.

Usually, a social ethic of great cohesiveness and strength is driven by spiritual, religious, or sacred customs. However, the old-time religion of the slaves is diverse, fragmented, and much weaker in the urban environment. Also, traditional Black religious expression exhibits the problem of double-consciousness, which serves to perpetuate White supremacy. Most importantly, mainstream African American religious beliefs embody no ethic or consciousness that can be used to guide health-related behavior among African Americans. Further, secular sources for such an ethic are scattered and overshadowed by massive consumer advertising that encourages health-threatening habits of consumption.[1]

Social tendencies to negate a progressive Black social ethic are particularly strong under current economic conditions. In the context of shrinking markets, Blacks represent an important profit margin. Thus, in this era, White elites are most focused on capturing the consumer potential of African Americans while maintaining a posture of neglect with regard to economic development and parity. The capture of Black minds and markets is paramount during this epoch of chronic overproduction.

What must be understood as a fundamental principle is that the health of a people is a function of the viability and positive adaptability of their culture. For example, family functioning, which includes an appropriate social ethic, is critical in directing health behavior and insulating the individual from negative consumer habits. The idea of an ethic implies creating and sustaining a tradition, but tradition is an impediment to radical consumption. It is in this sense that economic forces contribute to cultural negation, and capitalist culture is inherently health-negating because it promotes unrestrained consumption. At its very best, capitalist culture seeks to absorb health-related activities previously controlled by individuals, families, and communities into industrial products and profits. The results, unfortunately, are not health-driven but market-driven. Cultural hegemony as a social problem makes the health status of African Americans much more tenuous and problematic. African Americans have less institutional insulation against efforts to control their consumer patterns, less institutional viability because of economic dislocation, and less ability to produce and sustain a countervailing, health-promoting social ethic because of the potential challenge to White cultural dominance.

EXPLOITATION, CULTURE, AND HEALTH

Over the years, ethnographic, statistical, and historical studies of African Americans have pointed to the critical importance of ecological, environmental, and social factors affecting their health status. E. Franklin Frazier, for example, provided significant insight into the way in which European contact seriously disrupted African culture and contributed to health problems of massive proportions among Africans in Africa and in the New World. These cultural alterations not only affected African health but also the health of all peoples who were subjugated and exploited by Europeans. Europeans introduced new plant and animal life to satiate their social, cultural, and economic needs, thereby disrupting the traditional organization of African work and family. We know, for example, that the cultivation of coffee, cocoa, sugar, rice, tobacco, and cotton contributed to the use of slave labor. Subsequent institutional ruptures contributed to soil erosion in Africa and in the New World, and they disrupted long-established African dietary habits. Diversified African diets became more restricted and limited, seriously lowering the resistance of Africans to disease.[2]

Europeans were responsible for introducing venereal diseases, tuberculosis, smallpox, measles, pneumonia, strong alcoholic beverages, firearms, and the like, which ravaged Africans in both Africa and in the Americas. Africans were faced not only with lowered resistance to disease because of poorer nutrition but also with new diseases for which they had no natural immunity. Europeans used alcohol (drugs) to facilitate the enslavement of Africans, and alcohol became an important impetus for increased African mortality. Supplying slaves with tobacco they could sniff, chew, or smoke was useful in keeping them pacified. The introduction of firearms by Europeans in Africa changed the character of warfare, making it more devastating, and accelerated the slave trade.[3] Ironically, alcohol, tobacco, sugar, and firearms, which were all integrally associated with the motivation for the slave trade and slavery, represent major challenges to the health and well-being of African Americans today. In short, the disruption of African culture to serve the economic needs of Europeans caused profound and negative changes in the health of Africans in Africa and in the New World.

One of the great human tragedies of history that rivaled the slave trade was the pain and suffering of enslaved Africans as they were ravaged by disease, malnutrition, and inadequate protection from the elements. For example, the slave quarters were separated and isolated from those of the slave owner, and slaves suffered from a vast array of infectious and parasitic diseases associated with housing that had inadequate ventilation, insufficient windows for sunshine, and damp earthen floors, a haven for bacteria and fungus. Slaves also had to contend with contaminated water, poorly cooked food, larvae-infested soil, and inadequate clothing, including limited access to shoes. Respiratory illnesses were characteristic of the winter months. Dysentery and digestive ailments were warm-weather maladies. Parasitic worms were a problem all year long. Contagious diseases spread rapidly, and the slave owner and his family sometimes left the plantation during epidemics. Because of poor sanitation, overcrowded dwellings, and a lack of effective public health measures, infectious conditions such as malaria, yellow fever, smallpox, cholera, body lice, impetigo, typhus, tetanus, yaws, hook worms, syphilis, and the like were common.[4]

African Americans suffered a variety of other health problems. Industrial accidents and job-related hazards, such as the inhalation of tobacco fumes and nicotine poisoning, were examples. Coal mining brought the dangers of gas explosions, black lung disease, drowning from flooded shafts, and flash fires. Typical working conditions brought constant exposure to the extremes of climate.[5] Pregnancy was an intensely dangerous event for mother and child.[6] Neonatal tetany occurred from the improper handling of the umbilical stump, and new mothers could be threatened by the dangers of puerperal fever.[7] Punishment by whippings, which left severe scars, was another significant health hazard.

Chronic nutritional deficiencies were major health problems that were left unaddressed by slave owners. They had little knowledge in this regard, and owners were more interested in minimally satiating slave hunger in order to preserve their chattel while keeping profits up. Stealing by slaves was usually associated with trying to acquire food.[8] Fat pork and corn meal were the usual staples and constituted a poor diet. African slaves typically suffered from deficiencies in calcium, magnesium, vitamin C, protein, and B-complex vitamins. Slaves suffered high incidences of dental caries, crooked appendages, stooped shoulders, jaundiced complexions, splotchy skin, inflamed and watery eyes, partial blindness, rotten and missing teeth, and other nutritionally related deformities.[9] No doubt there were slaves who exhibited poor mental development and a lack of vitality because of malnutrition.

Besides the fact that knowledge of nutrition and disease causation was not well developed or widespread among slave owners or physicians, medical treatment could be more dangerous than the disease. Bleeding and purging patients were common, and methods of anesthesia and surgery were primitive. In response, many Africans actively treated their own ailments in addition to the treatment obtained from physicians that served the plantations. Some slaves established themselves as effective healers and made significant contributions to the treatment of various medical problems.[10] At times, White physicians took advantage of slaves and used them for medical experimentation. As a consequence, slaves sometimes suffered numerous surgeries at the hands of physicians who were trying to perfect various surgical procedures. Black suffering was exacerbated by the fact that anesthesia was not very effective and antiseptic conditions were not characteristic.[11]

What is most significant is the enormous amount of time and energy that African Americans had to invest in dealing with sickness and death. Because public health and medical science were not well developed, all people were at a disadvantage, but oppression and exploitation placed a profound burden on the health status of

African Americans that was not shared by Whites. Additional medical care, if it could have offered more enlightened treatment, would have been an aid to Black suffering. However, the most critical challenges to health were public health problems and not simply medical ones. Medical care was most useful for injury and trauma, but public health remedies were needed to eliminate or control infectious diseases and to provide a firm nutritional base upon which to strengthen the individual against disease.

Subsequent to the slave experience, poor health continued to be tied substantially to the exigencies of economic and racial oppression. Beyond the fact that racism denied Black people equal access to medical care, their subordinate relationship to the polity, economy, and social order subverted health-promoting institutional responses. These failed institutional responses revolved around the disorganization of family life and maladaptation to work. In addition, no pervasive social ethic existed that could stimulate self-conscious health promotion. For Blacks, poor health exacerbated existing social problems, lowered vitality and productivity, and disrupted the learning process among young people.[12]

One study of Blacks in the deep South discussed efforts in the late 1930s to instruct Black tenant farmers in the Yazoo-Mississippi Delta to plant vegetables and to diversify their crops. They were taught methods of canning vegetables and fruits so as to have such foods all year round. These efforts were necessary to improve the health of poor sharecroppers. Blacks of this region suffered from nutritional diseases like pellagra and were characteristically deficient in protein, calcium, phosphorus, and iron.[13] Another study of Black tenant farmers indicated that home-grown food, which could diversify and improve the nutritional quality of the diet, was essential to reducing their susceptibility to contagious diseases.[14]

Several social forces were at work simultaneously to disrupt the health of Black tenant farmers. First, tenant farmers had historically been required to grow one crop--cotton. Second, they depended on White land owners to direct their thinking and actions with regard to their livelihood and related activities. Third, health-negating habits were formed as a result of maladaptations to the structure of work and to available food sources. A progressive response to these circumstances required transforming existing cultural patterns, disengagement from the psychological domination of local White supremacy, and the discovery of viable, alternative health-promoting activities.

Other studies provided additional insights. For example, W. E. B. DuBois examined the relationship between environment and health in his *Philadelphia Negro*. This 1899 study of urban Black migrants associated high rates of infectious diseases and high infant mortality with poor sanitation, poor housing, and poor food. DuBois also observed that strong family organization with an appropriate ethic could have the effect of mitigating the unhealthy consequences of a poverty-stricken environment. DuBois made a distinction between poor health associated with racial prejudice and poor health associated with the accumulated habits and customs of the people.[15] We learned from this example that maladaptations to oppression and to urban life needed to be transformed. Thus, over a hundred years ago, DuBois understood the need for health promotion and encouraged African Americans to "start with a crusade for fresh air, cleanliness, healthfully located homes and proper food."[16]

Years later, E. Franklin Frazier would observe the disorganizing effects of oppression and urbanization on the Black family. For example, he noted that disorganized families seldom gathered for meals. Eating was an individual matter that gave little structure to food consumption and that seemed to indicate a situation in which there was little routine to family life that could teach appropriate habits. This dynamic, of course, is critical to family functioning, which contributes to health promotion.[17]

Through the slave period, postslavery rural period, and urbanization period, African Americans made both positive and negative adaptations nutritionally. Generally speaking, diversified diets with sufficient protein and liberal amounts of fresh fruits and vegetables were most healthful. The African American diet, with its variety of leafy greens, beans, grains, and green and yellow vegetables, contributed to health. Small servings of animal protein, which minimized fat consumption, were best. Substantial meals that could meet the caloric demands of hard physical labor supported the well-being of African Americans. Foods that were grown for self-consumption, varieties of fresh meat, fish, and poultry, and the use of natural sweeteners like molasses, which enhanced the mineral content of the diet, added to good nutritional health. The habits of boiling and baking foods were nutritionally superior to frying food. However, diets that lacked diversity, particularly with respect to fruits and vegetables, the practices of over-cooking vegetables, of using large amounts of fat and salt to prepare foods, of frying foods to the exclusion of other methods of food preparation, and of limiting vegetable consumption to a few starchy foods were maladaptive.[18] Eating based on taste, habit, convenience, or sociability rather than nutritional balance could prove problematic. Lifestyle shaped by oppression, poverty, urbanization, and marketing directed at Black consumer habits profoundly affected African American dietary conventions and health. These dietary conventions, whether positive or negative, were reproduced through patterns of sociability connected with family, church, recreation, and work.

In the twentieth century, there were two distinct phases of health problems that challenged the well-being of African Americans. The first phase involved the challenge of infectious and contagious diseases. The second involved the challenge of chronic diseases, so-called diseases of civilization. Early in the century, the primary causes of death were the infectious and contagious diseases of tuberculosis, pneumonia, influenza and typhoid fever, and the childhood diseases of scarlet fever, diphtheria, whooping cough, and measles. These diseases accounted for 37 percent of all Black deaths in 1910 but only 3 percent in 1974. Tuberculosis was the major cause of death for Blacks in the early 1900s. At this time, the life expectancy for Blacks at birth was around thirty-five years of age (fifty years for Whites). However, because of the public health movement and improved standards of living, contagious and infectious diseases and the diseases of childhood were brought under control. Significant and longterm improvements in life expectancy began in the late 1800s and continued through the 1920s and 1930s, but improvement was much slower in the 1950s, 1960s, and 1970s. The dramatic improvements in life expectancy were due primarily to substantial reductions in infant mortality. Declines in maternal mortality also were significant, raising life expectancy for Black women in their childbearing years.[19]

The health problems of African Americans were most responsive to public health measures, better nutrition and sanitation, and improvements in the standard of living. Health promotion efforts in the early 1900s included National Negro Health Week under the leadership of Tuskegee Institute and the National Negro Business League. For one week each year, ministers, doctors, and other qualified citizens would participate in activities to "urge cooperation with organized health agencies, emphasize mother and infant welfare work to reduce high mortality, and . . . lectures, health films and exhibits stress[ed] personal and home hygiene, social hygiene education and venereal disease control measures."[20]

As the infectious and contagious diseases of youth and middle age were brought under control, cancer and diseases of the heart increased. For example, these diseases accounted for 12 percent of Black deaths in 1910 and 46 percent of Black deaths in 1974.[21] Through the 1930s and 1940s, African Americans were living longer, and deaths from cancer for Blacks began to surpass those for Whites. Lung cancer increased among Blacks and Whites, but more so among Blacks. Also, while mortality from other kinds of cancer has been decreasing among Whites, it has been increasing among Blacks.[22]

Even though the gap between the mortality rates of Blacks and Whites from chronic diseases has declined, significant disparities remain, and new trends are emerging. As compared with

Whites, 86 percent of the excess deaths of Blacks can be accounted for by accidents, homicide, infant mortality, heart disease and stroke, cirrhosis, cancer, and diabetes.[23] Black women are plagued most by heart disease, cancer, cerebrovascular disease, diabetes, and accidents (including motor vehicle accidents), and Black men by heart disease, cancer, accidents (including motor vehicle accidents), homicide, and cerebrovascular diseases. From the latter part of the 1980s, AIDS has been increasing as a significant cause of death for African Americans.[24] Hypertension rates for Blacks have been higher than those for Whites for quite a long time and may account for 5,000 excess deaths a year. Hypertension is a significant risk factor in stroke due to the possibility of cerebral hemorrhage and end-stage renal disease.[25] By the mid-1980s, life expectancy began to decline for Black Americans, due largely to increased infant mortality and homicide. The fact that Black life expectancy has declined while White life expectancy has increased is perhaps one of the most poignant indicators that America offers a different reality for African Americans.[26]

Despite steady declines in infant mortality through the twentieth century, Black infant mortality has remained twice the rate of Whites. These rates vary by geographical region and are linked to socio-economic conditions and environment. Risk factors for infant mortality include poverty, low education, unmarried status, being African American, poor obstetrical history, high or low maternal age, urogenital infections, alcohol use, illegal drug use, smoking, absent or inadequate prenatal care, and exposure to toxic substances.[27] Some evidence exists to indicate that African Americans are substantially and perhaps disproportionately exposed to toxic environmental conditions.[28] Low birth weight is associated with high infant mortality, and Black women have the highest percentage of low birth weights. Poor nutrition, smoking, drinking, and substance abuse are significant risk factors. Over 50 percent of AIDS- and HIV-infected infants are Black. In addition, the same factors that affect infant mortality affect maternal mortality.[29]

Other health risks to young people and adults are quite varied. Malnutrition, anemia, lead poisoning, lack of immunizations, lack of dental care, child abuse, teenage childbearing (which includes higher risks for neonatal, infant, and maternal mortality), and cocaine, crack, alcohol, and tobacco use are particularly virulent problems. For example, from the mid-1980s, cocaine-related emergency room episodes increased and were highest among African Americans. Cigarette and alcohol advertising are directed at youthful Blacks, and African Americans spend disproportionately more money on alcohol and tobacco. Cigarettes account for almost 90 percent of all lung cancer, and Black men have 40 percent higher rates of lung cancer than White men. Alcohol use is significantly related to homicide, and homicides, which are predominantly intra-racial, are the leading cause of death for African American males fifteen to thirty-four years old. In addition, some argue that alcohol, because of its accumulated negative consequences, is probably the greatest contributor to poor health among African Americans.[30]

Being overweight is a significant risk factor in a range of chronic diseases. Diabetes, hypertension, and heart disease are examples. Black women tend to weigh much more than White women, even though there is no significant difference in height. Obesity is more prevalent in Black women above and below the poverty line; beyond the age of forty-five, well over 50 percent of all African American women are overweight. Also, Black men and women tend to have higher levels of serum cholesterol than the general population, a known risk for cardiovascular disease.[31]

Existing research shows a wide range of lifestyle and nutritional factors affecting chronic diseases. For example, there is strong evidence to indicate that lifestyle change alone without drugs or surgery can stop or reverse arteriosclerosis, a hardening of the arteries that can lead to heart attacks.[32] Increases in Black infant death rates are at least partially due to a rise in babies born to cocaine-addicted mothers.[33] Breastfeeding could contribute to better infant health and perhaps save infant lives. It provides nutrients and antibodies not found in cow milk or infant formula, and it encourages closer bonding between mother and child.[34] Proportionally, less Black people than White people are quitting smoking, and Black people are smoking cigarettes with higher nicotine. Smoking is rapidly becoming a habit of the least-educated segments of society. It is responsible for 400,000 deaths a year; by comparison, AIDS is responsible for around 25,000. Despite the fact that large numbers of people are ceasing to smoke, these numbers are offset by the numbers of young people who are persuaded to take up smoking.[35]

The powerful role of diet and lifestyle in chronic diseases is further exemplified by noting their role in several additional ailments that threaten the African American community. For example, high blood pressure and hypertension are related to stress, smoking, excess weight, and salt consumption. Diets high in potassium-rich fresh fruits and vegetables can help to prevent or lower high blood pressure.[36] Evidence suggests that high levels of fat in the diet make one more prone to cancer. Drinking contributes to cancers of the esophagus and pancreas, and smoking accounts for almost 90 percent of all lung cancers. Fibrous foods and foods such as broccoli, cauliflower, cabbage, and Brussels sprouts can help to prevent cancer. Vitamins A and C also enhance cancer protection. Stress, excessive consumption of sugar, and some prescription drugs can increase one's susceptibility to cancer.[37] Poor diet, stress, and excess weight can contribute to diabetes.[38] Nutrition, because of its role in helping the body to accommodate stress, can play a significant role in interpersonal relationships, as, for example, in domestic violence and the way that people decide to self-medicate themselves through alcohol and drugs. In short, there are many nutritional and lifestyle permutations that can contribute to heightening or reducing the prevalence of chronic diseases.

FAMILY AND HEALTH

The family is the primary institution for transmitting culture and for maintaining the health of the community. It is the first institution to respond to individual sickness. Important patterns of health behavior are established in the family and are of profound significance in promoting individuals who are highly resistant to disease and who are conscious of the complexities of lifestyle determinants for good health. For example, whether or not one learns appropriate dietary and nutritional habits is one such determinant of health. The kitchen, in a profound sense, is the primary medicine cabinet. The family that has acquired a sound knowledge of the properties of food, of proper food preparation, and of the appropriate balance in consumption has taken a major step toward solid preventive health measures.

The woman's role in childbearing gives her a strategic position in determining the health of her children and of subsequent generations. The mother may elect to breastfeed her child and provide it with nature's perfect food, or she may rely on manufactured substitutes. How the women prepares herself for childbearing is also important to the child's health and to her own. Whether mothers transmit knowledge concerning personal health care, childbearing, breastfeeding, and child care to their daughters will determine future child and maternal health.

The father has an equally important role in providing support for lifestyle patterns that promote health. There should be complementary and cooperative thought and action between spouses if positive health habits are to be maintained and internalized by the family as a whole. During childbearing the man must be able to provide instrumental and affective support to ensure the health of mother and child. Parents can consult one another to make important health-related decisions, and they can provide insulation against external stressors. Family meals, for example, are important events at which positive values and habits are reinforced through effective communication and the ritual of eating.

The Black family is under great duress, however. Black families headed by one parent (usually the women) are becoming the norm, and the number of African Americans who are living as singles is also rapidly increasing. These single-parent families and individuals are more and more living outside of extended family networks and therefore lack important social and financial supports. Over two-thirds of the Black children living in female-headed households live in poverty, and over one-half of all Black children live with their mothers and not with their fathers. Single parenting increases stress and is particularly difficult in combination with poverty. Married persons have fewer health problems than single people, and people who live alone have higher death rates than those who do not. Significant numbers of Black children are born to teenage mothers, which increases the health risks to both the mother and the child.[39]

Social factors contributing to economic dislocation and to increased singlehood and single-parent families are presenting significant challenges to the health of African Americans. The demands of work and the stresses of single parenting contribute to families being more dependent on external and often inappropriate sources of nutrition. People often respond to loneliness and stress in maladaptive ways. Even when family supports are in place through double-headed households or extended family structures, there still may not be a health promotion ethic that guides family activities and interactions. As a consequence, the African American family is not currently in a strong position to insulate its members against external forces that negatively shape health-related Black consumer patterns, to interpret illness experiences, to negotiate negative and conflicting aspects of the health care system, to provide a basis to dissipate stress, or to give direction to personal health habits. The linkages between cultural hegemony, family structure and function, and health are crucial ones.

THE LIMITS OF MEDICINE AND MARKET FORCES

Even though there is a profound need for more and better medical care in the Black community, medicine has reached its limits with respect to reducing the disparity between Black and White health.[40] Complex economic and socio-cultural factors must be challenged in order to create an appropriate cultural and institutional response to the character of chronic disease causation and the contradictions of capitalist culture. African Americans must realize that their well-being ultimately resides in their ability to take responsibility for their own health. This requires, among other things, demystification of the medical care system and consumer empowerment. For African Americans, such a process necessitates challenging existing forces of cultural hegemony and promoting cultural revitalization.

The mythology surrounding the hegemonic existence of medical care resides in the erroneous belief that more and better medical care can improve the mortality of large populations and is synonymous with improving the biological, psychological, and spiritual well-being of individuals and groups. People generally seek medical care for curative purposes, and medical care is more properly a form of sickness management and control. It is one type of health care, and although dominant in the marketplace, we cannot assume that such dominance has been purely the result of a superior ability to significantly and unilaterally improve the health of a population. Much of medicine's dominance is associated with its effective political organization and its ability to limit or eliminate competing health care systems. Also, the medical establishment has successfully limited the size, race, and sex of the physician population, and it has historically restricted African Americans and women from its centers of power. The union between corporate and industrial control, White male elites, the university system, and state power has virtually assured the medical care system of hegemony in the marketplace and of White male domination.

Moreover, there are clear limits to medical care. Improvements in the major indicators of health, that is, decreased infant mortality, longer average life span, and substantial reductions in infectious diseases, occurred before modern medicine had risen to prominence. These improvements in mortality and morbidity were associated with improvements in sanitation, nutrition, and key health-related behaviors. Disease and health are more a function of the social configurations of society and the adaptations or maladaptations to social life.[41]

Medical hegemony utilizes its impressive curative and sickness-management ability to obscure its considerable coercive, exploitative, and anti-health characteristics. The medical industrial complex, which is distinct from the altruistic motives of individual health professionals who strive to bring comfort and aid to the sick, is characterized by widespread contradictions. Medical care is plagued by rising costs, maldistribution of services, over-specialization, overproduction (medicalization), and iatrogenesis.

The medical industrial complex is one of the most profitable enterprises in the world and is challenged only by military spending in terms of the singular concentration of societal resources. In addition, the laws of supply and demand do not apply to medical production. Medical production (supply) tends to create its own demand by defining when, what, and how much patients should consume. The process of medicalization or the extension of medical markets involves more and more medical intervention into daily life. Heroic methods to treat dying people are one example.

The medicalization of life is an extension of the postcapitalist problem of overproduction and limited markets. The system of medical care resolves this problem by redefining patient needs in order to expand its markets, limiting competition from nonmedical health care systems, and raising prices for a captive market. Elective procedures become routine, unnecessary surgical procedures increase, and diagnostic tests proliferate. The coercive power of the state is used to define new reasons for medical intervention and to restrict the emergence of competing health care systems. Costly medical technologies, which frequently have little value in preventing disease, are routinely introduced and absorbed as new products in the medical marketplace. Federal payments for medical care and insurance companies provide ready funds to satiate medically defined demand. The results are spiraling increases in medical costs and diminishing returns to improving health. There is little incentive for the medical industrial complex to shift to low-cost health care methods regardless of their effectiveness in improving health.

Medicalization, the extension of medical products beyond consumer needs, contributes to iatrogenesis, or medically created diseases. The side effects of excess medical care have become so large that they produce sufficient sickness to fuel a new market of medical sickness. This sickness becomes an additional market for medical products and serves to mitigate the problem of falling profits and shrinking markets in a cluttered and over-medicated marketplace. Furthermore, medical care becomes maldistributed and available only to those who can pay. Costs spiral upward as the medical industry pursues profits at the expense of human health needs.

The contradictions of medical hegemony do not take place in a vacuum but are supported by an accommodating cultural ethos. The normative belief system in American society supports the idea that health is something to buy in the marketplace and not something that resides in the configurations of social, economic, and political institutions, and personal health behaviors. A radically commodified and convenience-oriented economy encourages cultural answers that seek consumption as a solution to human problems. Drug consumption, for example, whether prescription, over-the-counter, or illegal, is a natural extension of this belief system. Thus, the ability of people to knowledgeably take responsibility and control of their health through their families, religious institutions, and cultural practices atrophies. In fact, society sees as deviant attempts to take such control. African Americans are faced with the added problem of systemic institutional instability and subordination created by cultural hegemony. Lowered institutional insulation, greater economic dislocation, and a social system that encourages dependency on a Eurocentric, market-driven, consumer culture for ideas about how to live diminishes the capacity of African Americans to meet head-on the contradictions of medical care and to develop an enduring and appropriate self-conscious ethic for health promotion.

CONCLUSION

In sum, the poor health of African Americans is substantially linked to European contact and chronic cultural disruption as a consequence of serving the economic needs of White elites. Cultural hegemony as a systemic social problem emerged to sustain African malleability, dependency, and subordination in the light of economic exploitation. The resulting conditions have made it difficult for African Americans to respond to their existing health problems. These difficulties include maladaptations to oppression, which have become rooted in the fabric of African American life, lowered institutional insulation against market forces that promote unhealthy consumer habits, and patterns of thinking that tend to negate the development of an independent (nonmarket-dominated), countervailing health ethic. During the late 1960s, for example, African Americans were developing countervailing health promotion strategies as part of the broader Black consciousness movement. Unfortunately, these strategies failed to achieve widespread institutionalization and were absorbed and dissipated by hegemonic societal forces.

We have learned that despite the enormous need for more African American health providers and certain types of medical services, African Americans are threatened by the system's own contradictions. Cost, maldistribution, iatrogenesis, and misdirected priorities are salient issues. Medical care does not have to be costly, elitist, or elusive to those who cannot pay. Also, improving health must be addressed in a broader fashion. Poor health is a function of the structural sicknesses and maladaptations of postindustrial society, which for African Americans includes the social problem of cultural hegemony. This problem, because it is connected to exploitation derived from the economic and cultural aspirations of White elites, cannot be separated from the contradictions of the medical care system or from the contradictions of the capitalist culture at large. Cultural hegemony, through its promotion of African American cultural negation, contributes to the subversion of health-promoting institutional responses by the African American community.

NOTES

1. Jannette L. Dates, "Advertising," in Jannette L. Dates and William Barlow, eds., *Split Image: African Americans in the Mass Media* (Washington, D.C.: Howard University Press, 1990), p. 436.

2. E. Franklin Frazier, *Race and Culture Contacts in the Modern World* (Boston: Beacon Press, 1957), pp. 54-73.

3. Ibid.; Todd L. Savitt, *Medicine and Slavery: The Diseases and Health Care of Blacks in Antebellum Virginia* (Chicago: University of Illinois Press, 1978), pp. 7-47; Eugene D. Genovese, *Roll Jordan Roll: The World the Slaves Made* (New York: Vintage, 1976), p. 644; Basil Davidson, *The African Slave Trade: Precolonial History 1450-1850* (Boston: Little Brown, 1961), pp. 153-62;

4. Savitt, *Medicine and Slavery*, pp. 50-82; Kenneth M. Stampp, *The Peculiar Institution: Slavery in the Ante-bellum South* (New York: Vintage, 1956), pp. 297-307; William D. Postell, *The Health of Slaves on Southern Plantations* (Gloucester, Mass.: Peter Smith, 1970), pp. 1-30.

5. Savitt, *Medicine and Slavery*, pp. 107-9.

6. Ibid., pp. 111-48; Postell, *Health of Slaves,* pp. 111-41.

7. Savitt, *Medicine and Slavery*, p. 120; Postell, *Health of Slaves*, p. 117.

8. Savitt, *Medicine and Slavery,* p. 97; Genovese, *Roll Jordan Roll,* p. 603.

9. Kenneth F. Kipple and Virginia H. Kipple, "Slave Child Mortality: Some Nutritional Answers to a Perennial Puzzle," *Journal of Social History* 10 (March 1977):284-309; Stampp, *Peculiar Institution,* pp. 297-307.

10. Savitt, *Medicine and Slavery,* pp. 149-84; Herbert Morais, *History of the Negro in Medicine* (Washington, D.C.: Publishers Company, 1967).

11. Savitt, *Medicine and Slavery,* pp. 281-307.

12. Hylan Lewis, *Blackways of Kent* (New Haven, Conn.: College and University Press, 1964), pp. 14-15; Charles S. Johnson, *Growing up in the Black Belt: Negro Youth in the Rural South* (New York: Schocken Books, 1967), p. 112.

13. Hortense Powdermaker, *After Freedom: A Cultural Study in the Deep South* (New York: Russell & Russell, 1968), p. 80.

14. Arthur F. Raper, *Preface to Peasantry: A Tale of Two Black Belt Counties* (New York: Atheneum, 1968), p. 52.

15. W.E.B. DuBois, *The Philadelphia Negro: A Social Study* (New York: Schocken Books, 1967), pp. 156-63.

16. Ibid., p. 163.

17. E. Franklin Frazier, "Problems and Needs of Negro Children and Youth Resulting from Family Disorganization," in G. Franklin Edwards, ed., *E. Franklin Frazier on Race Relations* (Chicago: University of Chicago Press, 1968), p. 231.

18. Raper, *Preface to Peasantry,* p. 52; Clovis E. Semmes, "Toward a Theory of Popular Health Practices in the Black Community," *Western Journal of Black Studies* 7 (Winter 1983):207-8.

19. U.S. Department of Commerce Bureau of the Census, *The Social and Economic Status of the Black Population in the United States: An Historical View, 1790-1978.* Special Studies Series, P-23, no. 80, pp. 117-18.

20. Charles S. Johnson, *The Negro in American Civilization: A Study of Negro Life and Race Relations in the Light of Social Research* (New York: Henry Holt & Company, 1930), p. 194.

21. Bureau of the Census, *Status of the Black Population,* p. 117.

22. National Research Council Committee on the Status of Black Americans, *A Common Destiny: Blacks and American Society* (Washington, D.C.: National Academy Press, 1989), pp. 396-97.

23. Ibid.

24. National Center for Health Statistics, *Health, United States, 1990* (Hyattsville, Md.: Public Health Service, 1991), p. 80.

25. National Research Council, *A Common Destiny,* p. 422.

26. Bureau of the Census, *Status of the Black Population*, p. 117; "Life Expectancy for Blacks Drops," *The Detroit News*, March 16, 1989, p. 18A; National Center for Health Statistics, *Health, United States, 1990*, p. 12.

27. National Research Council, *A Common Destiny,* pp. 398-400; Dwight E. M. Angell, "City's Poor and Black Faced with Inadequate Medical Care," *Detroit News,* February 12, 1989, p. 1A; "Infant Death Rates in D.C. Increases Almost 50 Percent," *Ann Arbor News,* October 1, 1989, p. B9.

28. James H. Johnson and Melvin L. Oliver, "Blacks and the Toxics Crisis," *Western Journal of Black Studies* 13 (Summer 1989):72-77.

29. National Research Council, *A Common Destiny,* pp. 400-403; National Center for Health Statistics, *Health, United States, 1990,* p. 10.

30. National Research Council, *A Common Destiny*, pp. 412-19; Dates, "Advertising," in Dates and Barlow, eds., *Split Image,* p. 428; Frederick D. Harper, "Alcohol Use and Abuse," in Lawrence E. Gary, ed., *Black Men* (Beverly Hills, Calif.: Sage, 1981), pp. 169-77.

31. Reynolds Farley and Walter R. Allen, *The Color Line and the Quality of Life in America* (New York: Oxford University Press, 1989), p. 56; National Center for Health Statistics, *Health, United States, 1990*, p. 133.

32. Daniel Coleman, "Study: Lifestyle Changes Can Halt Hardening of Arteries," *Ann Arbor News,* November 15, 1988, p. A1, A4.

33. "Infant Death Rates," *Ann Arbor News,* p. B9.

34. Alan Berg, *The Nutrition Factor: Its Role in National Development* (Washington, D.C.:

Brookings Institution, 1973); Dan Sperling, "Breast-feeding Still the Ideal Formula," *USA Today,* June 26, 1990.

35. Larry Owens, "Blacks Smoking More, Stronger Cigarettes," *Michigan Chronicle,* June 12-18, 1991, p. 1C; Allan Parachini, "Smoking Becoming Habit of Poorly Educated," *Ann Arbor News,* January 6, 1989, pp. A1, A4; National Center For Health Statistics, *Health, United States, 1990,* pp. 30, 110.

36. George Berkley, *On Being Black & Healthy* (Englewood Cliffs, N.J.: Prentice-Hall, 1982), pp. 18-45.

37. Ibid., pp. 60-61; "Study Says Cancer Risk Double with `Pill' Users," *Ann Arbor News,* January 5, 1989, pp. A1, A6; National Center for Health Statistics, *Health, United States, 1990,* p. 18.

38. Berkley, *On Being Black & Healthy,* pp. 68-69.

39. National Research Council, *A Common Destiny,* p. 523; Robert Staples, *The World of Black Singles: Changing Patterns of Male/Female Relations* (Westport, Conn.: Greenwood Press, 1982), pp. 14, 208; Elmer P. Martin and Joanne Mitchell Martin, *The Black Extended Family* (Chicago: University of Chicago Press, 1978).

40. National Research Council, *A Common Destiny,* p. 440.

41. The following sources exemplify the range of works that have informed my discussion of the limits and contradictions of the medical care system: John Powles, "On the Limitations of Modern Medicine," in David S. Sobel, ed., *Ways of Health: Holistic Approaches to Ancient and Contemporary Medicine* (New York: Harcourt Brace Jovanovich, 1979), pp. 61-86; Howard Waitzkin, *The Second Sickness: Contradictions of Capitalist Health Care* (New York: The Free Press, 1983); Leonard A. Sagan, *The Health of Nations: True Causes of Sickness and Well-Being* (New York: Basic Books, 1987); Peter Conrad and Rochelle Kern, eds., *The Sociology of Health and Illness: Critical Perspectives,* 2nd. edn. (New York: St. Martin's Press, 1986); Ivan Illich, *Medical Nemesis: The Expropriation of Health* (New York: Pantheon, 1976); Morais, *History of the Negro in Medicine.*

8

Revitalization Tendencies

The problem of cultural hegemony has over the years precipitated several major cultural movements by African Americans. These movements are significant attempts to revitalize African American culture, and they reflect a search for identity, self-definition, and a more satisfying way of life. They also reveal African American sensitivity to the plethora of social forces directed at African American cultural negation and how Black people self-consciously act to generate responses that are empowering and humanistically transformative. Given the type of oppression experienced by African peoples who were brought to the Americas, one enduring tendency among African Americans is to seek to reconstruct themselves as human beings and to erect institutional barriers against continued exploitation and oppression. The purpose is to garner group power to dissipate structured inequality and to regain self-respect in the human family.

The need for independent and self-defined action by African Americans points to the fact that it is too much to expect mainstream America to change on its own. Obviously, however, efforts to reform mainstream America must continue, but African Americans also know that they must change negative elements of their culture that years of oppression have produced. Social processes that tend to reproduce oppression, inequality, and White supremacy still exist and are quite strong. These processes take various forms over time and are generally supported via the processes of cultural hegemony. Cultural hegemony produces a social malaise among African Americans that is not always understood. However, cultural movements are self-conscious efforts to cure this malaise and to revitalize one's daily existence. Because of the profundity, complexity, and culture-specific character of cultural hegemony, it is not likely that even progressive segments of the dominant society can overcome their culturally and institutionally structured drive to deny cultural democracy and economic and social equality to non-White and non-European peoples.

The following chapter explores various dimensions of African American efforts at cultural revitalization. The first part examines the revitalization movement of the Harlem Renaissance. It scrutinizes questions regarding the origins, demise, and significance of the Renaissance. The second part probes a neglected manifestation of cultural revitalization associated with the Black Consciousness movement of the 1960s and 1970s. It examines the role and significance of health beliefs and practices in processes of culture building. The third part investigates the contributions of one man, a community artist, who symbolizes the submerged potential in the Black community for cultural liberation. Such individuals are necessary in order to transcend the broader social forces of cultural negation, preserve the progressive elements of African American culture, and offer new possibilities for living. The question becomes one of creating and institutionalizing progressive cultural configurations, despite the distorting tendencies of market forces that select and legitimate cultural forms based on profit and not human need. I conclude with a brief commentary on the themes of Black Consciousness movements.

THE HARLEM RENAISSANCE

During the decade of the 1920s, a flowering of artistic creativity became centered in the Black community of Harlem. This creative spirit had earlier antecedents but did not become a recognized, self-conscious movement until this decade. While important advances were being made in all Black creative forms (dance, theater, the visual arts, etc.), the Harlem Renaissance was primarily a literary movement.[1]

Over time, certain complex socio-historical events combined to create the conditions for a concentration of artists and writers in one location. Linkages (face-to-face communications among artists and the creation of outlets for artistic creativity) that developed among creative artists and intellectuals fostered a group consciousness supported by the ethos and relative economic prosperity of the Harlem community. Similarly, other factors contributed to the decline of these linkages so that the Harlem Renaissance took on a less self-conscious and locally defined character. Creative activity among African Americans did not cease, but became more geographically and ideologically dispersed and less symbolic of a singular community (Harlem) ethos.

Among African Americans, the artistic flowering in the decade of the 1920s was important because it represented a countervailing force to the serious disruption and destruction of African cultural traditions and institutions resulting from the historical experience of chattel slavery, and the continued exploitation, oppression, and structured inequality embodied in the metaproblem of cultural hegemony. The Renaissance symbolized the fact that African Americans, freed from the constraints of chattel slavery, were now more capable of seriously grappling with the question of culture, a way of life, and a collective direction for themselves. Blacks, because of changes in the forms of oppression, had greater opportunity to move into colleges and universities and, for the first time, to create a substantial intellectual class.[2]

Charles S. Johnson, in his extensive study of Black college graduates, first published in 1939, provided some valuable information with respect to the rapid growth of the Black intelligentsia. He noted that from all available records from 1826 to 1936, there were 43,821 Black graduates of colleges and professional schools in America. The increase in the number of Black graduates did not really begin until about 1885 and accelerated considerably after 1920. These graduates were distributed between northern colleges and Black colleges in the South. Of the total number of Black college graduates (43,821), 14.7 percent (6,424) graduated from northern colleges and 85.3 percent (37,397) graduated from Black colleges in the South.[3]

The largest increase in the number of Blacks who graduated from northern and Black colleges occurred from 1920 onward. This increase was without a doubt a reflection of Black migration, urbanization, and industrialization. For example, there were more graduates during the eleven years from 1926 through 1936 than there were during the 100-year period from 1826 to 1926. Between 1920 and 1933, the annual number of Black graduates from northern colleges increased from 156 to 439, an increase of 181 percent. For the same period, the annual number of graduates from Black colleges increased from 497 to 2,486, or by 400 percent. There was a decline in the number of graduates listed for the years 1934, 1935, and 1936, partly because of the Depression and partly because of the difficulty in getting complete reports on graduates for this period.[4]

Besides the accelerated growth of college graduates in the 1920s, there was a much higher rate of growth in the number of Black graduates when compared to the rate of growth of all college graduates. In 1920, for example, there were 35,552 bachelor's degrees granted by all colleges and 381 degrees granted to Blacks. In 1928, there were 83,065 bachelor's degrees granted to all colleges and 1,152 granted to Blacks. Thus, there was a 115.5 percent total increase, compared to a 296.9 percent increase for Blacks.[5]

The development of a Black intelligentsia was a significant requisite to the cultural and artistic flowering that took place in Harlem. Much of the biographical material on major writers of this period showed that college training was a primary characteristic.[6] In addition, New York, Illinois, Ohio, and Pennsylvania, (in order) attracted the highest number of southern-born college graduates who went North to live.[7] Thus, we begin to see migratory trends that placed Black intellectuals in the North. In addition, colleges and universities, both Black and White, gained ascendancy as important socializing forces upon Black artists.

Educated Blacks who could embody Eurocentric cultural ideals were undoubtedly more acceptable to Whites who controlled artistic markets. In addition, the socializing impact of colleges and universities, which demanded the exclusive elevation of European artistic standards, contributed to much of the ambivalence of Black artists concerning their own identities and the direction and character of their art. Langston Hughes lamented, for example, a propensity to emulate White culture among some Renaissance artists. He observed a "desire to run away spiritually from [the] race."[8] White elites were interested in the so-called primitiveness of Black art and culture, and, through their patronage, also tended to shape an image of Black life that existed in their minds. Many Black writers, of course, wanted to prove their talent to White critics by demonstrating their ability to produce "high" art.[9] At the very least, the increase in college-trained African Americans stimulated the growth of creative intellectuals (artists) and reflected sociological conditions that freed, to a much greater extent, the creative potential of African Americans; a creative potential previously stifled by chattel slavery and a highly oppressive system of racial etiquette, segregation, and White supremacy.

The Harlem Renaissance, a northern and urban phenomenon, could not have taken place without the rapid northern and urban migration from the rural South. This migration was the result of push-and-pull factors, that is, the boll-weevil infestation, which sharply reduced cotton pro-

duction, segregation policies, lynching and
other violence directed against Blacks, and an
increasing job market in the North brought about
by the wartime requirements of increased industrialization and urbanization. A decreasing job
market in the South (Blacks were disproportionately tied to the declining cotton industry) and
an expanding job market in the North provided
the greatest impetus for Black migration. Few
Blacks left the South immediately following the
Civil War.[10]

During World War I, the gross national product and manufacturing jobs increased by about
one-quarter. From 1910 to 1914, European immigration to the United States had averaged over
one million persons per year. This level of immigration ended in 1916 (a combination of the
war and changing immigration laws). Because the
reduction in White immigrant labor occurred when
the demand for labor was increasing, labor re-
cruiters came into the South to secure Black labor to fill shortages for unskilled jobs. The
emigration of African Americans from the South
continued after the war and into the 1920s because of ongoing prosperity in the North and
economic depression in the South. In fact, during the 1920s, the number of Blacks who left the
South was greater than during the previous
decade. Within the northern and western states,
the Black population grew more rapidly than in
the southern states, and there was also a movement to the cities. By 1940, the greatest
concentration of Blacks was in New York and
Chicago.[11]

The experiences of the war, urbanization, and
northern migration were important factors shaping the lives of African Americans. Those experiences included rejection and discrimination by
White-controlled unions and extreme violence
from Whites as evidenced by the so-called "red
summer" of 1919, when race riots occurred in 25
cities. Also, substantial numbers of African
Americans who served in the military and who
traveled abroad experienced, for the first time,
social relationships that acknowledged them as
human beings. This new vision of self-respect
was again challenged when "during the first
years of post-World War I whites lynched seventy

blacks--ten of the group being soldiers still in
uniform. Fourteen blacks were publicly
burned--eleven while still alive."[12]

Opportunities for employment were the dominant factor in bringing African Americans of all
strata to the urban North. The writer and artist
were attracted to New York because it offered
the best publishing opportunities. Downtown, major publishing houses such as Alfred A. Knopf,
Boni and Liveright, Harper, Viking Press, and
Harcourt Brace were opening up to Black writers.[13] Other attractions were the theaters on
Broadway and in Greenwich Village and the
charisma and market potential of Harlem itself.[14]

Once the African American writer or artist
reached New York, the only place to live was
Harlem. The creation of Black Harlem was only
one example of the general development of large,
segregated Black communities in American cities
across the country. Given the nature of race relations, existing power relationships, the economic and residential conditions specific to New
York, and the thousands of African Americans
streaming to New York who needed a place to
live, the creation of Black Harlem was inevitable. Harlem not only became the largest
Black community in the country, but it also became a uniquely diverse and cosmopolitan community with a distinctive lifestyle and ethos.[15]

In the late nineteenth century (1890s),
Harlem was a prosperous White community of lux-
ury and wealth. Three decades prior to this, it
had been an isolated and poor community. Paral-
leling the general development and prosperity of
New York, Harlem was transformed into New York's
first suburb. This prosperity was the result of
an urban revolution characterized by improvements in the methods of transportation, sanitation, water supply, communication, lighting, and
building. The expansion of New York's population
(in 1880 the population of Manhattan alone
passed the one million mark, with 1,164,673) co-
incided with an expansion of business and industrial activity. This expansion created the need
for people to move beyond New York's bustling
inner core, and Harlem was to become a choice
residential section.[16]

One obstacle to Harlem's development in the early nineteenth century had been its distance from lower Manhattan. However, the expansion of subway routes into Harlem between 1879 and 1881 solved much of this problem. The character of Harlem began to change when a rash of land speculation and over-construction of apartment buildings was brought on by the anticipation of new subway routes in the 1890s. Not enough people were attracted to the area, and landlords began to compete for tenants, cutting rents.[17]

It was this period that created the conditions for Blacks to gain a foothold in Harlem. Rather than face financial ruin in Harlem's deflating real estate market, some White landlords and corporations were willing to rent to African Americans. They received the added bonus of collecting the higher rents that Whites traditionally charged Blacks. Others used the threat of bringing in Black renters to get their White neighbors to buy them out at a higher than market price. Nevertheless, in Harlem, many Blacks found decent living conditions for the first time in New York, and they flocked to Harlem and filled its houses as fast as they became available.[18]

James Weldon Johnson indicated that the move to Harlem by Blacks was largely engineered by Philip A. Payton, a Black real estate man. Payton was determined to obtain better housing for Black people in New York. This "became the dominating idea of his life, and he worked on it as long as he lived."[19] Payton approached landlords and presented them with the proposal to fill their empty houses. Thousands of Blacks poured into Harlem each month, creating a physical pressure for room. New York was riding a wave of prosperity. Newcomers found work as fast as they arrived at wages they had never dreamed of before. There was plenty of money for renting and for buying property, which Blacks did in force. African Americans lived in 1,100 different houses in a twenty-three-block area of Harlem in 1914 and numbered just under 50,000. In 1910, the population of Blacks in Manhattan had been 60,000. Thus, the tremendous concentration of Black people in one community is evident. By 1920, Harlem's northern border was 145th street and southern border was 130th street. The population had reached 80,000. By 1930, Harlem had reached its southern limit, the northern boundary of Central Park, and its population was 200,000.[20]

The White residents of Harlem showed little concern about the expansion of Blacks into their community until they began to spread west and across Lenox Avenue. Whites took steps to block this expansion by formulating a financial concern with the expressed purpose of purchasing from the Hudson Realty Company all property occupied by Blacks and then evicting them. Payton responded by organizing the Afro-American Realty Company, which would buy and lease houses to be let to Black tenants. This held Whites in check for several years. However, the Afro-American Realty Company lacked large amounts of capital and became defunct. Nevertheless, several African American individuals carried on. Philip A. Payton and J. C. Thomas bought two five-story apartments, evicted the White tenants and gave housing to Black ones. John B. Nail purchased a row of five apartments and did the same. St. Philips Episcopal Church, which had one of the wealthiest and oldest Black congregations, bought a row of thirteen apartments in Harlem and rented them to Black people. Whites propagated the myth that Blacks lowered property values, and they began to flee. A single Black family, even if well educated and of sufficient means, was cause for White flight.[21]

Harlem's White residents organized formal opposition to Black settlement through a number of local associations and landlords. Some were committees representing individual blocks, and others were community-wide in structure. Between 1907 and 1915, the last years in which there was significant opposition to Blacks who settled in Harlem, a number of protective associations were founded. Property owners on West 140th, 137th, 136th, 131st, 130th, 129th streets (in descending order as the Black community spread southward and along the avenues) signed agreements (restrictive covenants) not to rent to Blacks for ten or fifteen years. All of these efforts eventually failed because no single organization was able to gain total support of all White property owners in the neighborhood.[22]

Once the takeover of Harlem was complete, it exhibited a unique feature absent from other Black ghettos. Harlem was not a slum, but a symbol of prosperity and elegance. Thus, significant numbers of Blacks in New York were able to live in decent housing in a respected neighborhood. As a result, Harlem became a magnet attracting all types of Black-owned and Black-oriented economic, social and political organizations within its boundaries. The YMCA, YWCA, Urban League, and NAACP, in addition to an array of churches, insurances companies, small businesses, real estate firms, fraternal orders, settlement houses, and social service agencies, moved within Harlem's boundaries. Harlem's Negro National Guard, the "Fighting Fifteenth," was outfitted in 1916, and Harlem elected its first African American assemblyman in 1917. Also, Harlem hospital hired its first Black nurse and physician in 1919.[23] Harlem, in short, became a bustling city within a city.

Harlem remained prosperous, and an extraordinarily diverse Black population moved within its geographic boundaries. It attracted the African, the West Indian, the Southerner, the Northerner, the man from the city, the man from the town, the student, the businessman, the artist, the writer, and so on. Foreign-born Blacks (West Indians and Africans) formed a little less than 20 percent of the total Black population of New York, and Harlem contained substantially more foreign-born Blacks than any other Black community in the country.[24]

Harlem developed a distinctive cultural ethos. For example, the Marshall Hotel, a symbol of fashionable life on West 53rd Street, became famous as a headquarters for Black talent. The first modern jazz band ever heard in New York was organized there. This band, called the Memphis Students, was a playing, singing, and dancing orchestra that made the first combined major use of banjos, saxophones, clarinets, and trap drums. These and other musical innovations made their way to Harlem as New York's Black population shifted to the Harlem community.[25] Sociologist Ira De A. Reid conducted research for the

National Urban League that showed a rapid growth
in religious sects that "studied and practiced
esoteric mysteries."[26] Also, church life, beyond
its religious and spiritual functions, was at
the center of Black social life and flourished
in Harlem.

Harlem had developed a substantial elite
stratum, a proletariat, an underworld, and an
intellectual class all within its geographical
boundaries. Its spirit was reflected in a distinctive street life and developing cultural
forms (e.g. jazz, ballroom dancing, etc.). During the first two decades of the twentieth century, Harlem acquired an African consciousness,
as evidenced by the literature sold on the
streets of Harlem and the character of many religious, political, economic, and social organizations. Harlem was also a parade ground during
the warmer months of the year. No Sunday passed
without a parade (parades were not limited to
Sunday), and almost any excuse, such as "the
funeral of a member of the lodge, the laying of
a corner-stone, the annual sermon to the order,
or just a desire to `turn out,'" was suf-
ficient.[27]

In the next few years following the war, radicalism flourished in Harlem. Indicative of the
spirit of the times, Harlem took pride in the
fact that its famed regiment, the Fifteenth, was
shipped out of Spartanburg, South Carolina, when
its members became enraged over the treatment of
one of their men by a White hotel owner
(November 12, 1917). On July 28, 1917, 10,000
Blacks (men, women, and children) silently
marched down the streets of New York to protest
lynching, segregation, and racial injustice.
This was the famous "Silent Parade." Also, by
the second decade of the twentieth century, radical newspapers such as *The Messenger*, *Challenge*, *The Voice*, *The Crusader*, *The Emancipator*,
and *The Negro World* had sprung up in Harlem.[28]
The span of time following the war and extending
into the 1920s saw the growth of the Garvey
movement, the largest mass movement to occur
among African Americans. Conservative estimates
of membership in Garvey's Harlem-based organization, the Universal Negro Improvement Associa-

tion, placed the number at three million, and Garvey himself claimed six million.[29]

By the time Whites began flocking to Harlem in droves in the 1920s, it had developed an ethos and an identity created by a history of political struggle, radicalism, cultural diversity, and artistic innovation. It was this artistic innovation and cultural diversity that set the stage for the Harlem Renaissance. Whites were fascinated with Harlem's "exotic" character, and Black creative artists came in demand. Whites were particularly interested in Harlem's music and dance. African American domestics, for example, who could teach their employers and their employers' friends to do the latest dances were at a premium. Further, the great success in 1921 of the musical comedy, *Shuffle Along*, restored authentic Black music and dance to Broadway that had been missing for a decade. The interest in Black creativity paralleled a period of alienation by White writers and artists from their own cultural roots. This alienation also led some White intellectuals to take a deeper look at African American life and White American hypocrisy. Also, White curiosity about Black culture was precipitated by White authors who treated Black themes in their own work.[30] White interest in Harlem did much to open the door for Black writers to prestigious publishing houses since Black literary themes now had a substantial market.[31]

Langston Hughes, one of the younger but no less important Renaissance writers, related in his autobiography that White people came to Harlem in droves. They packed the expensive Cotton Club and saw the best Black entertainment that money could buy. White gangsters and monied Whites regularly attended the Cotton Club, but Blacks from Harlem could not attend this Jim Crow establishment in their own community. Harlemites were not pleased with this state of affairs and, according to Hughes, did not

> like the growing influx of whites toward Harlem after sundown, flooding the little cabarets and bars where formerly only colored people laughed and sang, and where now the strangers were given the best

ringside tables to sit and stare at the
Negro customers--like amusing animals in a
zoo.[32]

Harlem's nightlife became an important tourist
attraction, and Lindy-hoppers at the Savoy became more acrobatic and extreme for the entertainment of Whites. Some Blacks became entrepreneurs and went into the business of teaching Whites the latest dances.[33]
The ingredients of a distinctive cultural
ethos already existed among Manhattan's Black
population before the shift to Harlem, but the
sheer size and increasing diversity of Harlem
added to the dynamism and intensity of its cultural ferment. From the tradition of James Reese
Europe's Clef Club and Tempo Orchestras to the
stride piano virtuosity of James P. Johnson and
Willie (the Lion) Smith, and the jazz sounds of
Duke Ellington, African Americans became totally
responsible for the formation and character of
American dance music. They also produced America's major popular dances and dance innovations. Participation in these cultural forms required live performances in dance halls,
ballrooms, concert halls, clubs, cabarets, and
private parties. White elites, socialites,
celebrities, and creative artists looked to
African Americans for their popular music and
dance, and Harlem became their playground. The
underworld used Black music, dance, and comedy
to sell liquor (a most fruitful enterprise
during Prohibition) and other vices. In
addition, a developing mass communications
media, Broadway, music publishing houses,
advertisers, and the like fed off the Black
creative spirit symbolized by Harlem. European
audiences and artists abroad rapidly embraced
Black musical forms and began to imitate them.
Nevertheless, the Harlem community continued to
suffer economically and socially from racial
oppression, while 90 percent of its clubs and
cabarets were owned by Whites and downtown
racketeers.[34]
Harlem was clearly in vogue by the 1920s and
was synonymous with the Jazz Age. This fact,
combined with growing patronage for Black
artists and writers, the formal and informal

mechanisms for bringing the Harlem writers into face-to-face contact with one another, the previously mentioned ethos, cultural diversity, and segregated geography of Harlem, produced a self-conscious movement known as the Harlem Renaissance. The earliest acknowledgment of this movement appears to have been in 1924. By 1925, Alain Locke had compiled an edited volume, *The New Negro*, that contained a representative number of Renaissance writers and statements on the philosophy of the movement. Some of the notables chronicled in this volume were Jean Toomer, Zora Hurston, Eric Walrond, Countee Cullen, Claude McKay, Arna Bontemps, Angelina Grimke, Jessie Fauset, and many others. The drawings and decorative designs of the book were by Aaron Douglas, the visual artist who became most identified with the Harlem Renaissance.[35]

Alain Locke's acknowledgement of the "New Negro" as a force behind the Harlem Renaissance symbolized efforts by people of African descent, in the American context, to gain respect. They also grappled with reconstructing an identity unencumbered by negative, White-imposed images of Black life, which, unfortunately, many Blacks accepted. Blacks examined their cultural roots, which included Africa and African American folk life, rural and urban. Charles S. Johnson observed, "The Negro writers, removed by two generations from slavery, are now much less self-conscious, less interested in proving that they are just like white people, and . . . care less about what white people think."[36] This attempt by Renaissance writers to shake free of being defined by Whites was not successful, but the attempt was no less important. What was most significant was the recognition and the willingness to challenge cultural oppression. The "New Negro" was, as Locke had stated, "an attempt to repair a damaged group psychology and reshape a warped social perspective."[37]

In the days of the 1920s, there were a great many parties given in and out of Harlem that brought Black writers and artists together. In addition, these parties included White writers, artists, celebrities, and patrons of Black art. The most important party-giver outside of Harlem was Carl Van Vechten, a White writer who had devoted his life to promoting Black writers.[38] James Weldon Johnson, another important Renaissance writer, stated,

> Carl Van Vechten had a warm interest in colored people before he even saw Harlem. In the early days of the Negro literary artistic movement, no one in the country did more to forward it than he accomplished in frequent magazine articles and by his many personal efforts in behalf of individual Negro writers and artists.[39]

In Harlem the most important African American party-giver and promoter of the arts was A'Leilia Walker, heiress to millionaire Madame C. J. Walker (famous for her method of straightening hair). A'Leilia Walker gave lavish parties that were usually crowded because she wanted to give artists a chance to meet people who could help them. She sought out wealthy men and women who would become patrons of Black creative intellectuals, and she invited agents, producers, and publishers to encourage their interest in Black artists and writers. Among her properties, A'Leilia Walker owned a house on 136th Street, where she welcomed writers, sculptors, musicians, and so on.[40] There were other lesser parties given in and out of Harlem, but Van Vechten and Walker were the most well known and were symbolic of the spirit of the times.

Crisis and *Opportunity* magazines, official publications of the National Association for the Advancement of Colored People and the National Urban League, respectively, were important supporters of the Renaissance. During the movement's early stages, these publications provided the greatest exposure for young Black writers. W. E. B. DuBois became editor of *Crisis* at its inception in 1910. In an autobiographical sketch, he told of his desire to promote young Black writers through the pages of *Crisis*. DuBois was proud to have published such talents as Claude McKay, Langston Hughes, Jean Toomer, Countee Cullen, Anne Spencer, Abram Harris, and Jessie Fauset. Through the support of Amy Spingarn (wife of Joel), *Crisis* was able to offer young Black writers a series of prizes. *Opportu-*

nity, the organ of the Urban League, offered similar prizes. DuBois directly attributed the Harlem Renaissance to the efforts of these two publications.[41]

Similarly, Charles S. Johnson became editor of *Opportunity* at its inception in 1923. Johnson immediately moved to promote Black writers and artists through the pages of *Opportunity* and acted deliberately to bring White publishers and Black writers together.[42] However, Johnson was most successful as a promoter through the literary contests and dinners sponsored by his magazine. The first of the dinners was in 1924. Johnson commented in the May 1924 issue of *Opportunity* that

> Interest among the literati in the emerging group of younger Negro writers found an expression in a recent meeting of the Writer's Guild, an informal group whose membership includes Countee Cullen, Eric Walrond, Langston Hughes, Jessie Fauset, Gwendolyn Bennett, Harold Jackman, Regina Anderson, and a few others. The occasion was a coming out party at the Civic Club.[43]

The entire May 1924 issue of *Opportunity* was devoted to African American art, with special emphasis on the debut of Harlem's young writers. At least one scholar of this period has noted that *Opportunity* captured more of the spirit of the Renaissance than *Crisis*.[44] The former's pages, from 1924 to the early 1930s, contained many literary articles. However, *Opportunity* had a much smaller circulation than *Crisis*; by 1919, *Crisis* had reached a circulation of 104,000, while *Opportunity's* peak circulation in 1927 and 1928 was only 11,000.[45]

Following the initial support by these publications, wealthy philanthropist William C. Harmon became one of the first benefactors to recognize this group of young writers, and in December 1926, the first Harmon Foundation awards were announced. Thus, by the second decade of the twentieth century, the Harlem writers had acquired entrepreneurial support, a market largely among Whites, and a collective self-consciousness.

The decline of the Harlem Renaissance is usually associated with the Depression of the 1930s. A depressed economy quickly discouraged Whites from spending money on the night life of Harlem and from buying the products of Black writers and artists. More definitive studies are needed on the demise of the Renaissance, but in all likelihood there was a gradual erosion of the sources of support for Black writers, including their outlets for publication.

In 1928, Charles S. Johnson left as editor of *Opportunity* to take a position at Fisk University. In addition, *Opportunity* lost its funding from the Carnegie Foundation and was in financial difficulty. A'Leilia Walker died in 1931; the end of Prohibition deprived Harlem of much of its exclusive appeal; and there was some indication that Harlem's writers began to spread out over the country and abroad in pursuit of employment and additional educational opportunities. In the 1930s, some artists and writers continued under different sponsorship and promotion, for example, by the Works Progress Administration (WPA) and the Communist Party.[46]

In sum, the rise and decline of the Harlem Renaissance were in many ways linked to broader socio-historical events (e.g., World War I, migration, forced segregation, and the Depression). However, there were specific and unique determinants to the movement, such as, the circumstantial development of Harlem as a Black community. The Harlem Renaissance became possible because shifts in social structural variables removed some constraints to Black creative expression and brought Black creative products into the market place. However, this same dynamic presented a new set of challenges to Black creative processes because they were now subject to the whims of White-controlled market forces. Blacks lacked a market and they lacked control of their art products.

The Harlem Renaissance was related fundamentally to the expansion of an intellectual and middle class. This expansion was associated with changes in the characteristics of the economy that militated against the most severely restrictive forms of racial and cultural oppression. There was a shift from an authoritarian mode of oppression to a more liberal mode. The authoritarian mode requires overt subordination of African Americans in all social relationships, as well as very limited access to education, semi-skilled, skilled, and professional jobs, and the ownership of capital. The liberal mode of oppression liberalizes social relationships but functions to shape more intensely the cultural outlook of the subordinated strata that are most upwardly mobile. It seeks to marginalize this group in order to direct their quest for status and deflect challenges to White supremacy. Thus, while a break with authoritarian oppression precipitated a new personality, in this case the "New Negro," cultural questions, which were related to psychological control, became more intense. Although a literary tradition had already begun to develop among African Americans, the Renaissance brought a more focused discourse around the form and substance of the written word as a vehicle of cultural expression.

Harlem was a community in transition, like other Black communities, from the authoritarian to the liberal mode of oppression. Violence, custom, and law were still used to restrict Black people geographically, socially, economically, and politically, but social intercourse became more fluid. Both modes of oppression exist simultaneously, but their relative strength in relationship to one another changes based upon the requirements of Eurocentric domination. The Harlem community was a promised land for southern migrants, but it still suffered from domestic colonialism. Ghettoization brought higher rates of unemployment, overcrowding, poorer health, higher rents, and the like. The resources of Harlem flowed out of Harlem. Like other Black communities, its real estate, businesses, and politics were primarily controlled by Whites who lived elsewhere. Similarly, the valuable cultural products of Harlem were controlled by Whites who used what they wanted, when they wanted them, and for purposes that they defined. An upwardly mobile, Black, college-educated stratum became ambivalent about its relationship to the masses of African Americans. Given the nature of cultural hegemony, this is an understandable dilemma. Nevertheless, marginality also generated movement toward cultural revitalization and cultural unity.

Cultural unity, however, is not sufficient for progressive social change, because the development and evolution of African American cultural forms are not always positive. Cultural hegemony penetrates all strata of Black life. In addition to its tendency to marginalize, it also contributes to an array of maladaptive cultural responses. Unless African Americans are able to examine and define themselves and institutionalize progressive cultural forms, social change, human elevation, and empowerment are not possible.

HEALTH BELIEFS AND CULTURAL REVITALIZATION

This section explores how naturalistic health beliefs and practices emerged as an integral part of a self-conscious movement by African Americans to develop a more satisfying culture.[47] An important dimension of the Black Consciousness movement of the mid-1960s and 1970s was the fact that large numbers of African Americans were trying to construct a mode of life that could elevate their status in society and assist them in transcending what they considered to be oppressive and exploitative features of American life. A corollary to this movement was the issue of which lifestyle embodied the desirable and ideal characteristics of a new African American personality. As a consequence, many social change-oriented African Americans sought "natural" approaches to health care as a method to achieve these ends.

By "natural" approaches to health care, I mean the range of formally organized or professional health care systems that do not (and legally cannot) use drugs, surgery, or radiation to treat health problems. Instead, they may use spinal manipulation, nutritional therapy and counseling, colon irrigation, massage, physiotherapy, fasting, herbs and herbal supplements, acupressure and acupuncture, and the like. The types of health practices that use such methods of treatment include but are not limited to chiropractors, naturopaths, naprapaths, and colon therapists. A preference for natural health care also includes people who prefer naturalistic self-care. These people utilize herbal remedies, fasting, vitamins, dietary and lifestyle change, enemas and colonics, massage, and such health arts as meditation, yoga, and Tai Chi to prevent disease to correct various health problems or to improve their mental and spiritual well-being.

There is evidence of a growing distrust of orthodox medical care among various segments of the population.[48] Some have moved toward using alternative, nonmedical health practices in response to perceived deficiencies in medical treatment. For many, these moves have strong roots in the heightened radical consciousness and counterculture movements of the 1960s and 1970s.[49] Unfortunately, few studies have explored the manifestations of this phenomenon in the African American community.[50] This discussion helps to rectify this empirical void.

The examples provided here were drawn from a larger project that studied why some African Americans in Chicago decided to utilize formal, natural health care systems in place of or in conjunction with orthodox medical care.[51] What emerged during this research was the presence of a small but strongly organized segment of the African American community that linked naturalistic health beliefs and practices to their struggle to create a more desirable identity and culture. To illustrate this phenomenon I draw upon ethnographic interviews, field notes, public lectures, newspapers, magazines, miscellaneous documents, and oral histories.

Identity and Naturalistic Health Practices

The Black Consciousness movement of the mid-1960s and 1970s was characterized by an outpouring of artistic and creative products. The voice of the African American poet reached a crescendo, and the sight of young poets selling their small collections of poetry was quite common.[52] The poetic songs of African America expressed the diversity, breadth, and depth of the cultural strivings of this group. Collectively, African American creative intellectuals explored the possibilities of an ideal African personality. One poet of the period, Sister Zubena, in her collection of poems, *Calling All Sisters*, captured a nascent, naturalistic health consciousness and a critique of orthodox medicine when, in one poem called "The Miracle Lifetakers," she discussed how birth control pills were used to limit the African American population. She also noted their harmful effects, which included blood clots, cancer, migraine headaches, and, in some cases, the partial loss of vision and hearing. In her poem, "Hospitals," she decried genocidal practices against Black women through forced sterilization and medical poisoning. Sister Zubena gave us an answer to medical oppression through natural remedies. She wrote in her poem, "Medicine," that nature had an herbal remedy for every ailing part of the body. After listing herbs that were useful to treat various ailments in her poem, she exhorted the reader to reject chemical drugs in favor of herbal remedies.[53]

In the quest for the "right" way to live, food and dietary habits became powerful, cultural symbols for many African Americans. The African American poet and essayist, Don L. Lee, now Haki Madhubuti, expressed this broader quest when he wrote in the early 1970s that

> The major cause of illness in this country is insufficient diets. We have moved from real foods (organic and natural grown fruits and vegetables) to "foods" that contain additives, to "foods" that are processed, to "foods" that are chemically produced.[54]

He argued that the North Vietnamese and the revolutionary Toussaint L'Ouverture were successful in their military struggles because of their primarily vegetarian diets. Correspondingly, African American cuisine, "soul food," with its roots in the condition of slavery and it emphasis on pork, became targets for change. A change in one's dietary habits paralleled a broader transformation in one's self-image. The "right" diet and lifestyle became associated with a more conscious and aware African personality.

Comments from two ethnographic interviews further illustrate the above. Lorna, a thirty-one-year-old librarian and natural health-care advocate, commented on her decision to restrict the consumption of pork, "I . . . went through the phase that a lot of people in the Black community have gone through about the restriction on pork. I think that was probably true for me in the early seventies, my early college days."

Cheryl, a thirty-five-year-old employee of the state, commented on her efforts at dietary change before going to a natural health care practitioner: "Seventy was a time . . . of Black consciousness. . . . And you know, this thing could come up about pork . . . and that swine ain't no good for you. . . . I started to listen, . . . and I started to read to try and find out more about it."

Identity-Conscious Centers of Naturalistic Health Beliefs

Three types of core groups emerged that had an important impact on the health beliefs and practices of the broader African American community with respect to legitimating naturalistic approaches to health care and with respect to stimulating dietary and lifestyle change. They were the Nation of Islam (Black Muslims), headed by the late Elijah Muhammad, various Hebrew Israelite groups (Black Jews), and ethnic-(African) conscious artistic/spiritual groups. Members of these groups were not mutually exclusive and frequently interacted with one another via community businesses, forums, and activities.

The common element that united these groups was their emphasis on developing and perpetuating a lifestyle and culture that they believed would enhance the status and well-being of the African American community. They often saw mainstream American culture as a negative way of life. Furthermore, these core groups saw various aspects of the culture of African Americans as a direct result of their previous and current oppression in America. The belief was that the culture (diet and lifestyle) of African Americans had to change before their condition and status in America could change. For example, there was a way to eat that was "natural" (read as positive) and there was a way to eat that was "unnatural" (read as negative). For many African Americans who believed in naturalistic approaches to living, eating and self-help health care, formal, natural health care systems like chiropractic, naprapathy, colon therapy, and naturopathy became more attractive and desirable. Moreover, these groups were instrumental in stimulating naturalistic health beliefs and practices among others who were not tied to specific ethnic conscious ideological, philosophical, or theological beliefs. For example, in another interview, Harry, a thirty-six-year-old guidance counselor, explained the context in which he discovered and began to use naprapathy: "It was something new and different back then, maybe not now, but then it was a little circle of folks . . . the Black nationalist, cultural nationalist type of Black person."

The Nation of Islam. The dietary principles of the Nation of Islam were set forth in the book, *Eat to Live.*[55] The teachings of the late Elijah Muhammad, spiritual leader of the Nation of Islam, espoused the benefits of a vegetarian diet. Meat eating was against life, but meat was not so bad if eaten once a day or every other day. Eating pork, however, was against divine law and was considered a result of the condition of enslavement. The relevance of dietary change to a nascent Black identity was exemplified by Malcolm X, who became one of the most well-known ministers of the Nation of Islam. Malcolm described his rejection of pork as an important turning point in his conversion to the Nation of Islam while in prison:

> It was the funniest thing, the reaction, and the way that it spread. In prison, where so little breaks the monotonous routine, the smallest thing causes a commotion of talk. It was being mentioned all over the cell block by night that [I] didn't eat pork.

It made me proud, in some odd way. One of the universal images of the Negro, in prison and out, was that he couldn't do without pork. It made me feel good to see that my not eating it had especially startled the white convicts.

Later I would learn, when I had read and studied Islam a good deal, that, unconsciously, my first pre-Islamic submission had been manifested. I had experienced, for the first time, the Muslim teachings. "If you will take one step toward Allah--Allah will take two steps toward you."[56]

There were a number of foods that Elijah Muhammad considered taboo, but the main ingredient of his dietary techniques was to eat one meal of the "right" food every twenty-four hours. He felt that one should eat only simple, fresh foods, and eat only when fully hungry. He taught that artificial flavoring and coloring were slow death. He saw proper food as central to self-sufficiency, nation building, and spiritual development. Eating the right foods was following divine law. For Muhammad, eating right was living right, and if we live right, we do not need drugs and will live a long life. He also advocated breastfeeding, discouraged drugs during pregnancy, and opposed all intoxicants. He believed that good thoughts were also important to good health.

In a previous speech, one of Muhammad's top ministers admonished his audience for their dietary habits: "I know some of you love your chittlin's, and you love your fatback, but you're killing yourselves." In the same speech the minister urged his audience to eat less often but to eat the right foods: "When you eat all day and in between meals, your stomach has no chance to rest, therefore you waste yourself. By 47 or 50 you are ready to die when you should be ready to live. Why? Because you don't know the proper food to eat."[57]

The dietary techniques of Elijah Muhammad and the Nation of Islam had profound influences on non-Muslim African Americans. Muslim grocery stores, bakeries, and restaurants were springing up in African American communities all over the country, and these structures functioned to spread Muhammad's philosophy of diet and health to the broader African American community. Muhammad spread his views through radio broadcasts directed at the African American community. *Muhammad Speaks*, the official newspaper of the Nation of Islam, had a national circulation that touched major sectors of the African American community.[58] This newspaper consistently elaborated and reinforced the Black Muslim dietary and health philosophy. It provided consumer-oriented articles on nutrition and health, food selection, and food preparation. It also featured authoritative articles by people with doctoral and medical degrees whose research findings and perspectives supported the Muslim approach to health. For example, one 1963 article interviewed a prominent African American cardiologist who placed "the blame for heart diseases upon the foods we eat."[59] A 1975 article indicated that "all soul food is high in salt and this could be a contributing factor to the high hypertension death rate [among African Americans]."[60]

Cherry, a thirty-eight-year-old artist described an experience that eventually led her to change her diet and to use natural health care. Her experiences illustrated an important link between Muslim restaurants (institutions) and changing health beliefs and practices.

> I used to sell jewelry, and I went into a shop one day. I think that's when the transition, the Black, the dashikis, the whole thing, the Black awareness, about 1970, was popular then--changing foods, vegetarian diet. Well, I went to this shop [where they sold African garments], and I started talking to these "sisters." . . . This one "sister" says, . . . after I had gone there a couple times, . . . "Why don't you come and go to lunch with me?" . . . She was about forty then, but I could never see that on her. It made me real curious. . . . So we went on up to 71st to

the Muslim restaurant. . . . She ordered.
We had bean soup, a salad, some steamed
vegetables. I said, "Wow! you didn't order
any meat, any poultry, any fish or any-
thing." She said, "No, I haven't had any-
thing like that for ten years." That made
me real curious.

In other interviews with natural health care
users, a thirty-three-year-old postal worker
commented on her dietary change and her transition to natural health care use: "It all started
when I was still at home with my mother and some
seventeen years ago when she started listening
to Muhammad, the Muslim doctrine, that you
should not eat pork or white bread."

Sarah, a thirty-seven-year-old homemaker,
commented on the influence of the teachings of
Malcolm X, as well as the general 1960s and
1970s atmosphere of change, on her dietary
habits.

Malcolm [X]. That's about the only one
that influenced . . . my way of thinking.
Like the people I was around was speaking
about food and what we eat. . . . Don't be
eating pork. . . . Try not to deal with
too much meat. They was all into that type
of eating. It was your vegetables, you
know. . . . They really helped me to . . .
come to myself as far as . . . realizing
about the food thing--what you eat, you
know.

Hebrew Israelites. Hebrew Israelites, or
Black Jews, had a similar effect on the broader
African American community, but these groups
were not as prominent as the Nation of Islam.[61]
Nevertheless, many African Americans were attracted to their philosophy and way of life during the Black Consciousness movement of the
mid-1960s and 1970s. Some Hebrew Israelites emi-
grated to Israel and parts of Africa during the
late 1960s and 1970s with the hope of establishing a homeland. However, through their restaurants, business establishments, and proselytizing activities, Hebrew groups that remained in
this country continued to make an impact on the

health consciousness and dietary patterns of the African American community. For example, an article in the prominent African American newspaper, the *Chicago Defender*, described one of the Hebrew Israelite establishments: "If you want some `serious' vegetarian food made without any dairy or meat products and minus sugar or white flour, you've got to visit the Soul Vegetarian Restaurant located at 205 E. 75th Street."[62]

Hebrew Israelites believed and taught that they were God's chosen people mentioned in the Old Testament of the Bible.[63] Moreover, they believed that African Americans had experienced slavery and oppression because they had fallen from God's favor as a result of violating divine law. They argued:

The Bible was written by Black men who because of their disobedience and violations of the Laws (instructions) lost favor with God. Consequently, they yielded the rule of dominion of the world to the Euro-gentiles for an appointed period of time. During the gentile reign, the African Hebrews (children of Israel) underwent a chastisement (slavery) that caused them to descend to the lowest ebb of existence among the people of the world. . . . With the truthful interpretation of the Holy Scriptures and its prophecies, the season of salvation is set in motion.[64]

Thus, the concept of divine law was central to the lifestyle and dietary approach of Hebrew Israelite philosophy. It was only through living correctly, which also meant eating correctly, that one could then live in accord with divine law. Hebrews advocated "natural" foods and vegetarianism, sometimes to the exclusion of all dairy products. As in the case of the Nation of Islam, Hebrew Israelites considered pork to be a symbol of enslavement and an abomination to God. They explained: "Many defy the Creator and manage to break the law, as exemplified by breaking the dietary law, given our fathers in the wilderness; wherein, they were commanded by God to abstain from eating swine."[65] Further, Hebrew Israelites considered food preparation and consumption to be "at the highest level of mankind's development."[66] Many Hebrew Israelites advocated wearing only garments made from natural rather than synthetic materials; for example, cotton clothing was encouraged. They also encouraged "natural" childbirth and breastfeeding and discouraged abortion. Most were opposed to tobacco and drugs of all types. Similar to the Nation of Islam, many Hebrews counseled against excessive television, which they argued destroyed the body and the mind. Hebrews, again, as in the case of the Nation of Islam, encouraged self-sufficiency, and health problems were often addressed within the group, using herbal remedies.[67]

Again, the proselytizing of some Hebrew Israelite groups stimulated change among nonmembers, as this nurse and natural health care advocate testified: "One person that really influenced me. . . . My husband's best friend is a Black Hebrew." Another respondent explained that changes in diet seemed to have political ramifications and during the 1960s and 1970s: "People were vying for the attention, the heart and the mind of Black folks. . . . The Black Hebrew group was one of the groups."

Artistic/Spiritual Groups. Other individuals and groups that emerged during the 1960s and 1970s affected the dietary habits of African Americans and served to legitimate and promote a natural health philosophy in the African American community. Similar to the Nation of Islam and the Hebrew Israelites, they encouraged movement toward alternative lifestyles for African Americans. They were often, but not necessarily, guided by a spiritual philosophy regarding the "right" way to live. These artistic/spiritual individuals and groups frequently provided interpretations of the role of traditional and ancient African culture in the context of their current lives, and they often promoted a vision of how African Americans ought to live. Many were creative artists in the sense that at least part of their livelihoods was based on the fact that they were singers, dancers, musicians, visual artists, jewelers, sculptors, writers, actors, cooks, fashion designers, and the like. Some people became involved with formal spiritual communities that promoted alternative lifestyles structured around distinctive dietary and health practices. Therefore, the category artistic/spiritual was generally more diverse, fluid, and eclectic.

Several key institutions helped to galvanize a health-conscious and African-conscious artistic/spiritual community. One such institution was the Affro-Arts Theater, a community theater that opened on the South Side of Chicago.[68] It attracted significant numbers of the core groups mentioned above, as well as the broader African American community. The theater quickly became a nationally recognized mecca for Black culture and provided further prominence for a natural health care approach. The theater offered classes that promoted naturalistic health practices and that advocated vegetarianism. These classes reinforced the concept that the "right" diet was necessary for spiritual and cultural development. They also promoted the view that there were natural laws that defined how one should live.

Although the theater was shortlived (about two years), it made a significant impact on many African Americans with respect to introducing an alternative concept of health care. Some people who came out of this experience later became users of formal systems of natural health care, and some became practitioners. For example, one respondent commented that his wife had been referred to a natural health care practitioner as a consequence of taking health classes at the theater. The founder of the Affro-Arts Theater (composer and musician Phil Cohran) explained that he had begun to promote public classes on Black health in 1964, an idea that he later incorporated into the theater. He commented that prior to the opening of the theater,

We had all the "sisters" to fix different dishes and things to prove to the people that this food [vegetarian or health food] could taste just as succulent as that trash they was eatin'. . . . And it did start a lot of people to go and start exploring into health. So that's where you

got your whole Black Chicago comin' out of
a health thing.

Subsequent to the Affro-Arts Theater, another
educational and cultural institution, the Institute of Positive Education (directed by the poet
and essayist Haki Madhubuti), emerged. It also
provided a meeting place for the various core
groups mentioned previously. This institution
officially promoted vegetarianism and a naturalistic approach to health care.[69] It also functioned as a community center where lectures and
forums included presentations by naturopaths,
herbologists, naprapaths, and chiropractors. One
public lecture given in November 1979 by a
naturopath to a packed house at the institute
clearly linked naturalistic health beliefs and
practices with the quest for a new and more desirable African personality. The speaker stated:

The way that we're going to teach you, the
ancient system that we utilize is an ancient or Eastern way of looking at things.
And this way of looking at things is based
on the fact that man is a seed and God is
the tree. . . .

This is the Afrocentric cosmological hi-
erarchy. This is the way our forefathers
looked at life. . . .

Our forefathers recognized that they were
seeds, seeds from the fruit of God Himself. When they looked at nature, they
recognized that nature was broken down according to rank. And that rank was a spiritual rank. It was a rank based on energy,
energy being the Western word for spirit.
And when they looked at things, they
looked at things according to the spiritual capacity of a thing. . . .

The European distorts and destroys nature.
. . .

The European has taught you to utilize as
nutritional substances those life forms

that are detrimental to spiritual consciousness.

There were other centers of activity that
sprang up and promoted a natural health consciousness in the African American community.
Some were restaurants that offered vegetarian
cuisines and that also became outlets for
African American artistic expression. Others
were community centers and classes that provided
lectures, forums, and instruction in such health
arts and activities as yoga, Tai Chi, herbology,
natural or prepared childbirth, African dance,
and so on. For example, one community-based,
self-help health organization with a distinctly
African consciousness offered a "rejuvenation
workshop" in September 1979. Its objectives
printed in a promotional flier were as follows:

> This class is especially designed to serve
> the needs of the aware woman of today as
> she achieves her goals of total beauty,
> relaxation and radiant health through men-
> tal and physical balance. In it we utilize
> concepts of natural diet, Hatha Yoga exer-
> cises, meditation, auto-suggestion and in-
> ternal purity to prevent or eradicate most
> common physical ailments, including excess
> weight, flabbiness, colds, constipation,
> menstrual irregularities, gas, depression,
> tiredness, tension, and skin problems.

In addition to organized efforts, loose networks of individuals, particularly African American creative artists, propagated naturalistic
health beliefs and practices. One African-conscious musician and visual artist talked about
his dietary changes and how he learned of natural health care:

> There was this musician. . . . He and
> about three other musicians were real
> "tight" and we used to "hang" together all
> the time. This "brother" was the first one
> who actually told me about another way.
> One time we went into this restaurant, and
> he didn't order anything but vegetables. .
> . . As he ate he told me about the various

properties of vegetables. He said that we
needed to eat lighter foods. This way they
would pass through your system with little
trouble. Meat clogs up the system. This
made sense to me.

Another African-conscious musician explained
that

The first people that I knew who were
talking about [natural health care] were
[three musician friends]. . . . The first
vegetarian I had heard about was a
[musician friend]. . . . I thought maybe I
would cut down on eating meat so much. . .
. That's how I really got into [vegetari-
anism].

A jeweler and graphic artist commented on her
health and spiritual beliefs and African consciousness:

I believe myself to be a spiritual person,
which I believe is being religious from
what I consider a traditional frame of
reference in understanding the greatness
of my people and from a historical perspective, you know, my tradition in
Africa, the ancient Egyptians, and the
contributions that we have made--the fact
that we have survived all this time--and
our whole culture. . . . They both
[spirituality and health] go hand in
hand; I realize that. . . . The diet that
I deal with is . . . a first diet--when
there was not processed foods, when there
was . . . nothing but vegetables, fruits,
berries, nuts, water.

As this respondent indicated, a fundamental
belief of certain key sectors of a natural
health- and African-conscious community was that
naturalistic health beliefs and practices were
central to revitalizing spiritual development
and an ancient and lost culture. An editorial
statement by a publication of an African American spiritual and health collective drove home
this point:

This is a magazine of spiritual culture. A magazine dedicated to the upliftment and perfection of the spiritual awareness and capability of black people and through black people all people. We have named this magazine after Thoth, which in the ancient African tradition of Kemit (Egypt) was a symbol for the divine principle of wisdom.

A final example illustrates the important role that dietary change and naturalistic health practices had for some African Americans. This woman had become a part of the spiritual community mentioned above and reflected upon whether or not her Black militancy at the time could have influenced her decision to become a vegetarian. She explained: "It very well could have because I was around twenty-one; a lot could have been rebellion at the time. . . . I didn't like the way society was run and the way they treated Black people; so I just became different."

Implications and Conclusions

This section reveals the role of naturalistic health beliefs and practices in the Black Consciousness movement of the mid-1960s and 1970s. Three groups emerged from the African American community that contributed significantly to promoting naturalistic health beliefs and practices and to stimulating more generalized efforts to revitalize and transform African American culture. These groups were the Nation of Islam, Hebrew Israelites (Black Jews), and artistic/spiritual groups, which included creative artists and people who sought alternatives to mainstream American culture and to the negative features of African American culture.

Naturalistic health beliefs played an important role in efforts to develop an ideal African American personality and to stimulate group cohesion. They promoted group cohesion by providing a distinctive lifestyle, shared sacred beliefs, and a common moral order. These transcendent movement goals functioned to unify divergent groups. In addition, naturalistic health beliefs and practices provided a practical model for self-determination, self-help, and personal empowerment. They also functioned to reorient the self-image of a people who were seeking to rise above a traumatic history of oppression and exploitation. This reorientation provided a vehicle to break with the past and to project a vision of the future (albeit through a return, for some, to an idealized African past). In sum, naturalistic health beliefs and practices had an important galvanizing effect on identity formation and re-formation among some African Americans and was an important dimension of the social change and revitalization tendencies of the mid-1960s and 1970s.

CULTURAL SURVIVAL AND THE COMMUNITY ARTIST

The expropriation of African American culture by European American institutions of ideation is a well-established fact and cultural dilemma facing African American creative artists and intellectuals.[70] This dilemma is linked to the cultural dialectic that has pervaded the African American experience, which is the problem of cultural hegemony, the systemic negation of one culture by another.[71] For example, the venerable anthropologist St. Clair Drake has observed, "Since black communities have been, and are, relatively powerless, their cultural products are constantly being `co-opted' for ends other than those they set for themselves."[72]

Cultural products, particularly music, language, dance, and stylistic norms, are absorbed into the broader White-controlled commodity system, redefined, and used to advance the economic dominance of mainstream institutions. The result is to exploit African American creativity and markets, to expand non-Black markets domestically and globally, and to solidify the subordinate economic status of the African American community. Economic equity in the cultural arena for the African American community is stifled since African American creative artists perennially lose control of their cultural products, which includes their meanings, messages, images, and uses. As a further consequence, the humanizing and galvanizing dimensions of culture that serve to promote the group interests of African Americans are negated.

However, the African American community has always been able to respond to this dilemma through further creative innovation and efforts at institution building.[73] In short, the African American community continues to profoundly reshape the cultural fabric of American society even though there exists a tendency to deprive this community of control, economic benefit, legitimacy, and self-consciousness. The problem is not whether or not such efforts will continue but to what extent their progressive elements will be institutionalized.

What emerges, I believe, in the context of the above dynamic is the important role of the community artist in advancing the social progress of the African American community. In light of the need for progressive creativity in opposition to cultural negation and community disintegration, there are at least three aspects of the tendency toward negation that we need to consider. First, the African American community spawns and shapes its creative agents, who in turn express and advance the cultural ethos and aspirations of that community. The market for these creative agents is first an internal one. Second, as others outside of the community recognize and perceive social (and economic) benefits from these cultural products, a new external market develops. The artist begins to service this market but remains focused on his or her root, internal or home market. Third, as the external market becomes dominant, the artist tends not to focus on the home market and begins to alter his or her cultural products to accommodate the perspectives, expectations, economic potential, and legitimating power of the external market. At this point, external or mainstream markets begin to imitate, co-opt, and expropriate African American cultural products. The root market continues to experience these cultural products through the mass media but only in a commercial and negated form. The loss to the tradition, social cohesion, development, and self-consciousness of the root market is immense. In addition, economic control and benefit is most likely transferred out of the root market (community), if in fact such control or benefit ever existed.

The African American community artist functions primarily in the first mode and may periodically extend into the second--particularly for economic survival or humanistic reasons--but must resist the third for fear of distortion, absorption, and negation. Indeed, without the community artist, there would be no third mode because there would be no African American tradition to stimulate creative impulses uniquely different from European-based American culture. Thus, a critical strategy is to strengthen the position of the community artist who promotes and extends the traditions and progressive elements of the community.[74]

In light of the above dynamic, the role of the community artist who carries progressive African American traditions must be elevated as an object of study and as a priority for preservation, support, and development.[75] Phil Cohran is just such an artist who exemplifies a self-conscious commitment to uplifting the quality of African American life and intellect, while resisting countervailing political and market forces. I examine his example here, not only to illustrate an existing vehicle for community self-development, but also to emphasize the need for African Americans to look within their midst and select, support, and legitimate their progressive artists, teachers, and leaders who have rejected commercial co-optation in behalf of community development.

In 1967, the Affro-Arts Theater, founded by Phil Cohran, opened in the old Oakland Square Theater at 3947 South Drexel Boulevard on Chicago's South Side. At this time, the theater became a focal point for a growing Black consciousness among African Americans in Chicago. More than this, the Affro-Arts Theater symbolized the national aspirations of African Americans who sought to revitalize and elevate their social and cultural status.[76] Phil Cohran, who had already established himself as a respected musician, emerged as a mystic and visionary who saw divine purpose in music as a medium for inspiration, intellectual and spiritual elevation, and social development. Because Cohran had a well-defined concept of cultural progression and saw the creative and performing arts as having an edifying purpose beyond entertainment, he could instill deeper meaning and lend direction to the revitalization impulses emerging from the African American community. Cohran's efforts stimulated Pulitzer Prize-winning poet Gwendolyn Brooks to write about Phil Cohran in her poem, "The Wall."[77]

Later, when Phil Cohran produced his record, "The Malcolm X Memorial (A Tribute in Music)," through his own record company, Zulu Records, music critic Phyl Garland of *Ebony* magazine expressed the following:

> For some time, there have been black musicians in our midst who have realized the power of music as a force that might be used to galvanize the black community. . . . As might be expected, they have steered clear of affiliation with commercial firms that might restrict the depth and breadth of their expression. . . . Foremost on this front has been Chicago's Phil Cohran.[78]

In 1984, when *Down Beat* magazine decided to acknowledge Phil Cohran's artistry, the writer commented, "If Phil Cohran's name remains little known, it's by choice. For the past 20 years he has concentrated upon applying his music as a force for good within his community."[79]

Phil Cohran was born May 8, 1927, in Oxford, Mississippi.[80] Before reaching his teens, Cohran moved with his family to St. Louis and then to a location near Troy, Missouri, to escape the oppressive conditions of Mississippi. As a boy, Cohran sang the old spirituals in a segregated school every morning. As a consequence, the spirituals emerged as an important vehicle through which Cohran would later teach his ethical and aesthetic concepts. As a teenager, Cohran attended Lincoln University Laboratory High School in the 1940s. In high school, Cohran continued the musical training that he had begun when he was about five years of age, first on the piano, and later, at nine or ten, on the trumpet. Cohran subsequently branched off into other brass, string, and percussive instruments.

At Lincoln University Laboratory High School, Phil Cohran came under the tutelage of outstanding musicians, including Dr. O. Anderson Fuller, the first African American to earn a doctoral degree in music in the United States.[81] One typically found numerous outstanding African American teachers at Black high schools, colleges, and universities, a situation that was buttressed by the racist exclusionary policies of White institutions. Even though these accomplished African American intellects received little opportunity and recognition in White America, they established their mark through their students, their accomplishments in Europe, and their performances in front of African American audiences. Cohran explained:

I was under Dr. O. Anderson Fuller. There was Ruby Harris Gill and F. Nathaniel Gatlin. . . . They were some "sho nuff" people. Mrs. Gill was an authority on spirituals. She played violin and taught choral [techniques] and harmony. . . . Gatlin was a first-chair clarinetist at the festivals in Europe. He went over there for those summer festivals. . . . He couldn't even get a job here in this country because that was the 1940s. But I used to notice that . . . his house would be full of White students.

After high school, Cohran attended Lincoln University (Missouri) for one year but dropped out for financial reasons. He continued his musical development and eventually became the leader of a twelve-piece dance band called the Rajahs of Swing in St. Louis in 1948. In 1950, he was picked up by Jay McShann's band, one of the foremost exponents of the Kansas City style of blues and jazz and part of the ferment that spawned Charlie Parker. Traveling with McShann introduced Cohran to new and stimulating experiences that enlarged his understanding of the sensibilities of African American audiences. He observed, for example, their responses to blues singer Walter Brown, whom Cohran said could stop dance hall fights when he broke into song. Mc-Shann's group also played as a house band for pioneering, African American record producer Don Robey, a force behind the nascent musical style of rhythm and blues, or rock n' roll, as it was called when geared to a White market.[82]

Just as Cohran was becoming financially successful as a musician, he was drafted into the Army during the Korean conflict. He avoided combat when he was selected for intensive musical training at the Naval School of Music at Anacostia, near Washington, D.C. Here Cohran gained further exposure to the European classics and advanced his own facility with composition. After the Army, Cohran worked with a number of accomplished musicians (e.g., Oliver Nelson) but found his greatest growth through rehearsing, performing, and recording with Sun Ra in Chicago. Cohran explained:

> From Sun Ra, I grew by leaps and bounds. Because my history and all the music that I had been writing and studying had really come to a head--kind of an apex. . . . I had begun to develop my modal concept around '58. I started with Sun Ra in '60. And what he was doing blew my mind.

Cohran was further impressed by the discipline of the group.

After leaving Sun Ra, Cohran rededicated himself to developing an understanding of how African music was linked to world history and civilizations. As he studied world civilizations, Cohran concluded that, "since Africa was the root or source, . . . then I had to look at everything for its African [elements]."[83] Cohran decided that his music should reflect his African consciousness and that he should become multifaceted in order to elevate his music. He explained:

> I learned that the old African was everything. He was a scientist, a magician. He knew everything. If he didn't know everything, he didn't know anything. So then I began to study like that. I had never

> painted; I began to paint. I began to
> carve. I began to do everything.

Cohran also began to construct his own instruments.

Most significantly, Cohran struggled to put together a disciplined group to express his ideas and to achieve what he felt was the original purpose of the music, "a divine language to speak into the hearts of people." Cohran almost achieved the nucleus of such a group in the Afro-Arts Theater, but it would take over twenty years before he could forge a truly disciplined nucleus of musicians, largely consisting of his immediate and extended family.

Phil Cohran required that the musicians who played with him become multifaceted. If they were singers, they were expected to master their voices and learn to perform with other instruments. If they were instrumentalists, they were expected to master their primary instruments, develop facility with other instruments, and develop their voices. The total group had to become adept at executing Cohran's rhythmic scheme and at utilizing a wide range of percussive instruments. Vocal expression and dance were always a part of the total performance. For well over twenty-five years, Phil Cohran supported himself and his family through good times and some very bad times as a community artist. Through it all, he produced and sold his own records and tapes and maintained control over his creative products.

In order to enhance his musical growth, Cohran advocated a healthy lifestyle and spiritual development. He changed to a vegetarian diet, seeking a healthier mind and body, and he studied various aspects of meditation. Cohran's spiritual studies paralleled the refinement of his modal concept of music. He also found greater expression in stringed instruments (harp and zither), in addition to the brass instruments on which he was proficient. Cohran eventually solidified his holistic view of African American music, his distinctive polyrhythmic concept and approach to tuning, and his conceptual linkages between the structure of African language and musical forms and African American dialect. The latter was embodied artistically and conceptually in the dialect poetry of Paul Lawrence Dunbar and the a capella projections of the spirituals.

One additional and significant interlude before Phil Cohran began to consistently operationalize his concept of music in the African American community was his involvement with helping to found the Association for the Advancement of Creative Musicians (AACM). This group became the most well-known professional, African American music collective in America and abroad, with many of America's best known jazz musicians as its members. Cohran later left this organization because he differed with the approach to rhythm and improvisation utilized by some prominent members. Also, according to Cohran, the organization did not adequately move toward developing a vehicle that could employ its membership. Finally, these musicians remained primarily within a jazz idiom, but Cohran embraced multiple facets of an African American musical tradition. After leaving the AACM, Cohran joined writer/singer/actor Oscar Brown Jr. to write music for the works of Paul Lawrence Dunbar. This led to a contract with the Chicago Board of Education and finally enough resources to purchase equipment to produce his own recordings.

By 1965, Phil Cohran had begun to direct a steady stream of music at African Americans in Chicago, which was designed to educate them about their cultural heritage.[84] Cohran would eventually take his music into elementary and high schools, colleges, universities, museums, churches, community organizations, prisons, and the Affro-Arts Theater. In August 1965, the *Chicago Tribune* reported on Cohran's performance at an African American arts festival in the West Woodlawn community of Chicago:

> Highlight of the festival was the performance of the Artistic Heritage Ensemble under the direction of Philip Cohran. This is a unique ensemble in that the arrangements of the music it performs are largely based on African or Negro folk tunes and rhythms. Cohran, who arranges the music,

is a skillful musician who appears to be steeped in Negro History and music. . . .

Cohran introduced and played two unusual instruments he made based upon African instruments. One, the thumb piano, was amplified while he stood up and played it. The other, a take-off of the historic psalter[y], that uses a bow, was fascinating to watch.

It is not unreasonable to predict that this group will make a big name in the United States some day.[85]

Cohran did make a name for himself as his popularity reached its zenith during the opening of the Affro-Arts Theater. Later, political harassment and the conscious rejection of commercial enticements would limit his exposure. Cohran's success came from his skill as a musician and his understanding of African American audiences. Also, Cohran had unique abilities as a teacher with a highly developed aesthetic and cultural philosophy. In the tradition of the griot, Cohran educated his audiences through musical and oral expression. He typically explained the meaning and significance of the musical compositions that he played. Cohran always bonded with his audiences and brought them to the center of each performance.

Cohran's musical presentations were guided by a strong cultural philosophy. In 1965, he summarized this cultural philosophy in a short unpublished essay, "The Spiritual Musician." In his essay Cohran argued that music plays an important role in all highly evolved cultures. It must be a medium for the knowledge acquired through nature, people, and spiritual enlightenment, and it must be a source of inspiration. Music is a science and must be used purposefully and with precision. However, the science of music reaches its highest development when it functions and communicates on a spiritual plane. The African American musician must strive to develop spiritually, and he or she has a special role, since Africa, the source of world civilization, is the "trunk of the musical tree."

For Phil Cohran, the spiritual musician has the obligation "to keep reality before the people." The cultural philosophy of Phil Cohran had reached full-bloom prior to the opening of the Affro-Arts Theater.

In one of several interviews with him, Cohran described the sequence of events that led to the emergence of the Affro-Arts Theater in 1967. As a consequence of his involvement in a community project during the summer of 1967, Phil Cohran and his group played regularly at the 63rd Street Beach on Chicago's South Side. Cohran explained:

> That was when Chicago first became Black, because . . . you couldn't get Blackness over until you had some vehicle for exposing a lot of people. Well, the "Outer Drive" (an expressway that runs along Chicago's lake front) was it. People would be driving along . . . and hear these sounds and would turn around and drive over in there. . . . They'd come back at night and we'd be over there jammin', see. . . . And I was breakin' down history to 'em, . . . you know, different things I was dealin' with. Like I had a song on the wigs, you know, "The Talking Drum." I'd sing that and the "sisters" would take their wigs off and hold it up and say, "I ain't going to wear it no more," you know.
>
> And then people started wearing dashikis and "sisters" started wearing robes and things. And they'd come over. . . . They had somewhere they could go and show this. So pretty soon it got so bad that people felt bad when they'd come over there in their regular dress. So . . . by the time we got to August everybody was coming over there in something. They'd go home and make 'em something--wrap up in something and come back over there. It really was the beginning of Blackness in Chicago.

The performances by Phil Cohran and his Artistic Heritage Ensemble became a popular at-

traction on the South Side of Chicago, and the
63rd Street Beach became a favorite spot where
Black people celebrated their cultural heritage.
After the last performance of the summer, Cohran
asked his audience whether or not they wanted a
place where they could gather year-round. The
response was overwhelmingly positive. Cohran described his efforts to raise money and to find a
theater:

> Ok, I said, "I'm going to find out how
> many of you are for real!" I announced a
> meeting, "Tomorrow night over at the St.
> John Grand Lodge at six o'clock. I'll see
> how many of you are going to be there." .
> . . About eighty people showed up. And I
> was pretty encouraged by that. . . . I
> gave them statements. I ran off copies of
> statements [that said] "I authorize this
> person to solicit money to build a Black
> theater in my name--Phil Cohran." I signed
> it. They took it around and raised $1,300
> just asking, walking up and down the
> street. . . . We got the $1,300 plus my
> record money, and other things that we had
> done.

Cohran went on to say that he eventually settled on one of two Jewish-owned theaters in the
Black community. The rent was $1,000 a month.
The structure needed extensive repairs before it
could be opened, but the Black community responded by donating the time and necessary materials. Thus, the old Oakland Square Theater at
3947 South Drexel Boulevard was renovated
through an extensive community effort. The ad-
vertisement for the opening of the Theater read:
"All Up In Heah, The Affro-Arts Theater Presents
in Concert The Artistic Heritage Ensemble,
Philip Cohran--Director, Performing Black
Magic--Black History, Black Knowledge And Black
Truth, A Community Cultural Center--Rededicated
The Affro-Arts Theater." Public dedication of
the theater took place on December 2, 1967, at
8:00 p.m. The theater was widely supported by
the African American community and opened to an
impressive crowd of over 700 people.

The African and Eastern motif of the theater captured the spirit of the rising Black consciousness of the times and became a showcase for every form of Black cultural expression. The colorful wall murals, Eastern/African garb, and unique musical sounds, which drew heavily from the root tones and rhythms of Black music around the world, portended a different mode of life for African Americans. The theater projected a warmth and sense of spirituality. One could find support for a new identity that extended unbroken from the present into a rich ancient past.

The Affro-Arts Theater attracted such leading African American spokespersons as Stokely Carmichael, LeRoi Jones, and Rev. Albert Cleage, as well as noted artists, such as Oscar Brown Jr., Oletunji, Syl Johnson, Gwendolyn Brooks, and the Ghana Dance Ensemble. The emerging young poet, Don L. Lee (Haki Madhubuti) gained significant exposure through the theater. The gospel singing and theatrical presentations of the Rev. Spenser Jackson family were regular contributions to the theater. Darlene Blackburn and her dance troupe became regulars and set the standard for the rebirth of traditional African dance in Chicago. The theater presented the film, *The Battle of Algiers* and Jimmy Garret's play, *We Own the Night*, on its stage. The Organization of Black American Culture (OBAC), an important and developing collective of African American writers and artists, also gained a creative outlet through the theater.

The Affro-Arts Theater paralleled, and in most cases predated, the Black Studies movement, which was to take place on predominantly White college and university campuses. It provided a community-based vehicle to educate and enrich African Americans. A message of culture building was set within the framework of self-conscious creative expression. Cohran spoke to this aspect of the theater: "We had music classes. We had dance classes. And we had a womanhood and a manhood class to teach the people health and to teach them order and civilization."

Unfortunately, the Affro-Arts Theater fell on hard times. Internal dissension, financial problems, and political harassment brought an end to the theater by 1970. Phil Cohran left the theater before its ultimate demise, however. Most of the group that had constituted Cohran's Artistic Heritage Ensemble remained after he had left, but changed its name to the Pharoahs. The Pharoahs kept the theater going for a short period and continued to draw upon the tonal and rhythmic concept introduced by Cohran.

Several members of this group later helped to form the rhythm and blues/rock group known as Earth, Wind and Fire. Maurice White, the leader of Earth, Wind and Fire, never played with Phil Cohran. However, as Cohran pointed out, White spent a great deal of time observing at rehearsals and performances. White eventually attempted to recreate Cohran's electrified African thumb piano. Cohran had called his invention the Frankiphone (named after his mother, Frankie), an instrument that became his calling card. White referred to this instrument as the Kalimba, and his group recorded a popular song by the same name. Quite significantly, Earth, Wind and Fire initially projected an African/Eastern rhythmic, tonal, and spiritual concept in its music similar to that of Phil Cohran and the Affro-Arts Theater. However, even though there have been others who have emulated various aspects of the Phil Cohran concept, none have totally or consistently captured his sound or his approach to performance.

In performance, Cohran endeavored to teach the African American community about itself and how to live. Health, love of self, spiritual reality, historical connections, and so on were common themes. Cohran combined jazz, blues, gospel, spirituals, rhythm and blues, and rock in distinctive ways that illustrated the common thread that ran through all of Black music. Folktales, poetry, dramatic presentations, vocalizing, and dance had important roles in the total Cohran performance. Music, as the spirit of Black people, became the medium for the message.

After observing scores of Phil Cohran performances over twenty years, I have never observed a performance that did not uplift, educate, or inspire the audience. Each performance seemed to have profound meaning and continuity. Cohran carefully designed instrumental, vocal, and dance presentations to bring the audience to a spiritual cleansing. The hypnotic quality of the music along with a complex rhythmic structure subtly engaged and absorbed the body and the mind with predictable regularity. Most importantly, each performance projected a deep and abiding respect for the audience. Characteristic of African tradition and the African American church, the audience became one with the performance. Clapping, dancing, vocalizing were natural expressions of an audience that no longer saw itself as observer, but as participant.

The Affro-Arts/Phil Cohran example points to the significance of music for African Americans as a cohesive and galvanizing force.[86] All of the disparate threads of Black life are contained in this medium of expression. Cohran also helps us to realize the importance of the music as a vehicle for communicating messages. It attracts attention and engages the senses consciously and subconsciously. He exemplifies the community-based artist who circumvents the distorting character of the dominant mass media apparatus in order to feed the spirit of the masses.[87]

In sum, community-based art is a force that can touch the masses below the level of mass media structures controlled by the dominant society. Nevertheless, its preservation on a cultural and institutional level ensures continued production of cultural products that can be utilized by African American-controlled commercial endeavors. However, African Americans also need noncommercial, community-based, progressive artistic institutions to preserve the constructive and positive elements of African American culture; its liberating potential depends upon continued existence beyond the distorting power of market exploitation. Realization of this scenario means that African Americans must diligently work to identify methods to support and expand centers of progressive artistic and cultural production in the African American community.

A CONCLUDING COMMENT: THEMES OF BLACK CONSCIOUSNESS MOVEMENTS

The Harlem Renaissance was eclipsed as a literary movement but re-emerged in a much broader sense through the Black Consciousness movement of the mid-1960s and 1970s. Too often the themes of these prominent self-conscious currents of change are viewed in a segmented fashion. They are examined, for example, in terms of their political, aesthetic, philosophical, economic, literary, or revolutionary import. However, upon deeper examination, it becomes apparent that the activities of these periods point to a much greater and a much more inclusive endeavor. African Americans are seeking to eliminate their subordinate status in the world through searching for a more enlightened and elevated way of life, not only materially but also spiritually. The question of how to live looms large in light of the perennial problem of cultural hegemony and the forces of cultural negation. What people of African descent are becoming and what should they become are not trivial questions.

Self-transformation, self-examination, and self-direction are necessary for empowerment, regardless of the externality of oppression. Oppression also contributes to a spiritual malaise as well as economic and political dislocation. The struggle to become a new human being is paramount for a people who cannot truly return to a past before the cataclysmic experiences that altered their development, but who also cannot embrace the world as it is; such a world is socially constructed to subordinate an African personality. Thus, certain human questions facing people of African descent are not comprehended by the dominating society and do not achieve visibility or importance. Explorations into diverse strategies for recreating family life, the examination of various religious modes of expression that can be made devoid of White supremacy, the attempts to construct a progressive and health-giving lifestyle, the debates over political strategies for empowerment, the pursuit of economic self-sufficiency, and the quest for identity, land, and collective security are part of the struggle to produce a culture. The reconstructivist issue, that is, the problem of cultural development, is a historically determined response to the kind of oppression experienced by African people. This means culture in its broadest sense and includes the integration of economics, politics, and aesthetic production. Additionally, there is the issue of spiritual rebirth as African people seek to probe the meaning and purpose of their earthly sojourn and discover the universality (laws for living) of their experience.

The Black Consciousness movement that came to prominence in the late 1960s was part of an ongoing cyclical struggle for human rebirth. We know about the Harlem Renaissance of the 1920s. However, a less prominent artistic flowering occurred at the turn of the century (1900s), and the late 1980s and 1990s have seen some emergence of a Black cultural consciousness. These self-conscious cultural strivings never go away but seem to gain greater prominence at various times for various reasons. They are generational, occurring every twenty-five years, unless disrupted by major social upheavals like economic depression or warfare. Also, they are subject to counterinsurgency that is systemic. They undergo expropriation, co-optation, distortion, and commercialization by the dominating society. The struggle to transcend this process of negation necessarily involves the struggle to define, create, sustain, and institutionalize progressive cultural change. The objective is not simply to reform oppression and those who oppress but to create the ability to survive and prosper in spite of oppressive forces.

NOTES

1. See Alain Locke, *The New Negro* (New York: Atheneum, 1969); Charles S. Johnson, *Ebony and Topaz* (New York: National Urban League, 1927).

2. The first Black college graduate in the United States was John Russwurm, who founded the first Black newspaper in this country, *Freedom's Journal*. He graduated from Bowdoin in Maine in 1826. For twenty years after this, there were only seven more graduates of recognized col-

leges. In 1860, at the outbreak of the Civil War, there had been only twenty-eight. See Charles S. Johnson, *The Negro College Graduate* (New York: Negro Universities Press, 1969), pp. 7-21.

3. Ibid.

4. Ibid., pp. 9-10, 20.

5. Ibid.

6. See Locke, *The New Negro*; Nathan Huggins, *Harlem Renaissance* (New York: Oxford University Press, 1971); Roger Whitlow, *Black American Literature: A Critical History* (Chicago: Nelson-Hall, 1973); Lorraine Elena Roses and Ruth Elizabeth Randolph, *Harlem and Beyond: Literary Biographies of 100 Black Women Writers, 1900-1945* (Boston: G. K. Hall, 1990).

7. Johnson, *The Negro College Graduate*, pp. 54-55.

8. Langston Hughes, "The Negro Artist and the Racial Mountain," in John A. Williams and Charles F. Harris, eds., *Amistad I: Writings on Black History and Culture* (New York: Vintage Books, 1970), p. 301.

9. Huggins, *Harlem Renaissance*, pp. 190-243.

10. See Reynolds Farley, *Growth of the Black Population: A Study of Demographic Trends* (Chicago: Markham Publishing, 1970), pp. 44-46.

11. Ibid., pp. 47-48, 75.

12. George E. Kent, "Patterns of the Harlem Renaissance," in Arna Bontemps, ed., *The Harlem Renaissance Remembered* (New York: Dodd, Mead, 1972), p. 31.

13. See Richard Barksdale and Kenneth Kinnamon, eds., *Black Writers of American: A Comprehensive Anthology* (New York: Macmillan, 1972), p. 471.

14. See Bontemps, *The Harlem Renaissance Remembered*, pp. 1-26; Warrington Hudlin, "The Renaissance Re-examined," in Bontemps, *The Harlem Renaissance Remembered*, pp. 268-77.

15. See Jervis Anderson, *This Was Harlem: A Cultural Portrait, 1900-1950* (New York: Farrar Straus Giroux, 1981); James Weldon Johnson, *Black Manhattan* (New York: Alfred A. Knopf, 1930); Gilbert Osofsky, "Harlem: The Making of a Ghetto," in John Henrik Clarke, ed., *Harlem, U.S.A.* (New York: Collier Books, 1964), pp. 7-19.

16. Ibid.
17. Ibid.
18. Ibid.
19. Johnson, *Black Manhattan*, pp. 147-48, 153.
20. Osofsky, "Harlem," p. 19.
21. Johnson, *Black Manhattan*, pp. 148-50.
22. Osofsky, "Harlem," pp. 13-16.
23. Ibid., p. 18.
24. See W. A. Domingo, "Gift of the Black Tropics," in Locke, *The New Negro*, p. 341.
25. See James Weldon Johnson, "Harlem: The Culture Capital," in Locke, *The New Negro*, pp. 302-3.
26. Johnson, *Black Manhattan*, p. 165.
27. Ibid., p. 168; Richard B. Moore, "Africa-Conscious Harlem," in Clarke, *Harlem*, pp. 37-56.
28. Johnson, *Black Manhattan*, pp. 233-51.
29. C. L. R. James, *A History of Pan African Revolt* (Washington, D.C.: Drum and Spear Press, 1969), pp. 78-79.
30. See Whitlow, *Black American Literature*, p. 73; Huggins, *Harlem Renaissance*, pp. 288-289; Allon Schoener, ed., *Harlem on My Mind: Cultural Capital of Black America, 1900-1968* (New York: Random House, 1968), p. 66; Robert Kimball and William Bolcom, *Reminiscing with Sissle and Blake* (New York: Viking Press, 1973).
31. See Huggins, *Harlem Renaissance*; Kent, "Patterns of the Harlem Renaissance"; Harold Cruse, *Crisis of the Negro Intellectual* (New York: William Morrow, 1967).
32. Langston Hughes, *The Big Sea: An Autobiography* (New York: Hill and Wang, American Century Series, 1963), p. 225.
33. Ibid., p. 226.
34. Anderson, *This Was Harlem*, pp. 77-79, 153-79; Schoener, ed., *Harlem on My Mind*, p. 126.
35. Locke, *The New Negro*.
36. Johnson, ed., *Ebony and Topaz*, p. 13.
37. Locke, *The New Negro*, p. 10.
38. Hughes, *The Big Sea*, p. 243.
39. James Weldon Johnson, *Along This Way: The Autobiography of James Weldon Johnson* (New York: Viking Press, 1933), p. 382; also see Hughes, *The Big Sea*, p. 243; Huggins, *Harlem Renaissance*, p. 129.

40. See Anderson, *This Was Harlem*, pp. 225–31; Hughes, *The Big Sea*, p. 244.

41. W. E. B. DuBois, *Dusk of Dawn: An Essay Toward an Autobiography of a Race Concept* (New York: Schocken Books, 1968), p. 271.

42. See Patrick J. Gilpin, "Charles S. Johnson: Entrepreneur of the Harlem Renaissance," in Bontemps, *The Harlem Renaissance Remembered*, p. 224.

43. "The Debut of the Younger School of Negro Writers," *Opportunity* 2 (May 1924):143.

44. See Gilpin, "Charles S. Johnson."

45. Ibid., p. 223 (see footnote 27); *Opportunity* was supported by a grant from the Carnegie Foundation, while *Crisis* was self-supported.

46. See Huggins, *Harlem Renaissance*; Anderson, *This Was Harlem*.

47. Clovis E. Semmes, "Toward a Theory of Popular Health Practices in the Black Community," *The Western Journal of Black Studies* 7 (Winter 1983):206–13.

48. Michael Betz and Lenahan O'Connell, "Changing Doctor-Patient Relationships and The Rise in Concern for Accountability," *Social Problems* 31 (1983):84; Clovis E. Semmes, "Nonmedical Illness Behavior: A Model of Patients Who Seek Alternatives to Allopathic Medicine," *Journal of Manipulative and Physiological Therapeutics* 13 (October 1990):427–36.

49. See Howard S. Berliner and Warren J. Salmon, "The Holistic Health Movement and Scientific Medicine: The Naked and the Dead," *Socialist Review* 43 (1979):31–51; Michael Goldstein, Dennis T. Jaffee, Dale Garell, and Ruth Ellen Berke, "Holistic Doctors: Becoming a Nontraditional Medical Practitioner," *Urban Life* 14 (1985):317–44; Loretta Kopelman and John Moskop, "The Holistic Health Movement: A Survey and Critique," *The Journal of Medicine and Philosophy* 6 (1981):209–35; Meredith B. McGuire, *Ritual Healing in Suburban America* (New Brunswick, N.J.: Rutgers University Press, 1988); Mahesh S. Patel, "Evaluation of Holistic Medicine," *Social Science and Medicine* 24 (1987):169–175; Joel L. Telles and Mark H. Pollack, "Feeling Sick: The Experience and Legitimation of Illness," *Social Science and Medicine* 15A (1981):242–51.

50. See Clovis E. Semmes, "When Medicine Fails: Making the Decision to Seek Natural Health Care," *National Journal of Sociology* 4 (Fall 1990):175-98; and "Developing Trust: Patient-Practitioner Encounters in Natural Health Care," *Journal of Contemporary Ethnography* 19 (January 1991):450-70.

51. See Semmes, "Nonmedical Illness Behavior."

52. See, for example, Dudley Randall, ed., *Homage to Hoyt Fuller* (Detroit: Broadside Press, 1984).

53. Cynthia Conley (Sister Zubena), *Calling All Sisters* (Chicago: Free Black Press, 1970).

54. Don L. Lee (Haki Madhubuti), *From Plan to Planet--Life Studies: The Need for Afrikan Minds and Institutions* (Chicago: Broadside Press and Institute of Positive Education, 1973), p. 87.

55. Elijah Muhammad, *How to Eat to Live* (Chicago: Muhammad's Temple of Islam No. 2, 1972).

56. Malcolm X, *The Autobiography of Malcolm X*, with the assistance of Alex Haley (New York: Grove Press, paperback edition, 1964), p. 156.

57. Louis Farrakhan, *7 Speeches* (New York: Muhammad's Temple No. 7, 1974), pp. 24-25.

58. In a presentation at the 13th Annual Black Studies Conference at Olive-Harvey College, Chicago, in April 1989, Wali Muhammad, the current editor of the Nation of Islam's newspaper, *Final Call*, indicated that before its demise, *Muhammad Speaks* had reached a weekly circulation of over 800,000. One should also note that Elijah Muhammad regularly broadcast over thirty to forty radio stations directed at various African American communities from at least the early 1960s.

59. "Heart Attacks On the Rise, Negro Doctor Cites Causes," *Muhammad Speaks*, 4 February 1963, p. 6.

60. "Did You Know?" *Muhammad Speaks*, 29 August 1975, p. 21.

61. One publication from a Hebrew Israelite group in Chicago stated that there were over 250 Black Israelite congregations in the United States. See "Did You Know," *Return to the Source*, March 1982, p. 7.

62. "An Elegant Vegetarian Meal from Soul Vegetarian," *Chicago Defender*, 27 December 1984, p. 18.

63. Ben Ammi, *The Black Man and Truth* (Chicago: Communicators Press, 1982).

64. Ibid., p. 96.

65. Ibid., p. 112.

66. Ibid., p. 39.

67. Ibid.

68. "Mecca for Blackness," *Ebony*, May 1970, p. 96.

69. See Johari Kunjufu, *Commonsense Approach to Eating* (Chicago: Institute of Positive Education, 1973).

70. See, for example, Harold W. Cruse, "Black Studies: Interpretation, Methodology, and the Relationship to Social Movements," *Afro-American Studies: An Interdisciplinary Journal* 2 (1971):15-51; Jannette L. Dates and William Barlow, eds., *Split Images: African Americans in the Mass Media* (Washington, D.C.: Howard University Press, 1990); St. Clair Drake, *Black Folk Here and There*, vol. 1 (Los Angeles: Center for Afro-American Studies, University of California, 1987); Nelson George, *The Death of Rhythm and Blues* (New York: E. P. Dutton, 1989); LeRoi Jones (Amiri Baraka), *Blues People* (New York: William Morrow, 1963); Ortiz Walton, *Music: Black, White and Blue* (New York: William Morrow, 1972).

71. See Clovis E. Semmes (Jabulani K. Makalani), "Black Studies and the Symbolic Structure of Domination," *The Western Journal of Black Studies* 6 (1982):116-22; and "The Sociological Tradition of E. Franklin Frazier: Implications for Black Studies," *Journal of Negro Education* 55 (1986):484-94.

72. Drake, *Black Folk*, p. xv.

73. See George, *Death of Rhythm and Blues*; Jones, *Blues People*; Clovis E. Semmes (Jabulani K. Makalani), "Toward a Sociological Analysis of the Renaissance: Why Harlem?" *Black World* 25 (February 1976):4-13, 93-97.

74. It is the critical role of a business and middle class to provide philanthropic support to the noncommercial progressive traditions of its community. Indeed, if this class neglects such a role, its own economic base and markets will be

in jeopardy as its community's cultural foundations erode and the sources of creativity needed to maintain and broaden commercial markets dry up.

75. So-called "Black Belts" in numerous urban centers across the country produced community-type relationships in the midst of more impersonal urban structures. In these settings one always found community-based artists and intellectual (teachers) who served to motivate African American youth to achieve excellence, despite forced segregation, poverty, racism, oppression, and inequality. Today, market and political forces tend to separate carriers of progressive African American traditions from African American youth, a structural problem that contributes to the disintegration of primary institutions and the retardation of secondary institutional development. For examples of how segregated and poor Black urban communities spawned excellence, see Dempsey J. Travis, *An Autobiography of Black Chicago* (Chicago: Urban Research Institute, 1981); Arna Bontemps and Jack Conroy, *Anyplace But Here* (New York: Hill and Wang, 1966).

76. "Mecca for Blackness: Chicago's Affro-Arts Theater Celebrates African Culture," *Ebony* (May 1970):96–100.

77. Gwendolyn Brooks, "The Wall," in *In the Mecca: Poems by Gwendolyn Brooks* (New York: Harper & Row, 1968), pp. 42–43.

78. Phyl Garland, "Sounds," *Ebony* (November 1971).

79. "Profile: Phil Cohran," *Down Beat* (December 1984):54–55.

80. I obtained information on Phil Cohran's life from extended interviews with him in 1979 and 1980. I supplemented these interviews with documents from his personal files and from newspaper and magazine clippings, handbills, and other documents in the public domain. I have formally observed, recorded, and tracked Cohran's performances for a decade.

81. See Eileen Southern, *The Music of Black Americans* (New York: W. W. Norton, 1971), p. 452.

82. See George, *Death of Rhythm and Blues.*

83. For example, Phil Cohran teaches about the diffusion of Old World (African) culture into European culture by way of the Moorish conquest of Spain. This connection is symbolized through one of Cohran's signature compositions, "The Spanish Suite."

84. In 1965, Cohran's group was called the Artistic Heritage Ensemble. This was the name of the group that Cohran would take into the Affro-Arts Theater in 1967. Years later, Cohran would call his group the Circle of Sound. Subsequently, he developed the Phil Cohran Youth Ensemble and the group, Legacy.

85. "West Woodl'n Scene of New Black Arts Festival Fair," *Chicago Tribune*, August 2, 1965.

86. I have not discussed the political activism of Phil Cohran, which included fighting prostitution fueled by White conventioneers in the African American community, exposing merchants who sold bad food in the community, playing benefits for numerous worthy causes, and working with other artists to help elect the late Harold Washington, Chicago's first African American mayor.

87. Harold Cruse stressed the need to decentralize the administrative, economic, and technological structures that govern the production of material culture. The current technological revolution in audio and video production, which includes the proliferation of pay TV options, provides a critical opportunity for such decentralization to take place. It remains to be seen, however, whether or not African American artists and entrepreneurs can seize upon this opportunity and effectively negotiate existing forces of institutional negation. See Cruse, "Black Studies," pp. 44-50.

9

A Concluding Comment

The preceding chapters provide a way of seeing and understanding the African American experience by revealing fundamental historical imperatives facing people of African descent. A basic question is: Given the type of social reality confronting African Americans, what are the range and types of responses required as African Americans express their humanness? The metaproblem of cultural hegemony is antithetical to this humanness because it systemically preempts self-definition and institution building. To gain legitimacy, behavior must be directed in the interest of Euro-American elites. Therefore, the illusion of social freedom and individualism dissipates at the level of power and control and at the point that social formations are reproduced. This scenario is not an absolute process but reflects a tendency inherent in the existing social dynamic. This tendency is altered when African Americans are able to respond as a group and utilize cultural memory and critical thought to elevate their collective position in society. Individualistic social philosophies tend to stifle progressive change in light of the reality of group power and control. The resulting cultural negation helps to sustain political and economic impotence, and it inhibits the ability to transcend cultural maladaptation, including

maladaptations associated with economic dislocation.

A critical dimension of the metaproblem of
cultural hegemony is the distortion of the production of knowledge. As a part of this issue,
the training of African American scholars is
problematic, as is the framing and examination
of relevant questions of inquiry. Unless African
American scholars have a personal commitment to
becoming steeped in an existing African American
intellectual tradition, the reward systems in
graduate schools and in academe in general do
not force such immersion, even when there is a
focus on what are presumed to be African American issues. This shortcoming also ignores, of
course, the contributions that a Black intellectual tradition can make to comprehending social
phenomena in general. Most significantly, certain types of research questions are ignored and
for the most part never occur. Too many African
American scholars, to survive in mainstream
academe, become marginal to a theoretically productive African American intellectual tradition.
They are encouraged to perform safe and acceptable research, and they are selectively exposed
to theories, events, people, and issues that the
mainstream academy deems appropriate. The academic establishment has a tendency to select a
few Black scholars who are sufficiently alienated from or marginal to the Black community in
various ways, reward and support them, and hold
them up as intellectual icons. This process of
cultural negation will probably not change.
Thus, it is important for African American intellectuals to actively maintain a rigorous independent research agenda and to preserve and
cultivate an Afrocentric intellectual tradition.
A Black business and leadership stratum must
also support and draw sustenance from such
scholars.

To a great extent, culture is communication,
and levels of social organization are the vehicles through which cultural forms come into existence and are sustained. Thus, social organization and culture represent two sides of the
same coin. Structural changes or alterations in
required patterns of interaction contribute to
cultural change, but cultural processes also in-

volve thinking and reflection that direct the formation of social organization. There are multiple imperatives to which humans must adjust for which they develop social thinking; these include but are not limited to reproduction, death, disease, physical differences, food production, and so on. The critical issue for African American studies is how social organization and culture interact and affect institutional development in light of the metaproblem of cultural hegemony.

The social dynamic facing African Americans requires sustained examination of cultural maladaptations that encourage them to contribute to their own oppression and lack of empowerment. These maladapations may or may not be expressed as social problems as defined by mainstream America. In fact, such maladaptations are sometimes the result of conformity to Eurocentric norms. Cultural reconstruction, revitalization, and innovation are important to transcend maladaptive responses.

The African American experience also demands a different approach to the study of racism in the context of cultural hegemony. Simplistic notions of prejudice and discrimination are not adequate. Besides institutional racism, there is liberal and conservative racism. Also, there is the complex relationship of plantation racism, yet to be explicated in the scholarly literature or studied as a social problem, but well understood in the African American experience. This type of racism involves maintaining the control and oppression of African Americans, as well as their unequal status, through Black intermediaries.

For mainstream America to transform its hegemonic tendencies and structured inequality, it must incorporate the centers of nonmainstream thought and become open to critique and meaningful change. Equality must involve justice, the deconstruction of myths of superiority, shared power, and respect for difference, and not simply conformity, which, in this social context, is translated into cultural negation, political impotence, and economic dislocation. Explicating the metaproblem of cultural hegemony has implications for understanding the experience of other non-White, oppressed, exploited and under-represented groups. It also can expand our understanding of the human experience in general by dismantling the layers of socially constructed knowledge founded on hegemonic mythology and by providing a new opportunity for human discourse, vision, and advancement.

Bibliography

Akbar, Na'im. "Africentric Social Sciences for Human Liberation." *Journal of Black Studies* 14 (June 1984):395–414.

Anderson, Charles H. *White Protestant Americans: From National Origins to Religious Group.* Englewood Cliffs, N.J.: Prentice-Hall, 1970.

Anderson, Jervis. *This Was Harlem: A Cultural Portrait, 1900–1950.* New York: Farrar Straus Giroux, 1981.

Asante, Molefi Kete. *Afrocentricity: The Theory of Social Change.* Buffalo, N.Y.: Amulefi Publishing, 1980.

———. *The Afrocentric Idea.* Philadelphia: Temple University Press, 1987.

Barksdale, Richard, and Kenneth Kinnamon, eds. *Black Writers of America: A Comprehensive Anthology.* New York: Macmillan, 1972.

Barrett, Leonard E. *Soul-Force: African Heritage in Afro-American Religion.* Garden City, N.Y.: Anchor Press, Doubleday, 1974.

ben-Johannan, Yosef. *African Origins of the Major "Western Religions."* New York: Alkebu-lan Books, 1970.

———. *Black Man of the Nile and His Family.* New York: Alkebu-lan Associates, 1972.

Berg, Alan. *The Nutrition Factor: Its Role in National Development*. Washington, D.C.: Brookings Institution, 1973.

Berkley, George. *On Being Black and Healthy: How Black Americans Can Lead Longer and Healthier Lives*. Englewood Cliffs, N.J.: Prentice-Hall, 1982.

Blassingame, John W. *The Slave Community*, rev. edn. New York: Oxford University Press, 1979.

Bogle, Donald. *Toms, Coons, Mulattoes, Mammies and Bucks: An Interpretive History of Blacks in American Films*, expanded edn. New York: Continuum Publishing, 1989.

Bontemps, Arna, ed. *The Harlem Renaissance Remembered*. New York: Dodd Mead, 1972.

Bracey, John H. Jr., August Meier, and Elliott Rudwick, eds. *Black Nationalism in America*. New York: Bobbs-Merrill, 1970.

Chimuzie, Amuzie. *Black Culture: Theory and Practice*. Shaker Heights, Ohio: Keeble Press, 1984.

Clark, Cedric (Sayed Malik Khatib). "The Concept of Legitimacy in Black Psychology." In Edgar G. Epps, ed. *Race Relations: Current Perspectives*. Cambridge, Mass.: Winthrop Publishers, 1973.

Clarke, John Henrik. "The Fight to Reclaim African History." *Negro Digest* 19 (February 1970):10-15, 59-64.

Cleage, Albert B. Jr. *The Black Messiah*. Trenton, N.J.: African World Press, 1989.

Cone, James H. *For My People: Black Theology and the Black Church*. Maryknoll, N.Y.: Orbis Books, 1984.

————. *A Black Theology of Liberation*. Maryknoll, N.Y.: Orbis Books, 1986.

Cripps, Thomas. *Slow Fade to Black: The Negro in American Film, 1900-1942*. New York: Oxford University Press, 1977.

Cross, William E. Jr. *Shades of Black: Diversity in African American Identity*. Philadelphia: Temple University Press, 1991.

Cruse, Harold. *Crisis of the Negro Intellectual*. New York: William Morrow, 1967.

————. *Rebellion or Revolution*. New York: William Morrow, 1968.

————. *Plural but Equal*: *A Critical Study of Blacks and Minorities and America's Plural Society*. New York: William Morrow, 1987.

Dates, Jannette L., and William Barlow, eds. *Split Image: African Americans in the Mass Media*. Washington, D.C.: Howard University Press, 1990.

Davidson, Basil. *The African Slave Trade: Pre-colonial History 1450-1850*. Boston: Little Brown, 1961.

Davis, Allison, Burleigh B. Gardner, and Mary R. Gardner. *Deep South: A Social Anthropological Study of Caste and Class*. Chicago: University of Chicago Press, 1959.

Davis, Allison, and John Dollard. *Children of Bondage: The Personality Development of Negro Youth in the Urban South*. New York: Harper and Row, 1964.

deGraft-Johnson, J. C. *African Glory: The Story of Vanished Negro Civilizations*. Baltimore, Md.: Black Classic Press, 1986.

Doyle, Bertram W. *The Etiquette of Race Relations in the South: A Study of Social Control*. New York: Schocken Books, 1971.

Drake, St. Clair. *The Redemption of Africa and Black Religion*. Chicago: Third World Press, 1970.

————. *Black Folk Here and There: An Essay in History and Anthropology*, 2 vols. Los Angeles: University of California, Center for Afro-American Studies, 1987.

———— and Horace R. Cayton. *Black Metropolis: A Study*, 2 vols., rev. edn. New York: Harcourt, Brace and World, 1970.

DuBois, W. E. B. *The Souls of Black Folk*. Greenwich, Conn.: Fawcett Publications, 1961.

————. *The Philadelphia Negro: A Social Study*. New York: Schocken Books, 1967.

Edwards, G. Franklin, ed. *E. Franklin on Race Relations*. Chicago: University of Chicago Press, 1968.

Emory, Lynne Fauley. *Black Dance in the United States from 1619 to 1970*. Palo Alto, Calif.: National Press, 1972.

Essien-Udom, E. U. *Black Nationalism: A Search for Identity in America*. New York: Dell, 1964.

Ewen, Stuart. *Captains of Consciousness: Advertising and the Social Roots of the Consumer Culture*. New York: McGraw-Hill, 1976.

Fanon, Franz. *Black Skin, White Mask*. New York: Grove Press, 1967.

————. *Toward the African Revolution*. New York: Grove Press, 1967.

Farley, Reynolds. *Growth of the Black Population: A Study of Demographic Trends*. Chicago: Markham Publishing, 1970.

———— and Walter R. Allen. *The Color Line and the Quality of Life in America*. New York: Oxford University Press, 1989.

Fauset, Arthur Huff. *Black Gods of the Metropolis: Negro Religious Cults in the Urban North*. Philadelphia: University of Pennsylvania Press, 1944.

Ferguson, Blanche E. *Countee Cullen and the Negro Renaissance*. New York: Dodd, Mead, 1966.

Frazier, E. Franklin. *Black Bourgeoisie: The Rise of a New Middle Class*. New York: The Free Press, 1957.

————. *Race and Culture Contacts in the Modern World*. Boston: Beacon Press, 1957.

————. *The Negro Family in the United States*, rev. and abbr. edn. Chicago: University of Chicago Press, 1966.

————. *Negro Youth at the Crossways: Their Personality Development in the Middle States*. New York: Schocken, 1969.

————. *The Negro Church in America*, new edn. bound with *The Black Church Since Frazier*. New York: Schocken Books, 1974.

Frederickson, George M. *White Supremacy: A Comparative Study in American and South African History*. New York: Oxford University Press, 1981.

Gayle, Addison, ed. *The Black Aesthetic*. Garden City, N.Y.: Doubleday, 1971.

Genovese, Eugene D. *Roll Jordan Roll: The World the Slaves Made*. New York: Vintage, 1976.

George, Nelson. *The Death of Rhythm and Blues*. New York: E. P. Dutton, 1989.

Gutman, Herbert G. *The Black Family in Slavery and Freedom, 1750–1925*. New York: Pantheon, 1976.

Hale-Benson, Janice E. *Black Children: Their Roots, Culture, and Learning Styles.* Baltimore, Md.: John Hopkins University Press, 1986.

Hare, Nathan. "What Black Intellectuals Misunderstand About the Black Family." *Black World* 25 (March 1976):4-14.

Hazzard-Gordon, Katrina. *Jookin': The Rise of Social Dance Formations in African-American Culture.* Philadelphia: Temple University Press, 1990.

Hayes, Floyd W. III. "A Bibliographical Essay: The African Presence in America Before Columbus." *Black World* 22 (July 1973):4-22.

Hernton, Calvin C. *Sex and Racism in America.* New York: Grove Press, 1965.

Herskovits, Melville J. *The Myth of the Negro Past.* Boston: Beacon Press, 1958.

Holloway, Joseph E., ed. *Africanisms in American Culture.* Bloomington and Indianapolis, Ind.: Indiana University Press, 1990.

Huggins, Nathan. *Harlem Renaissance.* New York: Oxford University Press, 1971.

Hughes, Langston. *The Big Sea: An Autobiography.* New York: Hill and Wang, 1940.

Illich, Ivan. *Medical Nemesis: The Expropriation of Health.* New York: Pantheon, 1976.

Jacques-Garvey, Amy, ed. *Philosophy and Opinions of Marcus Garvey*, 2 vols. in one. New York: Arno Press and the New York Times, 1969.

James, C. L. R. *A History of Pan African Revolt.* Washington, D.C.: Drum and Spear Press, 1969.

Johnson, Charles S., ed. *Ebony and Topaz: A Collectanea.* New York: The National Urban League, 1927.

————. *The Negro in American Civilization: A Study of Negro Life and Race Relations in the Light of Social Research.* New York: Henry Holt and Company, 1930.

————. *Patterns of Negro Segregation.* New York: Harper and Brothers, 1943.

————. *Growing Up in the Black Belt: Negro Youth in the Rural South.* New York: Schocken Books, 1967.

————. *The Negro College Graduate.* New York: Negro Universities Press, 1969.

Johnson, James Weldon. *Along This Way: The Au-
    tobiography of James Weldon Johnson*. New
    York: Viking Press, Viking Compass Edition,
    1968.
————. *Black Manhattan*. New York: Atheneum,
    1972.
Jones, LeRoi (Amiri Baraka). *Blues People*. New
    York: William Morrow, 1963.
Jones, Reginald L., ed. *Black Psychology*. New
    York: Harper and Row, 1972.
Jordan, Winthrop D. *White Over Black: American
    Attitudes Toward The Negro 1550-1812*. Bal-
    timore, Md.: Penguin Books, 1969.
Kaiser, Ernest. "The History of Negro History."
    Negro Digest 27 (February 1968):10-15, 64-
    80.
Karenga, Maulana. "Kawaida and Its Critics: A
    Sociohistorical Analysis." *Journal of Black
    Studies* 8 (December 1977):125-48.
————. *Introduction to Black Studies*. Ingle-
    wood, Calif.: Kawaida Publications, 1982.
————. "Black Studies and the Problematic of
    Paradigm: The Philosophical Dimension."
    Journal of Black Studies 18 (June
    1988):395-414.
Kimball, Robert, and William Bolcom. *Reminiscing
    with Sissle and Blake*. New York: Viking
    Press, 1973.
Kiple, Kenneth F., and Virginia H. Kiple. "Slave
    Child Mortality: Some Nutritional Answers
    to a Perennial Puzzle." *Journal of Social
    History* 10 (March 1977):284-309.
Kochman, Thomas. *Black and White Styles in Con-
    flict*. Chicago: University of Chicago
    Press, 1981.
Ladner, Joyce A. *Tomorrow's Tomorrow: The Black
    Woman*. New York: Anchor Books, Doubleday,
    1971.
————, ed. *The Death of White Sociology*. New
    York: Vintage, 1973.
Landry, Bart. *The New Black Middle Class*. Berke-
    ley and Los Angeles: University of Califor-
    nia Press, paperback, 1988.
Lincoln, C. Eric. *The Black Muslims in America*.
    Boston: Beacon Press, 1969.
———— and Mamiya, Lawrence H. *The Black Church
    in the African American Experience*. Durham,
    N.C.: Duke University Press, 1990.

Levine, Lawrence W. *Black Culture and Black Consciousness: Afro-American Folk Thought from Slavery to Freedom*. New York: Oxford University Press, 1977.

Lewis, Hylan. *Blackways of Kent*. New Haven, Conn.: College and University Press, 1964.

Locke, Alain, ed. *The New Negro*. New York: Atheneum, 1974.

MacDonald J. Fred. *Blacks and White TV: Afro-Americans in Television Since 1948*. Chicago: Nelson-Hall, 1983.

Mckay, Claude. *Harlem: Negro Metropolis*. New York: Harcourt Brace Jovanovich, 1968.

MacRobert, Iain. *The Black Roots and White Racism of Early Pentacostalism in the USA*. New York: St. Martin's Press, 1988.

Mapp, Edward. *Blacks in American Films: Today and Yesterday*. Metuchen, N.J.: Scarecrow Press, 1972.

Marsh, Clifton E. *From Black Muslims to Muslims: The Transition for Separatism to Islam, 1930-1980*. Metuchen, N.J.: Scarecrow Press, 1984.

Martin, Elmer P., and Joanne Mitchell Martin. *The Black Extended Family*. Chicago: University of Chicago Press, 1978.

Martin, Frank. "The Egyptian Ethnicity Controversy and the Sociology of Knowledge." *Journal of Black Studies* 14 (March 1984):295-325.

Martin, Tony. *Race First: The Ideological and Organizational Struggles of Marcus Garvey and the Universal Negro Improvement Association*. Westport, Conn.: Greenwood Press, 1976.

Morris, Aldon D. *The Origins of the Civil Rights Movement: Black Communities Organizing for Change*. New York: The Free Press, 1984.

Mowry, George E., ed. *The Twenties: Fords, Flappers and Fanatics*. Englewood Cliffs, N.J.: Prentice-Hall, 1963.

National Research Council Committee on the Status of Black Americans. *A Common Destiny: Blacks and American Society*. Washington, D.C.: National Academy Press, 1989.

Newman, Mark. *Entrepreneurs of Profit: From Black-Appeal to Radio Soul*. New York: Praeger, 1988.

Park, Robert. "The Conflict and Fusion of Cultures with Special Reference to the Negro." *Journal of Negro History* 4 (April 1919):111–33.

Pinkney, Alphonso. *Red, Black, and Green: Black Nationalism in the United States.* New York: Cambridge University Press, 1976.

Platt, Anthony M. *E. Franklin Frazier Reconsidered.* New Brunswick, N.J.: Rutgers University Press, 1991.

Porter, James A. *Modern Negro Art.* New York: Arno Press and the New York Times, 1969.

Postell, William D. *The Health of Slaves on Southern Plantations.* Gloucester, Mass.: Peter Smith, 1970.

Powdermaker, Hortense. *After Freedom: A Critical Study in the Deep South.* New York: Russell and Russell, 1968.

Raboteau, Albert J. *Slave Religion.* New York: Oxford University Press, 1978.

Raper, Arthur F. *Preface to Peasantry: A Tale of Two Black Belt Counties.* New York: Atheneum, 1968.

Rodney, Walter. *How Europe Underdeveloped Africa.* Dar-es-Salaam, Tanzania: Tanzania Publishing House, 1972.

Rogers, J. A. *World's Great Men of Color,* 2 vols., rev. edn. New York: Collier Books, 1972.

Roses, Lorraine Elena, and Ruth Elizabeth Randolph. *Harlem Renaissance and Beyond: Literary Biographies of 100 Black Women Writers 1900–1945.* Boston: G. K. Hall, 1990.

Savitt, Todd L. *Medicine and Slavery: The Diseases and Health Care of Blacks in Antebellum Virginia.* Chicago: University of Illinois Press, 1978.

Schoener, Allon, ed. *Harlem on My Mind: Cultural Capital of Black American, 1900–1968.* New York: Random House, 1968.

Semmes, Clovis E. (Jabulani K. Makalani). "Foundations of an Afrocentric Social Science: Implications for Curriculum-Building, Theory, and Research in Black Studies." *Journal of Black Studies* 12 (September 1981):3–17.

————. "Black Studies and the Symbolic Structure of Domination." *The Western Journal of Black Studies* 6 (Summer 1982):116-22.

————. "The Sociological Tradition of E. Franklin Frazier: Implications for Black Studies." *Journal of Negro Education* 55 (Fall 1986):484-94.

Smitherman, Geneva. *Talkin and Testifyin: The Language of Black America*. Detroit, Mich.: Wayne State University Press, 1977.

Southern, Eileen. *The Music of Black Americans: A History*. New York: W. W. Norton, 1971.

Spear, Allan H. *Black Chicago: The Making of a Negro Ghetto: 1890-1920*. Chicago: University of Chicago Press, 1967.

Stampp, Kenneth M. *The Peculiar Institution: Slavery in the Ante-Bellum South*. New York: Vintage, 1956.

Stanfield, John H. *Philanthropy and Jim Crow in American Social Science*. Westport, Conn.: Greenwood Press, 1985.

Staples, Robert. *Introduction to Black Sociology*. New York: McGraw-Hill, 1976.

————. *The World of Black Singles: Changing Patterns of Male/Female Relations*. Westport, Conn.: Greenwood Press, paperback, 1982.

————. *The Urban Plantation: Racism and Colonialism in the Post Civil Rights Era*. Oakland, Calif.: Black Scholar Press, 1987.

Sutherland, Robert Lee. *Color, Class, and Personality*. Washington, D.C.: American Council on Education, 1942.

Thompson, Vincent Bakpetu. *The Making of the African Diaspora in the Americas 1441-1900*. New York: Longman, 1987.

Van Sertima, Ivan. *They Came Before Columbus*. New York: Random House, 1976.

————, ed. *African Presence in Early Europe*. New Brunswick, N.J.: Transaction Publishers, 1985.

————, ed. *Egypt Revisited*, 2nd edn. New Brunswick, N.J.: Transactions Publishers, 1989.

———— and Runoko Rashidi, eds. *African Presence in Early Asia*, rev. edn. New Brunswick, N.J.: Transaction Books, 1988.

Walton, Ortiz. *Music: Black, White and Blue: A Sociological Survey of the Use and Misuse of Afro-American Music*. New York: William Morrow, 1972.

Washington, Joseph. *Black Sects and Cults*. Garden City, N.Y.: Anchor Books, Doubleday, 1973.

Welsing, Frances Cress. *The Isis Papers: The Keys to the Colors*. Chicago: Third World Press, 1991.

Whitlow, Roger. *Black American Literature: A Critical History*. Chicago: Nelson-Hall, 1973.

Williams, Chancellor. *Destruction of Black Civilization*. Chicago: Third World Press, 1974.

Williams, George Washington. *History of the Negro Race in America: From 1619 to 1880*, 2 vols. New York: G. P. Putnam's Sons, 1883; reprint edn., New York: Bergman Publishers, 1968.

Wilmore, Gayraud S., ed. *African American Religious Studies: An Interdisciplinary Anthology*. Durham, N.C.: Duke University Press, 1989.

Woodson, Carter G. *The Mis-Education of the Negro*. Washington, D.C.: Associated Publishers, 1933.

———. *The History of the Negro Church*, 2nd edn. Washington, D.C.: Associated Publishers, 1945.

X, Malcolm. *The Autobiography of Malcolm X*, with the assistance of Alex Haley. New York: Grove Press, 1964.

Index

African American
 studies, 15; pa-
 rameters of, 32-
 33; Yale sympo-
 sium, 74
African-centered
 thought: Black
 universities and,
 18; biogenetic ar-
 guments and, 22-
 23; Center for In-
 ner City Studies,
 19; Ethiopianism
 and, 15; focus of,
 20, 37 n.54;
 Harlem Renaissance
 and, 16; histor-
 ical basis, 12-15;
 1960s social move-
 ments and, 16-17;
 problems of meta-
 physical dualism
 and, 20-22; roots
 of nomenclature,
 19-20; social or-
 ganization and
 culture and , 23,
 30-32; variations
 of, 15-16;

vindicationist
 tradition, 15
African heritage,
 transformation of,
 6-8
African Methodist
 Episcopal Church,
 146
African Orthodox
 Church, 148, 153
Afrocentric forms,
 24-30
Akbar, Naim, 23
Ali, Noble Drew, 148
Allen, Armstead, 19
Amos 'n' Andy, 112,
 128
Anderson, Regina 210
Assimilation. *See*
 cultural negation
Association for the
 Advancement of
 Creative Musicians
 (AACM), 235
Augustine, St., 161,
 162

Baraka, Amiri. *See*
 Jones, LeRoi

ben-Jochannan, Yosef,
19, 162
Bennett, Gwendolyn,
210
biculturality, 28
Black arts movements,
16, 28
Black brokers, 119–
123
Black consciousness
movements, 16, 21,
28–29; cultural
revitalization
and, 242–43;
naturalistic
health beliefs
and, 213–28. *See
also* Black power
Black consumer mar-
kets, 116; Black
women and, 124–25;
mainstream economy
and, 118; values
and consumption
patterns, 125–26
Black culture: and
Africanization of
America, 126; and
popular culture,
117; problems of
control, 130–33;
role in expanding
markets, 126–30
Black images: in ev-
eryday life, 111–
12; minstrelsy and
White supremacy,
111–13, 127; tech-
nology, mass media
and, 112–13, 126–
28
Black intelligentsia:
in Harlem Renais-
sance, 199, 211–
13; rise of, 198
Black Jews, 27, 60,
148, 153, 154, 167
n.36.

Black labor, 115–16,
118
Black power, 156–57
Black theology, 157
Black universities.
See under Afri-
can-centered
thought
Blackburn, Darlene,
239
Blake, Eubie, 129
Blassingame, John, 7,
13
Bontemps, Arna, 208
Brooks, Gwendolyn,
231, 239
Brown, Oscar, Jr.,
235, 239
Brown, Walter, 233

capitalism, contra-
dictions of, 116–
18
Carmichael, Stokely,
239
Carruthers, Jacob, 19
Charles, Ray, 133
Charleston, 129
Christianity: accul-
turation, oppres-
sion and, 13–14;
African American
culture and, 7–8;
and social cohe-
sion, 6. *See also*
religion; reli-
gious thinking
Clark, Cedric (Sayed
Malik Khatib), 93,
97–99
Clarke, John Henrik,
19
Cleage, Albert, 157,
239
Cohran, Phil: and Af-
fro-Arts Theater,
223, 237–40; con-
tributions to cul-

tural survival, 241; and health, 223-24; life and philosophy of, 230-37

color stratification, 4-5

Cone, James, 157, 160

consumption, radical, 174

Cosby, Bill, 133

counterculture movements, 214

crime, and health, 172-73

Cross, William, 109-10 n.11

Cruse, Harold: and African-centered thought, 17; and Black leadership, 82-85; and crisis of Black intellectual thought, 77-81; and group power, 114-15; and integrationist ethic, 74-77; theoretical contributions to African American studies, 71-74, 89-90; theory of the cities, 85-89;

Cullen, Countee, 208, 209

cultural competition, 115-16

cultural hegemony: and Afrocentric forms, 24-30, 33; countervailing force to, 124; and cultural movements, 195-96; cultural products and, 212, 228-29, 241; defined, 1-3; institutional weakness and health, 172; language and, 9-10; and liberal and authoritarian modes of oppression, 212; plantation experience and, 4-6; response to 242-43; role of religion in, 6-9, 139-43; systemic tendencies of, 120-24

cultural mode of production, 81

cultural negation, 7-8, 30-31, 111, 124-26; and commodity formation, 130-31

cultural survival: control of Black culture and, 228-30; requirements for, 253-54; and role of community artist, 230. *See also under* Cohran, Phil

Darktown Follies, 129

Delaney, Martin, 77

Diop, Cheikh Anta, 19, 25

Divine, Father, 148

double-consciousness, 16, 30, 158, 173

Douglass, Frederick, 77

Doyle, Bertram, 101

Drake, St. Clair, 10, 15, 25, 146, 228

DuBois, W. E. B., 16, 179, 209

Dunbar, Paul Lawrence, 235

Earth, Wind and Fire, 240
economic development: and culture, 123–24; restrictions on, 119–22; role of Black brokers, 122–23
Ellington, Duke, 207
Ellison, Ralph, 2
Ethiopianism, 15, 146, 148
Europe, James Reese, 207

Fanon, Franz, 150
Farrakhan, Louis, 155
Father Divine Peace Mission, 60
Fauset, Jessie, 208, 209, 210
Fourteenth Amendment, 83, 85
Frazier, E. Franklin, 6, 21, 119–20, 123; on African Americans and ruling elites, 73; on Black youth and personality development, 60–63; on comparative cultures and assimilation, 63–66; contributions to African American studies, 41–43, 66; criticisms of, 43–44, 68–69 n.5; on family and assimilation, 43–51; on health, 175, 179; on middle-class dependency, 79; on middle-class formations, 51–57;

on nationalistic movements, 75; on religious values and social organization, 57–60, 144
Fuller, Hoyt, 19
Fuller, O. Anderson, 232
fundamentalist religious expression, 60

Garland, Phyl, 231
Garnet, Henry Highland, 15
Garofola, Reebee, 9
Garret, Jimmy, 239
Garvey, Marcus, 77, 152–53
Garvey Movement, 27, 148, 152, 153, 155, 205
Gatlin, F. Nathaniel, 232
Gayle, Addison, 17
Gender, 5
Ghana Dance Ensemble, 239
Gill, Ruby Harris, 232
Grace, Daddy, 148
Griffith, D. W., 127
Grimke, Angelina, 208
group power: challenges to African American, 115–16; White Anglo-Saxon Protestant domination, 114–15

Hammer, 133
Harlem: development of, 201–2; growth of Black population, 202–4; radicalism of, 205–6;

White interest in,
206–8
Harlem Renaissance,
16, 27, 79, 81,
87–89, 128–29,
196, 197, 206–11.
See also migration
Harmon, William C.,
210
Harris, Abram, 209
health: and cultural
ethos, 189–90; and
cultural hegemony,
190; drugs, crime
and, 172–73; and
European contact
with Africa, 175–
76; and family
stability, 172;
and institutional
weakness, 172–73;
medical limi-
tations, market
forces and, 187–
88; medicalization
and, 188–90; need
for a health
ethic, 173–75; and
postslavery ex-
perience, 178–80;
relationship to
oppression and
liberation, 171;
role of the fam-
ily, 185–86; and
slavery, 176–78;
types of health
problems, 180–84;
the viability of
culture and, 174.
See also
revitalization
movements
Hebrew Israelites.
See Black Jews
Herskovits, Melville,
21, 43

Hughes, Langston,
199, 206, 209, 210
Hurston, Zora, 208

Institute of Positive
Education, influ-
ences on health
practices, 224
integrationist ethic.
See under Harold
Cruse

Jackman, Harold, 210
Jackson, Bo, 133
Jackson, Jesse, 85
Jackson, John G., 19
Jackson, Michael, 133
Jewish nationalism,
80
Johnson, Charles S.,
198, 208; and *Op-
portunity* maga-
zine, 210–11
Johnson, James P.,
207
Johnson, James Wel-
don, 202, 209
Johnson, John H. *See*
Johnson Publica-
tions
Johnson, Syl, 239
Johnson Publications,
19, 120–22
Jolson, Al, 127
Jones, LeRoi (Amiri
Baraka), 7, 239
Jones, Reginald, 17

Karenga, Maulana, 18,
28
Kemet, 25–26
Khatib, Sayed Malik.
See Clark, Cedric
King, Martin Luther,
Jr., 156
knowledge production,
problems facing
African American

intellectuals,
251-52

Ladner, Joyce, 17
Lafayette Theater,
129
language. *See under*
cultural hegemony
legitimacy: the
plantation proto-
type and color
stratification,
99-101; and racial
etiquette, 99-104;
role in cultural
negation, 96-99;
and segregation
and integration as
forms of domi-
nation, 105-8; as
a social problem,
93-94
Lincoln, C. Eric, 158
Locke, Alain, 16, 208
L'Ouverture, Tous-
saint, 215
Lyles, Aubrey, 129

Mckay, Claude, 208,
209
McShann, Jay, 232
Madhubuti, Haki, 215,
224, 239
marginality, 6, 32
Marshall Hotel, 204
Marxist thought, 72,
80-81
Memphis Students, 204
mental oppression, 1
metaphysical dualism.
See under Afri-
can-centered
thought
migration, 119, 198-
200, 211. *See also*
urbanization
Miller, F. E., 129

minstrel tradition,
as a prototype of
cultural nega-
tion, 10, 32. *See*
Black images
Moorish Science, 27,
60, 148
Moynihan, Daniel
Patrick, 42
Muhammad, Elijah,
153. *See also* Na-
tion of Islam
Muhammad, Wallace,
D., 155

Nail, John B., 203
Nation of Islam, 27,
77; as a counter-
vailing force to
cultural hegemony,
124, 148, 153-55;
health beliefs and
practices of, 217-
20
National Association
for the Advance-
ment of Colored
People (NAACP),
77, 84
naturalistic health
beliefs: and
artistic/spiritual
groups, 222-27;
and cultural
revitalization,
213-14; and Hebrew
Israelites, 220-
22; and identity,
214-16; and the
Nation of Islam,
217-20
*Negro Digest (Black
World)*, 19
Nelson, Oliver, 233
noneconomic liberal-
ism, 83-84, 89

Oletunji, 239

Olive-Harvey College,
19
oppression, authori-
tarian versus lib-
eral mode, 212
Organization of Black
American Culture
(OBAC), 239
Original Dixieland
Jass Band, 128

Park, Robert, 46-47
Payton, Philip A.,
202-3
Pentacostalism, 147
Peters, Erskine, 37
n.54
Pharoahs, 240
providential design,
148

Ra, Sun, 233
Raboteau, Albert, 7
racism, 1; how to
study, 253-54. See
also cultural
hegemony, defined;
oppression; Wels-
ing, Frances
Rajahs of Swing, 232
reconstructivist tra-
dition, 27-28, 33
Reid, Ira De A., 204
religion: and Ameri-
can creed, 141;
Black experience
in America, 141-
43; and Black
theology, 157-68;
and Civil Rights
movement, 156; and
Garvey movement,
152-53; and Nation
of Islam, 153-55;
and the psychology
of oppression,
149-52, 155-56;
role in European

imperialism, 140-
41; and social
organization, 139;
variations in
African American
expression, 143-
48. See Frazier,
E. Franklin, on
religious values
and social organi-
zation
religious myth, truth
in, 158-64
religious thinking:
challenges to
Western Christian-
ity, 160-62; dis-
tinctiveness from
institutional
forms, 158-60;
liberating and
humanizing aspects
of, 163-64
Rev. Spenser Jackson
family, 239
revitalization move-
ments, 195-96; and
Harlem Renais-
sance, 197-213;
and health beliefs
and practices,
213-28
Robey, Don, 233

Sissle, Noble, 129
Sister Zubena, 215
Smith, Willie (the
Lion), 207
social heritage, 6,
14. See also Fra-
zier, E. Franklin,
on family and
assimilation, on
middle-class for-
mations
social organization
and culture, 252-
53. See also under

African-centered thought

Spingarn, Amy and Joel, 209
Spencer, Ann, 209
Staples, Robert, 17
status and social control, 4-5, 9, 32
stratification: and dominating group, 3-5; and plantation system, 5-6
Stuckey, Sterling, 7

Thomas, J. C., 203
Thompson, Anderson, 19,
Toomer, Jean, 208, 209
Tucker, Sophie, 128
Turner, Nat, 146

unity of opposites, 21
Urban League, 77
urbanization, 48-51, 52-53, 57, 59-60. See also migration

Van Sertima, Ivan, 26
Van Vechten, Carl, 208, 209
vindicationist scholars, 19
vindicationist tradition. See under African-centered thought; St. Clair Drake

Walker, A'Leilia, 209-211
Walker, C. J., 209
Wallace, Walter, 30-31
Walrond, Eric, 208, 210

Warner Brothers, 127
Washington, Booker T., 77
Washington, Joseph, 157
Welsing, Frances, 23-24, 29, 150-51
West African focus, 24, 26-27, 33
White supremacy. See Black images; cultural hegemony; legitimacy; Welsing, Frances
Williams, Chancellor, 19
Williams, George Washington, 14

X, Malcolm, 153, 154, 155, 156, 157, 217, 220

Ziegfeld, Florenz, 129
Zulu Records, 231

About the Author

CLOVIS E. SEMMES (Jabulani Kamau Makalani) is associate professor of African American Studies at Eastern Michigan University. He has published widely in the areas of African American studies and sociology.